W9-AQG-841

The Debate over Slavery

The Debate over Slavery

Antislavery and Proslavery Liberalism in Antebellum America

David F. Ericson

NEW YORK UNIVERSITY PRESS
New York and London

NEW YORK UNIVERSITY PRESS
New York and London

Library of Congress Cataloging-in-Publication Data
Ericson, David F., 1950–
The debate over slavery : antislavery and proslavery liberalism in antebellum America / David F. Ericson.
p. cm.
Includes bibliographical references and index.
ISBN 0-8147-2212-1 (acid-free paper) —
ISBN 0-8147-2213-X (pbk. : acid-free paper)
1. Antislavery movements—United States—History —19th century.
2. Slavery—Political aspects—United States—History—19th century.
3. Slavery—Southern States—Justification. 4. Liberalism—United States—History—19th century. 5. Abolitionists—United States—History—19th century. 6. United States—Intellectual life—19th century. 7. Southern States—Intellectual life—19th century.
8. Southern States–Race relations. I. Title.
E449 .E73 2001
306.3'62'0973—dc21 00-010365

New York University Press books are printed on acid-free paper, and their binding materials are chosen for strength and durability.

Manufactured in the United States of America

10 9 8 7 6 5 4 3 2 1

To CL

Contents

Acknowledgments

I wish to thank the following scholars for their "friendly" comments on the many earlier versions of individual chapters of this manuscript—John Diggins, Louisa Green, Russell Hanson, Philip Klinkner, Robert Martin, Joanna Scott, the late Richard Sinopoli, and Rogers Smith—as well as several anonymous reviewers of the full manuscript. I also wish to thank the New York University Press "team"—Stephen Magro and Despina Papazoglou Gimbel—for their assistance in getting this manuscript into print. Finally, I wish to thank the National Endowment for the Humanities and Wichita State University for partially funding the research and writing of this book.

Portions of chapters 2 and 5 were published previously as part of my essay "Dew, Fitzhugh, and Proslavery Liberalism," in *The Liberal Tradition in American Politics: Reassessing the Legacy of American Liberalism*, ed. David F. Ericson and Louisa Bertch Green (New York: Routledge, 1999), pp. 67–98. I wish to thank Routledge, Inc., for permission to include that material in this book.

Part I

1 The Liberal Consensus Thesis and Slavery

This book is a study of American antislavery and proslavery rhetoric spanning the years from 1832 to 1861.[1] Throughout, I assume that rhetoric mattered. Rhetoric mattered in this period of American history not because the antislavery and proslavery arguments themselves abolished the Southern institution of racial slavery or prevented the institution from being abolished without a civil war or because those arguments themselves caused the Civil War. Rather, rhetoric mattered because the particular forms that the antislavery and proslavery arguments took during the antebellum period significantly affected the course of events that led to disunion, civil war, and emancipation.

The antislavery and proslavery arguments unsettled the public mind into believing that the nation was a house divided against itself that could no longer stand. Perhaps a nation half free and half slave could have continued to exist indefinitely into the future if sectional antislavery and proslavery rhetoric had not been introduced. When this sectional rhetoric was introduced, however, it deepened the divisions within the nation and made it less likely that the country could continue to exist as it had in the past.

The consensually and progressively liberal nature of antislavery and proslavery rhetoric contributed to this outcome. Because the two sides appealed to similar ideas for such divergent ends, it became increasingly apparent that the differences between them were fundamental. Because the two sides applied liberal ideas to the particular circumstances of their own society with such diverse results, it became more and more difficult to dismiss the conflict between them as peripheral to the future of a nation conceived in liberty.

The Civil War was a case in which rhetoric mattered. It was also a case in which consensus mattered, though in a different way than it was "supposed to." It was a case in which consensus exacerbated rather than tempered political conflict. Finally, it was a case in which liberal ideas mattered, making racial slavery vulnerable to attack and yet not foreclosing all avenues of defense.

Hartz and His Critics

In 1955, when he published *The Liberal Tradition in America*, Louis Hartz established a new consensus paradigm for understanding American political history.[2] He argued that American political history was best understood as the unfolding of a single, liberal tradition of political ideas, in contrast to the cyclical, conflictual model of history that Charles Beard and the other Progressive historians had favored.[3]

Since that time, Hartz's "liberal consensus" thesis has not gone unchallenged. Indeed, some scholars have claimed that another paradigm shift in our understanding of American political history occurred in the 1970s, following the publication of such major works of republican revisionism as Bernard Bailyn's *Ideological Origins of the American Revolution*, Gordon Wood's *Creation of the American Republic*, and J. G. A. Pocock's *Machiavellian Moment*. According to these historians, American political history, at least into the 1780s, was best understood as the unfolding of a republican tradition of "civic virtue" instead of a liberal tradition of "atomistic freedom."[4]

More recently, both historians and political scientists have favored a more philosophically synthetic approach, contending that American political history is best understood as the unfolding of not one tradition of political ideas but of many traditions. James Kloppenberg's 1987 article "The Virtues of Liberalism: Christianity, Republicanism, and Ethics in Early American Political Discourse" advocated a "discursive pluralism" of liberal, republican, and Protestant ideas.[5] Even more recently, Rogers Smith presented, in a variety of forums, a similar argument for "multiple traditions" of liberal, republican, and ascriptive ideas.[6] Yet I believe that Hartz's "liberal consensus" thesis, suitably modified, remains sound.

Two Issues of Interpretation

One of the issues distinguishing Hartz's consensus or single-tradition approach and his critics' multiple-traditions approach is methodological.[7] What are the relative merits for us, as social scientists, of using single-factor, as opposed to multiple-factor, analyses? A second issue is more empirical. Did historical actors strategically use ideas from various traditions of political ideas to serve an array of ulterior motives, regardless of the lack of coherence among those ideas, or did they seek and achieve some (or even a considerable degree of) coherence among the political ideas they used?

Obviously, there is no one right answer to the methodological issue. Whether a single-factor or -tradition approach is superior to a multiple-factor or -traditions approach depends on the phenomenon in question.[8] In effect, Hartz argued that a single-tradition approach was superior for understanding American political history from the Revolutionary War to the McCarthy era, whereas a multiple-traditions approach was superior for understanding European political history over the same time period.[9] His critics disagreed, stating that a multiple-traditions approach was also superior for understanding American political history during that time period. In effect, they claimed to be able to explain more "variance" (to use the factor-analysis term) in American political history using several different traditions of political ideas—liberal, republican, Protestant, and/or ascriptive–than they could using only one, liberal, tradition.

Hartz's critics were undoubtedly right about their ability to explain more variance in American political history by using several different traditions of political ideas than by using only one tradition. That superiority of a multiple-traditions approach, however, does not settle the methodological issue because we can explain more variance in a phenomenon without necessarily understanding it any better. In fact, it may well be the case that we understand American political history less well using a multiple-traditions approach than we do using a single-tradition approach.

Consider the following logic: If we can explain more variance in a phenomenon using three factors than we can using one factor, then presumably we can explain more variance in the phenomenon using more than three factors than we can using just three factors. If we were to add together all the intellectual traditions that scholars have used to explain the variance in American political history, we would have a very long list indeed, and presumably we could explain (almost) all the variance in American political history.[10] Yet no scholar would ever use all those traditions as explanatory factors because he or she would soon reach the point of diminishing returns. Instead of dissipating "the fog of history," he or she would be merely recreating it. Hence we, as social scientists, are admonished by the law of parsimony to simplify our explanations of social phenomena as much as possible on the premise that the simpler the explanation of a phenomenon is, the better we will understand it.

This superiority of a single-tradition approach also does not settle the methodological issue, because by using only one explanatory factor we may *over*simplify our explanation of a phenomenon and thus distort rather than improve our understanding of it. In terms of understanding American political history, then, the issue is settled neither by claiming that we gain "greater descriptive and explanatory power" by using a multiple-traditions approach nor by claiming that we can "drive a wedge of rationality" through American political history by using a single-tradition approach.[11] Instead, the issue is settled ultimately by the results. Frankly, I find Hartz's results much more compelling than those of his critics. The multiple-traditions approach may offer a more accurate picture of bits and pieces of American political history, but it offers a very obscure picture of the whole. Although Hartz's critics are suspicious of any metanarrative of American political history, they fail to explain the ebb and flow of the liberal, republican, Protestant, and/or ascriptive ideas that they would substitute for his metanarrative. As I see it, the multiple-traditions approach commits its practitioners to explaining not only why the mix between these different sets of political ideas took the particular form it did during any one historical epoch but also why that mix changed over time. Those tasks, however, remain unfulfilled.

The second issue that arises in evaluating the relative merits of the single-tradition or consensus approach and the multiple-traditions approach to American political history is intellectual coherence. This issue has both an intrapersonal and an interpersonal dimension.

On the intrapersonal level, the question is how much particular historical actors sought and achieved intellectual coherence. This question is, of course, empirical, with some actors seeking and achieving more coherence than others did. The consensus approach is superior to the multiple-traditions approach on this level because it is more open to the possibility of such coherence.

Scholars who use a multiple-traditions approach cannot seem to avoid treating historical actors as sieves of disembodied intellectual traditions. The image they present is of intellectual traditions, now hypostatized, channeling the ideas of historical actors into certain well-worn patterns of thought. Multiple-traditions scholars substantially, if not completely, reduce the agency of historical actors in synthesizing the ideas they have "inherited" from these various traditions into more or less coherent bodies of political thought. In practice, these scholars never seem to reach the political thought of any particular historical actor.[12]

The contrasting image that consensus scholars present is of historical actors actively participating in a process of seeking and achieving some degree of intellectual coherence or ideological constraint among their inherited ideas.[13] These scholars presume that some constraint exists among the ideas of particular actors, that some of their ideas are primary to others, and that those primary ideas provide a nucleus into which other, more secondary or tertiary ideas are synthesized to form more or less coherent bodies of political thought. Thus (re)formulated, the consensus view is that for most political actors throughout American history, one type of ideas provided this constraint and was primary to other types of ideas. The *liberal consensus* view is that liberal ideas provided this constraint and were primary to nonliberal ideas, whether they were republican, Protestant, ascriptive, or some other type.[14]

Scholars who use a consensus approach argue, therefore, not only that most individual actors throughout American history sought and achieved (within some range) ideological constraint among their political ideas but also that they did so in the same general way. The interpersonal claim seems more problematic than the intrapersonal one.[15] Perhaps the multiple-traditions approach is superior on the interpersonal level in reflecting the undeniable diversity that existed in the political ideas of individual actors throughout American history. How diverse those ideas really were is an empirical question, but it is also a matter of evaluating the results. On the interpersonal level, I again find Hartz's results much more compelling than those of his critics. To me, an analysis of American political history in terms of a liberal consensus that powerfully (though not hegemonically) discouraged the expression of nonmainstream, nonliberal ideas fits the data better than does an analysis of American political history in terms of individual actors (almost) indiscriminately picking and choosing from a smorgasbord of ideas and traditions. In addition, Hartz's critics face the formidable tasks of explaining why individual actors made the intellectual choices they did as well as why those choices might have changed over time.

Slavery as a Test Case

The superiority of the consensus approach cannot be settled by fiat, by Hartz, me, or anyone else. It must be tested. Accordingly, in this book, I test the "liberal consensus" thesis against its toughest case: the antebellum debate over the justice, expediency, and ultimate fate of the Southern institution of racial slavery. The historiographical significance of this case, however, was not the only reason that I chose it. I chose it also because of the continuing importance of issues of race to American politics and how those issues are rooted in the antebellum debate over the fate of Southern slavery. The United States never really solved the slavery issue; rather, the issue was "solved" for it on the battlefield. This resolution meant that all the wrenching decisions that had to be made about transforming a racially inegalitarian society into a racially egalitarian one were made, if they were made at all, after, not before, Southern slavery was abolished.[16] Those decisions were then imposed on a militarily defeated and increasingly recalcitrant South by Northern politicians, as if the North had not been implicated in the prior situation and already had become the racially egalitarian society that its Republican leaders somewhat halfheartedly, and ultimately unsuccessfully, tried to force the South to become. But this modus operandi may have been the only way that such decisions could have been made. The South, after all, was not prepared to make them on its own, and the North, at least, had abolished racial slavery. Nonetheless, the way that those decisions were made guaranteed that they would be made incompletely. As a result, the nation remains racially divided.[17]

But there has been progress. Few Americans today would publicly defend such extreme forms of racial inequality as racial slavery. Many Americans did during the antebellum period. The key historiographical question is in what way the antebellum defenders of slavery were committed to liberal ideas and were as committed to those ideas as were the abolitionists who attacked the institution, and as are Americans today who (perhaps wrongly) no longer feel any need to attack it. If any group in American history fits the illiberal or ascriptive mode, it was the defenders of slavery in the antebellum South. The antebellum debate over the fate of the institution is indeed a tough case for the "liberal consensus" thesis, especially on the proslavery side.[18]

In fact, it is such a tough case that Hartz himself did not interpret the proslavery movement in liberal terms. Instead, he saw the antebellum South as undergoing a "reactionary Enlightenment" in the course of defending its institution of racial slavery.[19] For the antebellum period, therefore, Hartz implicitly adopted a multiple-traditions approach, with the antislavery movement firmly in the liberal camp and the proslavery movement somewhat less firmly in the illiberal camp.[20] He then reasserted his "liberal consensus" thesis by showing how a putatively illiberal proslavery movement was vanquished completely, both militarily and ideologically, during the Civil War and Reconstruction.[21]

Especially because the movement had a much more lasting impact than he claimed that it did, I believe that Hartz undersold his own thesis when interpreting the proslavery movement.[22] Accordingly, I believe that both the antislavery and proslavery movements were fundamentally liberal in nature, that liberal ideas were primary for both sides and other, nonliberal, ideas were secondary and tertiary, and that both major antislavery figures and major proslavery figures attempted to achieve coherence on liberal ideas and were more or less successful in doing so. I then would not deny the illiberal elements that other scholars, including Hartz himself, emphasize in proslavery thought, but I would disagree with their emphasis on those elements. Asserting the "liberal consensus" thesis in a stronger form than Hartz himself did, I argue in this book that the Southern institution of racial slavery could be and was defended on liberal grounds. I also argue that the illiberal elements in proslavery thought were not "un-rationalized" but were integrated to a significant degree into the liberal elements.

Hartz Revisited

The key historiographical question now becomes why Hartz did not interpret the proslavery movement in this manner, since it would have advanced his thesis.[23] The first reason is that his understanding of liberalism was essentialist. He genuinely seemed to believe that liberal ideas were one thing and not another, that they were antislavery and not proslavery, and that they could not be both.[24] The second reason is that he viewed the proslavery dilemma as primarily psychological. He seemed much more interested in how proslavery figures could reconcile their liberal psyches with their defenses of the, to him, inherently illiberal institution of racial slavery than in how they in fact did defend the institution.[25]

Hartz's principal error was assuming that an American liberal consensus meant that most Americans subscribed to the same political ideas. He seemed to think that most Americans not only interpreted liberal ideas in the same way but also applied those ideas to their concrete social settings in the same way. A more nuanced, historically grounded understanding of the American liberal consensus, however, allows for significantly different interpretations and applications of liberal ideas. When we accept this possibility, we allow for both a proslavery and an antislavery liberalism as well as for serious political conflict, even a civil war, among a group of people who hold the same general set of political ideas.[26]

I think Hartz also erred in viewing the proslavery dilemma primarily as a psychological dilemma rather than a rhetorical one. Although the antebellum defenders of slavery did not question their commitment to the institution, they did question how they could defend that commitment to other Americans. Here, they found liberal *arguments* very useful for their purposes.

I would therefore recast Hartz's thesis in a rhetorical form, again in a stronger form than he himself cast it. Recast rhetorically, the "liberal consensus" thesis is that both proslavery and antislavery figures offered predominantly liberal arguments in conjunction with other types of arguments. Since according to this thesis, both sides offered predominantly liberal arguments, their arguments would become increasingly liberal over time. That is, liberal arguments would encourage responses in kind, leading to a dialectic of response and counterresponse of such arguments.[27] From the nature of their public arguments, we then could infer that antislavery and proslavery figures believed that their audiences generally subscribed to liberal ideas and that they themselves did, too. But these inferences could be wrong. Orators can misjudge their audiences, and they certainly can be disingenuous. In this case, it is hard to imagine that many of the proslavery arguments were not disingenuous, although I would not want to underestimate the human capacity of self-justification or overestimate the human capacity for self-deception. Even though making inferences about the mental states of political actors is irresistible and, to some extent, unavoidable, they still are inferences. Those mental states are ultimately inaccessible to others. The nature of their public arguments is not, however. As social scientists, I believe that our attention should be directed to analyzing the public dimensions of human behavior, not to psychoanalyzing the actors. In this book, my own attention is thus directed to judging whether antislavery and proslavery figures used liberal arguments, not to divining whether they had "clear" liberal consciences.

This rhetorical "turn" also has political justifications. Within a group of people generally committed to liberal ideas—as I think Americans were and are—the challenge for those people who believe that racial slavery or any other social practice is unjust or inexpedient is *not* to dismiss their opponents as racists or advocates of other illiberal ideologies. Rather, the challenge is to develop a more persuasive set of liberal arguments in opposition to the practice than their opponents can develop in support of it. I confess to being enough of a rhetorical "idealist" to believe that the latter strategy is the more effective one. In the case of the antebellum debate over the fate of Southern slavery, the abolitionists eventually did adopt just such a strategy. Today we should, too, when confronting contemporary forms of social oppression, racial or otherwise.

The Individual Cases

As a way of testing whether the antebellum debate over the fate of Southern slavery displayed the hypothesized traits of being predominantly liberal in nature and becoming increasingly so over time, I analyze the antislavery and proslavery arguments of several well-known antislavery and proslavery figures: Lydia Maria Child, Frederick Douglass, Wendell Phillips, Thomas R. Dew, George Fitzhugh, and James Henry Hammond. These cases are arranged to permit intrapersonal as well as interpersonal comparisons across time. In subsequent chapters, I make the following comparisons: Child's 1833 abolitionist primer, *An Appeal in Favor of That Class of Americans Called Africans*, with Frederick Douglass's 1852 antislavery jeremiad, "What to the Slave Is the Fourth of July?" (chapter 3); several of Phillips's major antislavery writings and speeches from 1837 to 1861 (chapter 4); Dew's 1832 antiabolitionist pamphlet, *Review of the Debate in the Virginia Legislature, 1831–32*, with Fitzhugh's 1857 proslavery polemic, *Cannibals All!, or Slaves without Masters* (chapter 5); and several of Hammond's major proslavery writings and speeches from 1836 to 1860 (chapter 6).

These cases and comparisons represent the antislavery and proslavery movements across time and points of view. On the antislavery side, Child sympathized with the New England circle of abolitionists led by William Lloyd Garrison, but she never formally joined any Garrisonian organization and some of her views were unorthodox from a Garrisonian perspective.[28] Douglass had once belonged to the Garrison circle, but by the time of his Fourth of July oration, he had broken with Garrison and become associated with the upstate New York circle of abolitionists led by Gerrit Smith.[29] Phillips was, in contrast, one of the most loyal and influential members of the Garrison circle.[30] On the proslavery side, Dew was a college professor who personally inserted himself into an unprecedented, and unrepeated, debate over the fate of racial slavery in his own state of Virginia.[31] Fitzhugh, in contrast, was a self-educated Virginian, minor Democratic Party functionary, and small slaveholder who tried to carve out a national reputation for himself as a proslavery polemicist.[32] Finally, Hammond was, unlike both Dew and Fitzhugh, from South Carolina and a prominent politician and planter whose proslavery statements were a matter of public record.[33]

In this book, I focus on the antislavery and proslavery arguments of individual antislavery and proslavery figures so that I can better assess—than I could using a more synoptic approach—how those arguments were synthesized into more or less coherent wholes, *ex hypothesi*, liberal wholes. My cases, therefore, are not intended to be statistically representative of antislavery or proslavery opinion in the antebellum United States. I do, however, canvass the antislavery and proslavery arguments more broadly in the second chapter of the book, which makes my analysis more generally representative of antislavery and proslavery opinion in the antebellum United States, at least on the elite level.[34] This broader canvass also permits me to construct a schema of antislavery and proslavery arguments for use in the later chapters in which I analyze my individual cases.

Earlier studies of the antebellum debate over the fate of Southern slavery almost invariably focus on one or the other side.[35] While it is understandable that Hartz and his critics disproportionately analyzed the proslavery side of the debate, given its more problematic status from a liberal point of view, we can truly test the validity of the "liberal consensus" thesis during the antebellum period only by considering both sides together. By considering both sides together in the same volume, I also am better able to show how the antislavery and proslavery arguments developed dialectically in relation to each other, bringing the nation to the brink of civil war. In the last chapter of the book, I return to the question of civil-war causation, a question that was not heavily debated by Hartz and his critics but that, of course, has been heavily debated by other scholars. I thus intend to accomplish several other things in this book beside test the "liberal consensus" thesis, although that remains my main objective.

The historiographical debate over the "liberal consensus" thesis is important because how we understand history affects how we act in history. Whether we understand particular historical cases as illiberal or liberal helps determine whether we react to those cases as aberrations or as integral parts of our national experience. It always is easy to dismiss the antebellum defenders of slavery as racists, which I am very willing to admit they were. It is much more difficult to recognize that they shared principles that we generally evaluate in positive terms and encounter these historical figures on grounds that no longer seem as comfortable or familiar to us as they once did. The antebellum debate over the fate of Southern slavery is a particularly good historical case for illustrating this point because the institution still generates political controversy, precisely because it was not an aberration but an integral part of our national experience.[36] The abolition of racial slavery in the Reconstruction South did not end racial oppression in this country, nor did it end other forms of invidious discrimination that can be, and have been, defended on liberal grounds. Fortunately, those practices also have been attacked on liberal grounds, although less fortunately by people who may have been equally racist to the people who defended them. The racist charge is undiscriminating. In many important ways, this particular historical case has lessons for all Americans, especially for those who have dedicated themselves, as the abolitionists did, to dismantling existing forms of social injustice.

2

The Antislavery and Proslavery Arguments

In this chapter, I develop a schema of antislavery and proslavery arguments for use in the following chapters that examine specific antislavery and proslavery figures. Since this schema is intended to support a "liberal consensus" thesis, I begin by distinguishing liberal from nonliberal ideas and liberal from nonliberal antislavery and proslavery arguments.[1]

Liberal and Nonliberal Arguments

I define liberal ideas as a general set of ideas that appeal to personal freedom, equal worth, government by consent, and private ownership of property as core human values. Conversely, nonliberal ideas appeal to some notion of natural inequality based on race, gender, ethnicity, religion, or birthright that denies those liberal values to significant numbers of human beings.[2] At the core of the liberal universe of arguments are those claiming that a certain social practice maximizes, or fails to maximize, the practical liberty of the men affected by that practice, and at the core of the nonliberal universe of arguments are those claiming that a certain social practice honors, or fails to honor, the eradicable inequalities among men. For example, a liberal antislavery argument would claim that the Southern institution of racial slavery was an unjust institution because it effectively denied that African Americans were men with a birthright to freedom equal to that of European Americans. A liberal proslavery argument, in contrast, would claim that the institution was a just institution because slavery was the status in which African Americans could enjoy the most practical liberty in light of their present circumstances, which rendered them incapable of prospering as free men alongside European Americans. A non-liberal antislavery argument would claim that the Southern institution of racial slavery was an unjust institution because it effectively denied African Americans the opportunity to work, worship, and learn at the feet of a superior white/Anglo-Saxon/Protestant race. Finally, a nonliberal proslavery argument would claim that the institution was a just institution because African Americans constituted an inferior race consigned by nature or God to be the slaves of a superior white/Anglo-Saxon/Protestant race.

Two points about these definitions require further comment. First, I have defined liberal and nonliberal ideas rather loosely. Since these are analytic categories, I could define them as loosely or tightly as I wanted, but defining them tightly would, I think, distort an important feature of politics. This feature is how political actors can, and often do, use a common set of ideas either to defend or attack the same institution. Those ideas then become quite flexible in their use. In this particular historical case, my hypothesis is that political actors in the antebellum United States used a common set of liberal ideas to either defend or attack the institution of racial slavery, regardless of whether they themselves referred to those ideas as liberal ones and regardless of whether they or their audiences actually believed in those ideas. As I have defined that liberal universe, it is not unbounded—its differences with its opposite are clear—but it is an amorphous universe that can comfortably support arguments both in defense of and in opposition to the institution of racial slavery. The "loose" definitions reflect how political ideas are typically used.[3]

Second, I acknowledge that it is easier to attack than to defend racial slavery using liberal arguments. Liberal ideas are *prima facie* antislavery, but that *prima facie* case can still be rebutted.[4] Again, this view reflects a certain historical reality. Proslavery figures did consider themselves on the defensive. Consequently, their arguments were of a qualifying nature: (1) *ceteris paribus*, racial slavery is an unjust institution, but the *ceteris paribus* clause does not hold in the case of the Southern institution of racial slavery; (2) all appearances to the contrary, the institution increases rather than decreases the practical liberty of the Southern slaves; and (3) the abolition of the institution would more adversely affect the liberties of both freemen and slaves than its continued existence would. The defenders of slavery in the antebellum United States obviously did not think they were in a hopeless polemical position in trying to defend the institution to their fellow Americans.[5] They had good arguments, by my definition, good liberal arguments. Even if we today believe that the abolitionists had better ones, we should not forget that antebellum Americans might have felt differently about the relative merits of the antislavery and proslavery arguments and that at the time they were the ones whose judgments about such matters carried political weight.

Deontological, Consequentialist, and Contextualist Arguments

In this and later chapters, I also distinguish antislavery and proslavery arguments as deontological, consequentialist, or contextualist arguments.[6] Antislavery deontological arguments condemned slavery as an unjust institution in itself; proslavery deontological arguments defended slavery as a just institution in itself (or as *not* an unjust institution). Antislavery consequentialist arguments condemned slavery as an unjust institution based on its harmful social consequences; proslavery consequentialist arguments defended slavery as a just institution based on its beneficial social consequences (or on the harmful social consequences of abolishing the institution). Antislavery contextualist arguments condemned slavery as a historically contingent institution that may have been appropriate to other times and places but that was not appropriate to this time and place; proslavery contextualist arguments defended slavery as part of a family of protective institutions and dependent statuses appropriate to all times and places (or that was *not* inappropriate to this time and place). If a liberal consensus had existed in the antebellum United States, then liberal arguments would have been predominant within each type of argument and increasingly so over time. I also substantiate a second rhetorical dynamic in the antebellum debate over the fate of the Southern institution of racial slavery. This dynamic occurred across types of arguments toward contextualist ones.

The explanation of the dynamic toward contextualist arguments is twofold. First, if we assume that the majority in both sections of the country took a relatively moderate "necessary evil" stance toward the fate of Southern slavery on deontological and consequentialist grounds—that it was an unjust institution in itself but that the social consequences of abolishing the institution would be less palatable than the social consequences of its continued existence—then contextualist arguments provided one way of breaking that impasse.[7]

The second explanation for this dynamic is the way that contextualist arguments associated antislavery and proslavery sentiments with other values that most Americans held dear, such as the union, human progress, and the nation's special mission in history. This aspect of contextualist arguments thus could have explained why Northern antislavery and Southern proslavery figures believed that those arguments would be particularly appealing to moderate public opinion within their respective sections of the country. The rhetorical superiority of contextualist arguments seemed especially strong on the antislavery side. The basic appeal was that if we Americans value the union, human progress, and the nation's special mission in history, then we cannot support the continued presence of racial slavery on our soil because it jeopardizes all those other values. The "house divided" argument—that the continued existence of the Southern institution of racial slavery and the preservation of the union were incompatible with each other—was a perfect example of this type of argument. Such contextualist arguments seemed to place the proslavery side in a more defensive position than the antislavery deontological and consequentialist arguments did. The defenders of slavery could only deny that the continued existence of the institution was antagonistic to those other values, as in insisting that the union was not really a house divided against itself or that a house divided against itself need not fall.[8]

The dynamic toward contextualist arguments had two consequences. It reinforced the first dynamic toward liberal arguments because most Americans defined the union, human progress, and the nation's special mission in history in liberal terms. The union was a union dedicated to liberty; human progress was progress toward liberal institutions; and the nation's special mission in history was a mission to spread the blessings of its uniquely liberal institutions to other countries around the world. The dynamic toward contextualist arguments also exacerbated the sectional conflict over the fate of Southern slavery by raising the stakes of the conflict and broadening its base. Increasingly, it involved more than "merely" the fate of Southern slavery. In a fascinating, though also tragic, case of reality mirroring rhetoric, it divided the house when the "middle" in each half of the country moved toward the antislavery and proslavery extremes.[9] The "house divided" argument thus became a self-fulfilling prophecy.

Deontological Arguments

On the antislavery side, the principal deontological argument was the liberal argument that slavery violated the natural rights and liberties of the slaves. Here the basic appeal was to the "self-evident" truths of the Declaration of Independence. As William Lloyd Garrison, in the inaugural issue of the *Liberator*, vowed,

> Assenting to the "self-evident truth" maintained in the American Declaration of Independence, "that all men are created equal, and endowed by their Creator with certain inalienable rights—among which are life, liberty, and the pursuit of happiness," I shall strenuously contend for the immediate enfranchisement of our slave population.[10]

The abolitionists also invoked self-evident truths of a more explicitly religious nature, such as a belief that slavery violated the Protestant principle that all men are equal before God. Yet they usually did not distinguish religious and secular languages in their antislavery appeals but, rather, fused the two together. For example, the 1833 Declaration of Sentiments of the American Anti-Slavery Society firmly planted the organization "upon the Declaration of our Independence and the truths of Divine Revelation." Earlier the document juggled the Old Testament and John Locke to contend:

> The right to enjoy liberty is inalienable. To invade it is to usurp the prerogative of Jehovah. Every man has a right to his own body—to the products of his own labor—to the protection of law—and to the common advantages of society. It is piracy to buy or steal a native African, and subject him to servitude. Surely, the sin is as great to enslave an American as an African.[11]

On deontological grounds, the abolitionists faced a relatively easy challenge. At least initially, their strategy was "merely" to persuade their fellow Americans to act on what they presumed to be uncontroversial, consensual values.[12] The defenders of slavery confronted a much tougher polemical challenge on deontological grounds. Both Protestant and liberal values, which they also presumed most Americans shared, seemed to clearly condemn the institution. On the face of it, the institution did appear to violate such widely shared American values as that all men were equal before God, that they were endowed by God or nature with inalienable rights to life, liberty, and property in themselves and the fruits of their labors, and that all legitimate forms of government, including, *in extremis*, slavery, were based on the consent of the governed. The defenders of slavery pursued a number of strategies to overturn the strong *prima facie* case against the institution.

At some point, probably every defender of slavery offered a biblical defense of the institution.[13] Proslavery figures emphasized the fact that the ancient Hebrews were slaveholders and had been charged by the God of the Old Testament with enslaving other nations. They also noted that the Jesus of the New Testament did not condemn Roman slavery, which, they all agreed, was a far crueler form of slavery than American slavery. As their trump card, they cited Paul's Letter to Philemon in which the apostle counsels a fugitive slave to return to his master and henceforth dutifully serve him. After presenting a series of such proslavery arguments in his well-publicized letters to the British abolitionist Thomas Clarkson, James Henry Hammond concluded that "American slavery is not only not a sin, but especially commanded by God through Moses, and approved by Christ through His Apostles."[14]

Typically, however, proslavery figures did not rely solely on a biblical defense of slavery. Like their antislavery counterparts, they combined religious and secular arguments.[15] As George McDuffie declared in his widely circulated 1835 gubernatorial message to the South Carolina legislature, "Whether we consult the sacred Scriptures, or the lights of nature and reason, we shall find these truths [to the effect that slavery is the status most conducive to the happiness of the African race] as abundantly apparent, as if written with a sunbeam in the heavens."[16]

With particular reference to the Declaration of Independence, which at the time reflected "the lights of nature and reason" for so many Americans, the defenders of slavery pursued two general strategies to try to blunt its antislavery appeal.[17] They either denied that the Declaration's self-evident truths applied to African Americans, or they claimed that those truths had to be carefully circumscribed in practice.

The first strategy was to exempt African Americans from the Declaration on the grounds that they were not qualified for self-government, in either the individual or the collective sense. In his contribution to the prominent proslavery compilation *Cotton Is King*, David Christy insisted that neither Thomas Jefferson nor the other signers of the Declaration of Independence could "ever have intended to apply its principles to any barbarous or semi-barbarous people, in the sense of admitting them to an equality with themselves in the management of a free government."[18] Yet Christy here, as elsewhere in his essay, does not make clear whether African Americans are exempted from the document because of their "inferior" nature or the "barbarous" environment from which they or their ancestors came.[19] Proslavery figures generally refused to choose between nature and environment because to choose nature would have displayed a racism that seemed fundamentally illiberal and to choose environment would have suggested that Southern whites were, again illiberally, enslaving people that they should have been educating to an equality with themselves.[20] As a result, the proslavery literature leaves the alleged inferiority of black to white Americans "tactfully" ambiguous.[21]

The preferred strategy was to attack the Declaration of Independence on more general grounds by broadening the exceptions from its self-evident truths beyond racial or ethnic criteria. In opposing a 1848 Senate bill to organize Oregon as a free territory, John C. Calhoun refuted the Declaration's central claim that "all men are created equal" by observing that "all men are not created. According to the Bible, only two—a man and a woman—ever were—and of these one was pronounced subordinate to the other. All others have come into the world by being born, and in no sense . . . either free or equal." He went on to expose "the most dangerous of all political errors" that, he thought, often was committed in appealing to the document: the presumption that "those high qualities [of liberty and equality] belonged to man without effort to acquire them, and to all equally alike, regardless of their intellectual and moral condition."[22] The intent of this proslavery strategy, however, was not to reject entirely the Declaration and its underlying liberal principles but to stress that those principles were abstractions that had to be adjusted to existing conditions. When those adjustments were made, proslavery figures were confident that liberal principles would call for the continued existence of racial slavery in the South rather than for its abolition. In his speech on the Oregon bill, Calhoun did not reject "the cause of liberty" but, to the contrary, contended that the campaign "to bestow on all—without regard to their fitness either to acquire or maintain liberty—that unbounded and individual liberty supposed to belong to man in the hypothetical and misnamed state of nature, has done more to retard" that cause "than [have] all other causes combined."[23] Accordingly, the defenders of slavery favored a circumstantial defense of the institution, arguing that under certain conditions and for certain people, liberal principles actually required slavery. This strategy was preferred precisely because it seemed more liberal than the first one. Even though the immediate purpose of the strategy was to defend the continued existence of "black slavery" in the South, the strategy worked only to the extent that it was open to defending other forms of slavery, even "white slavery."[24]

The defenders of slavery also confronted the liberal idea of property rights as the right to oneself and the products of one's labor. Again, the presumption was against the right of one man to hold property rights in another person, but again, proslavery figures had several counterarguments at their disposal. First, they maintained that even if it was unjust for one man to hold property rights in another person, the fact was that under Southern law, men did hold property rights in other men. It followed that Southern slaveholders committed no injustice in holding men in slavery, especially since they were not responsible for the original injustice of enslaving those men.[25] Hammond assured Clarkson that

> the means . . . by which the African race now in this country have been reduced to slavery, cannot affect us, since they are our property, as your land is yours, by inheritance or purchase and prescriptive right. You will say that man cannot hold *property in man*. The answer is, that he can and *actually does* hold property in his fellow all the world over, in a variety of forms, and *has always done so*.[26]

Proslavery figures had a second counterargument at their disposal. They contended that Southern slaveholders did not really hold property rights in men but only rights to the products of their labor. In this sense, Southern slaveholders were analogous to Northern capitalists who held rights to the products of their employees' labor. Unlike free laborers, slaves did not, of course, receive wages in return, but they did receive an equivalent in food, shelter, and clothing. The defenders of slavery argued that Southern slaves actually received a better exchange for their labor than Northern free laborers did, since they were guaranteed a subsistence for life, and free laborers were guaranteed a subsistence only as long as they produced a profit for their employers. In his contribution to *Cotton Is King*, Albert Bledsoe asked rhetorically,

> But may not one man have a right to the labor of another, . . . and yet that other a right to food and raiment, as well as to other things? May not one have a right to the service of another, without annulling or excluding all the rights of that other? . . . If it may exist for one period, why not for a longer, and even for life? If the good of both parties and the good of the whole community requires such a relation and such a right to exist, why should it be deemed so unjust, so iniquitous, so monstrous?[27]

This second counterargument was the preferred one because once again, it seemed the more liberal one. It portrayed slavery in Lockean, contractual terms, as an exchange of liberty for, at a minimum, subsistence, with correlative rights and duties on both sides of the exchange. It had the further advantage of favorably comparing the master-slave relations of the South with the employer-employee relations of the North.[28]

Finally, slavery appeared to violate the liberal idea of consent. As Bledsoe conceded, the institution established "a right to the labor or obedience of another without his consent."[29] Other connotations of consent were, however, more favorable to the proslavery cause. By portraying slavery in contractual terms, the defenders of the institution read the slaves' consent back into the relationship. They could proceed further along the same line of argument by positing the slaves' alleged contentment with and lack of resistance to their status as indicating their tacit consent to it.[30] Proceeding in another direction, proslavery figures could argue that the institution was based on the consent of the governed: the majority of the citizens of the Southern states who, through their representatives in government, continued to enact laws supporting it. In this sense, they could maintain that the abolition of the institution, not its continued existence, would violate the consent of the governed and especially of the slaveholders.[31] As with the liberal ideas of liberty, equality, and property, the defenders of slavery depicted it as an institution that was perfectly defensible on grounds of the liberal idea of consent.

Whether the Southern institution of racial slavery was so defensible was, of course, not a question decided ultimately by its defenders or its opponents. Most Americans probably continued to believe that the institution violated the nation's liberal founding principles. It is hardly surprising therefore that proslavery figures stressed the consequentialist arguments supporting the continued existence of the institution and, even more, the consequentialist arguments opposing its abolition. They enjoyed a stronger polemical position on consequentialist grounds than they did on deontological grounds. At least initially, they thus gravitated toward the "necessary evil" position. They admitted that the institution was evil on deontological grounds but contended that its continued existence was necessary on consequentialist grounds. Jefferson memorably expressed this position in the wake of the Missouri crisis: "We have the wolf by the ears, and we can neither hold him, nor safely let him go. Justice is in one scale, and self-preservation in the other."[32]

Consequentialist Arguments

Proslavery consequentialist arguments themselves seemed to fall into "necessary evil" and "positive good" categories. "Necessary evil" (antiabolitionist) consequentialist arguments catalogued the possible harmful social consequences of the abolition of Southern slavery, and "positive good" (proslavery) consequentialist arguments detailed the possible beneficial social consequences of the continued existence of the institution. Although the "necessary evil" arguments undoubtedly enjoyed more popular support in both the North and the South, the "positive good" arguments contained a greater potential for forging sectional solidarity in the South and converting more moderate proslavery opinion into more radical proslavery opinion. Proslavery figures, accordingly, faced a powerful incentive to offer "positive good" arguments. Over time, their arguments did tend to become more "positive good" in nature, a tendency that included an increasing reluctance on their part to admit that Southern slavery was an evil institution on deontological grounds. The "necessary evil" and "positive good" arguments, nonetheless, merged, and every proslavery figure was certain to offer both types of consequentialist arguments.[33]

In analogizing the continued existence of racial slavery in the South to holding a wolf by the ears, Jefferson took a "necessary evil" position. About the continued existence of the institution, he remarked:

> There is not a man on earth who would sacrifice more than I would to relieve us from this heavy reproach, in any *practicable* way. The cession of that kind property, for so it is misnamed, is a bagatelle which would not cost me a second thought, if, in that way, a general emancipation and *expatriation* could be effected; and, gradually, and with due sacrifices, I think it might be.[34]

Most Americans were much less sanguine about the prospects of African colonization. As a result, proslavery figures attacked abolition on the assumption that it could be accomplished only through other, more drastic means.[35] They then portrayed the consequences of a general emancipation of the Southern slaves in apocalyptic terms. The possibilities included incendiary race wars sparked by embittered freed slaves; a worldwide economic depression prompted by the loss of the millions of dollars that Southern planters had invested in their slaves and the alleged inefficiency of free black labor; and recurrent social unrest fueled by the impossibility of constructing a racially egalitarian society in a postemancipation South, which eventually would subvert republican government in the nation as a whole and require a despotic government in its stead.[36] The upshot of these "worst-case" scenarios was that the slaves would not benefit from their emancipation and everyone else would lose. In particular, the defenders of slavery argued that emancipation would make Southern blacks no more, and perhaps less, free while inevitably making Southern whites less free.[37] Here they invoked the core liberal argument that institutions should be arranged in such a way as to maximize the liberty of the people affected by those institutions. Broadly assuming that liberty was a zero-sum good, they claimed that this "maximum liberty" argument justified the continued existence of racial slavery in the South rather than its abolition. With the dire possibilities of abolition in mind, archcolonizationist Henry Clay insisted:

> The liberty of the descendants of Africa in the United States is incompatible with the safety and liberty of the European descendants. Their slavery forms an exception—an exception resulting from a stern and inexorable necessity—to the general liberty in the United States. We did not originate, nor are we responsible for this necessity. Their liberty, if it were possible, could only be established by violating the incontestable powers of the state, and subverting the union. And beneath the ruins of the union would be buried, sooner or later, the liberty of both races.[38]

These "necessary evil" consequentialist arguments blended into "positive good" ones. In proslavery rhetoric, the negative consequences of abolishing slavery were, in many cases, the positive consequences of its continued existence. Yet the purpose of the "positive good" consequentialist arguments was precisely to present the case for the institution more positively and more aggressively; to offer not merely antiabolitionist but also proslavery arguments. The defenders of slavery attributed to the institution a litany of beneficial consequences for both blacks and whites, the North and the South, the United States and the world. They argued that the Southern slaves were happy, contented, and better off than the free laborers of the American North and western Europe; that the institution was an extremely profitable one for the regional, national, and international economies; and that it provided a stable foundation for republican government in the American South by disenfranchising a lower class composed exclusively of blacks and elevating a middle class composed exclusively of whites.[39] Again, the "positive good" consequentialist arguments converged on the "maximum liberty" argument, this time framed in comparative terms: slave societies are actually freer than free societies. As McDuffie explained,

> But where the menial offices and dependent employments of society are performed by domestic slaves, a class well defined by their color and entirely separated from the political body, the rights of property are perfectly secure, without the establishment of artificial barriers. In a word, the institution of domestic slavery supersedes the necessity of . . . a hereditary system of government.[40]

McDuffie completed this argument with the statement for which his gubernatorial message became famous: "Domestic slavery, therefore, instead of being a political evil, is the corner-stone of our republican edifice."[41]

Proslavery figures also argued that the Southern institution of racial slavery "improved" the African American slaves by exposing them to a "superior" culture. The logical conclusion of this argument was that the institution was preparing the slaves for freedom and, consequently, was perfectly defensible on those liberal grounds. Not surprisingly, proslavery figures carefully hedged this conclusion and placed it well into the future. The only way that they could escape it, however, was by arguing that the African American slaves never would be fully prepared for freedom because as members of an allegedly inferior race, they were naturally incapable of governing themselves or anyone else. Not being eager to make this illiberal move, Chancellor Harper called in his contribution to *Cotton Is King* for the continued existence of racial slavery in the South into the indefinite future on the grounds that "if in the adorable providence of God, at a time and in a manner which we can neither foresee nor conjecture, they [the slaves] are to be rendered capable of freedom . . . they would be prepared for it in the best and most effectual, because in the most natural and gradual manner."[42]

The antislavery side also faced a dual challenge on consequentialist grounds. The abolitionists had to offer both antislavery consequentialist and proabolitionist arguments. They argued that the continued existence of racial slavery in the South really contained a host of harmful, rather than beneficial, social consequences. They also pointed out that all the imagined horrors that abolition would usher in were simply that: imaginary. Still, the abolitionists found themselves on the defensive when presenting the latter type of argument, especially because many people in the North, even many people in the North with antislavery leanings, appeared to accept the validity of at least some of the antiabolitionist arguments presented on the proslavery side. Proabolitionist consequentialist arguments were, furthermore, actually anti-antiabolitionist ones, plagued by all the polemical problems inherent to arguing a double negative. As a result, the abolitionists de-emphasized this type of argument and instead stressed the antislavery consequentialist arguments that chronicled the various social disadvantages associated with the continued existence of the Southern institution of racial slavery.[43]

The crux of the antislavery consequentialist arguments was that the proslavery consequentialist arguments seriously underestimated the negative consequences of the continued existence of Southern slavery for the slaves themselves and seriously overestimated the positive consequences of the continued existence of the institution for everyone else. The abolitionists then engaged in a series of denials of and counterassertions to proslavery consequentialist arguments. The Southern slaves were not happy, contented, and better off than Northern free laborers; they were ruthlessly exploited and brutalized and, unlike the free laborers, had no hope of improving themselves. The slave-labor system was not an extremely profitable one; it was a heavy drain on the regional, national, and international economies. The institution of racial slavery did not provide a stable foundation for republican government in the South; it empowered an imperious "slavocracy" that threatened the liberties of nonslaveholding whites, North and South.[44] The abolitionists were confident that any neutral observer would conclude the "maximum liberty" argument in favor of free societies, not slave societies, even without taking into account the massive deprivations that occurred in the latter to the natural rights and liberties of the slaves themselves.[45] As John Greenleaf Whittier, now known more for his poetry than his abolitionism, declared in "Justice and Expediency," "The slave-holding states are not free. The name of liberty is there, but the spirit is wanting. They do not partake of its invaluable blessings."[46]

The proabolitionist consequentialist arguments were even more defensive. In general, the abolitionists dismissed the "worst-case" scenarios of the proslavery figures as figments of their own prejudiced imaginations. William Jay, son of John Jay and a prominent abolitionist in his own right, sought to quell the widespread fears of immediate emancipation by stating the obvious: the freed slaves would, "like other persons, be subject to the control of law, and responsible for their conduct." In his influential antislavery treatise, *Inquiry into the Character and Tendency of the American Colonization and American Anti-Slavery Societies*, Jay went on to suggest that African Americans were fit for freedom, as fit as they ever would be while they remained in bondage. He ridiculed those who wanted to postpone a general emancipation of the Southern slaves "to wait for this fitness" as resembling "the conduct of the simpleton who loitered by the brook, expecting to pass dry shod, after the water had run off."[47]

More specifically, the proabolitionist arguments of antislavery figures were directed to controverting the antiabolitionist arguments of their proslavery counterparts. Emancipation will not spark race wars in the South; it will improve race relations in the region by dissipating the malice that slaves inevitably feel toward their masters. Emancipation will not prompt a worldwide economic depression; it will boost the economic performance of the South because the freed slaves will work more efficiently as free laborers than they did as slaves. Emancipation will not fuel recurrent social unrest in the South; it will spread the benefits of republican government to a greater portion of the Southern population by erecting a more egalitarian society in the region, both across and within racial lines.[48] Whittier thus concluded "Justice and Expediency" by claiming that things will "go well for America" only when the Southern slaves are emancipated and "under one common sun of political liberty the slaveholding portions of our republic shall no longer sit, like the Egyptians of old, themselves mantled in thick darkness, while all around them is glowing with the blessed light of freedom and equality."[49]

At its deepest level, antislavery rhetoric insisted that liberty was *not* a zero-sum good. A general emancipation of the Southern slaves would increase, not decrease, the aggregate liberty of the people of the South and of the nation as a whole, both blacks and whites. Soon after Maryland formally abolished slavery in the waning months of the Civil War, Frederick Douglass returned to his native state to bury the opposite premise:

> The old doctrine that the slavery of the black, is essential to the freedom of the white race, can maintain itself only in the presence of slavery, where interest and prejudice are the controlling powers, but it . . . belongs to the commercial fallacies exposed long ago by Adam Smith. It stands on a level with the contemptible notion, that every crumb of bread that goes into another man's mouth, is just so much bread taken from mine. Whereas, the rule is in this country of abundant land, the more mouths you have, the more bread you can put into your mouth, . . . As with political economy, so with civil and political rights. The more men you make free, the more freedom is strengthened.[50]

But the abolitionists still confronted the predicament that many Americans genuinely seemed to fear the "worst-case" scenarios that proslavery figures crafted of a racially embattled postemancipation South. Nor did many Americans seem to embrace the abolitionists' own "best-case" scenarios of a racially egalitarian postemancipation South.[51] These Americans took the position that Southern slavery was, at least for the foreseeable future, a necessary evil because they found the proslavery consequentialist arguments equally as compelling as the antislavery deontological arguments. In seeking to persuade these "middle" Americans to adopt stronger antislavery positions, the abolitionists increasingly turned to a third type of argument.

Contextualist Arguments

Over time, the abolitionists learned that antislavery contextualist arguments could be extremely effective in persuading Northern moderates to adopt stronger antislavery positions. Northern moderates and radical abolitionists could coalesce around antislavery contextualist arguments, since they appealed to values that both groups shared besides a common (though far from equally salient) antislavery disposition. Indeed, the great virtue of contextualist arguments was that they connected that disposition to widely shared liberal, Protestant, and nationalist values by portraying the continued existence of racial slavery in the South as a threat to those values. The abolitionists developed, in particular, three antislavery contextualist arguments: the "American exemplar," "human progress," and "house divided" arguments.

The "American exemplar" argument invoked the national faith that the United States was "a city on the hill" with a special mission in history to spread the blessings of its uniquely liberal institutions to other parts of the world. In the hands of the abolitionists, the argument became that the continued presence of such an illiberal institution as racial slavery on American soil undermined that mission and exposed Americans as hypocrites. The Declaration of Sentiments of the American Anti-Slavery Society called for immediate abolition in order "to wipe out the foulest stain which rests upon our national escutcheon." Whittier echoed that language in condemning slavery as "the stain on our own escutcheon." He demanded immediate abolition so that "political, religious, and legal hypocrisy should no longer cover with loathsome leprosy the features of American freedom."[52]

According to the "American exemplar" argument, the evils of the Southern institution of racial slavery were partly contextualist. However evil the institution may have been on deontological and consequentialist grounds, it was worse on contextualist grounds. Racial slavery would not have been as culpable in another context, in another nation without a world-historic mission for liberty. The "American exemplar" argument also cloaked the antislavery position with the liberal, Protestant, and nationalist values that most Americans shared. The original Puritan sense of mission in coming to a new world had been increasingly secularized over time. Nevertheless, the American sense of mission still retained much of its initial religious fervor, and even as originally defined, it included an important liberal component. The Puritans had come to a new world in search of both religious and political liberty.[53] The American sense of mission also was infused with a nationalistic fervor. Only one nation—the United States—had a world-historic mission to spread the blessings of its institutions around the world. Finally, the "American exemplar" argument gained strength from the way that it complemented the "human progress" and "house divided" arguments. The American mission placed the nation at the forefront of historical and transhistorical progress; disunion would abort that mission.

The "human progress" argument tapped into prevailing beliefs in the progressive nature of history.[54] The abolitionists fashioned those beliefs into a powerful argument against the continued presence of racial slavery on American soil by contending that the institution impeded progress and yet was doomed by the further march of progress. It was a dying institution. It was also an anachronistic institution. It was an institution that may have been appropriate to earlier, more benighted ages but that was not appropriate to, and could not long survive in, this new age of enlightenment. The "human progress" argument fortified the abolitionists to undertake a campaign against such a strongly entrenched institution as the Southern institution of racial slavery and buttressed their confidence in the ultimate victory of their cause. Through it, they sought to overcome resistance to their cause by dismissing such resistance as futile. In *The Sin of Slavery and Its Remedy*, Elizur Wright attempted to counter popular notions that the antislavery crusade was quixotic. To the contrary, he expected personally, "with God's good help, to hear the trumpet of the world's jubilee announcing that the *last fetter* has been knocked off from the heel of the *last slave*."[55]

Along with many other abolitionists, Wright was clearly inspired by the religious millennialism of the Second Great Awakening. This religious millennialism was reflected in the "human progress" argument. As the Declaration of Sentiments of the American Anti-Slavery Society sermonized,

> Our trust for victory is solely in God. We may be personally defeated, but our principles never! Truth, Justice, Reason, Humanity, must and will gloriously triumph. Already a host is coming up to the help of the Lord against the mighty, and the prospect before us is full of encouragement.[56]

The abolitionists, however, did not place their trust solely in God. Their religious millennialism was intertwined with a more secular belief in inevitable progress toward universal liberty. This progressive liberalism also was reflected in the "human progress" argument. Whittier's "Justice and Expediency" surmised that the Southern slaveholders "must know that the present state of things cannot long continue . . . [because] there is a love of liberty which the scourge cannot eradicate."[57] American nationalism was a final ingredient in the "human progress" argument. Like the "American exemplar" argument, it singled out the United States as the harbinger of a future world of liberty and equality for all. The "house divided" argument exaggerated the nationalistic tendencies of the antislavery movement, although it sometimes did so in peculiar ways.

Long before Abraham Lincoln etched the "house divided" argument into the national consciousness during his unsuccessful 1858 Senate campaign to unseat Stephen A. Douglas, the abolitionists had been promulgating the argument. In his 1834 "Lectures on Slavery and Its Remedy," Amos Phelps predicted that

> liberty and slavery are, from their nature, discordant elements. They can never harmonize. They can never, for any length of time, co-exist in the same political fabric. Sooner or later they will fly asunder. "Every kingdom divided against itself is brought to desolation, and every city or house divided against itself shall not stand."[58]

The "house divided" argument was probably the most effective of the antislavery contextualist arguments because it appealed so directly to American nationalism. The argument implied that the conjunction of racial slavery (for blacks) and liberal institutions (for whites) in the same nation was extremely volatile and might well destroy the nation. It also implied that racial slavery would not be as deleterious in another nation where it was more consistent with the broader institutional context and where it therefore would not threaten to destroy the nation. The "house divided" argument was a classic slippery-slope argument. It defined slavery as a cancer on the nation's liberal body politic.

For some abolitionists, the remedy was uniting the house against slavery and excising the cancer from the South. For other abolitionists, it was razing the house and quarantining the cancer to the South.[59] Whatever conclusion they chose, they used the "house divided" argument to link the fate of Southern slavery to the fate of the union. The abolitionists learned, often to their great chagrin, that more Americans cared about the latter than about the former. They also came to realize that whether or not the institution could be abolished outside the union, it would be abolished only within the union.[60]

The abolitionists thus realized that the key to the success of their movement was maintaining that the preservation of the union required dismantling Southern slavery. As early as 1834, Phelps argued that the continued existence of the institution "will originate collisions without end, and work out certain, if not speedy destruction to the Union and the nation."[61] The abolitionists increasingly turned to the "house divided" argument as a way of converting Northern moderates to the "weak" antislavery position that the safety of the union demanded the end of racial slavery in the South. This position was one on which Northern moderates and radical abolitionists could agree.[62] The "house divided" argument obviously appealed to American nationalism. But to the extent that American nationalism had assumed a missionary zeal by the antebellum period, the argument also appealed to consensual Protestant and liberal values. Disunion would not have seemed so horrible at the time to so many Americans if they had not believed that their nation was a city on the hill with a world-historic mission to spread the blessings of its uniquely liberal institutions to other parts of the world.

The antislavery contextualist arguments, again, placed proslavery figures in a defensive position. Their basic response was to deny, not affirm. Proslavery figures denied that the continued existence of racial slavery in the South impaired the American exemplar. Nor, according to them, did it obviate human progress or create a house divided. They also denied the main assumption of the antislavery contextualist arguments: that the institution of racial slavery was an illiberal one in its effects on the people of the South, black or white. Yet even in these negative forms, proslavery contextualist arguments could serve as a common rallying point for Southern proslavery figures and Southern moderates. In denying the antislavery contextualist arguments, the proslavery contextualist arguments denied that the South was the illiberal, backward, and parochial region of the country that the antislavery contextualist arguments asserted it to be.

Proslavery contextualist arguments also took more positive forms that associated proslavery sentiments more closely with consensual liberal, Protestant, and nationalist values. As such, they could help Southern proslavery figures pressure Southern moderates into adopting stronger proslavery positions. In their more positive forms, the proslavery contextualist arguments insisted that the abolition of the Southern institution of racial slavery, not its continued existence, was the real threat to the fulfillment of the American mission, the continuation of human progress, and the preservation of the union.

Instead of contending that Southern slavery was holding back the American mission, proslavery figures argued that Southern slaveholders were the principal carriers of that mission. As McDuffie observed,

> More than a half a century ago, one of the most enlightened statesmen who ever illustrated the parliamentary annals of Great Britain [Edmund Burke] . . . ascribed the high and indomitable spirit of liberty which distinguished the Southern Colonies, to the existence of domestic slavery; referring to the example of the free states of antiquity as a confirmation of his theory. Since those colonies have become independent States, they have amply sustained the glory of their primitive character. . . . impartial history will ratify, that the principles of rational liberty are not less thoroughly understood, and have been more vigilantly, resolutely and effectively defended against all the encroachments of power, by the slaveholding States, than by any other members of the confederacy.[63]

Here McDuffie brushed aside the hostile relationship between the spirits of slavery and liberty that was the central premise of the antislavery version of the "American exemplar" argument. He went on to accuse the abolitionists themselves of being the greatest threats to the fulfillment of the nation's world-historic mission for liberty in seeking to eradicate the institution on which its own spirit of liberty rested, at least in the South. He concluded that he "would as soon open a negotiation for selling the liberty of the State at once, as for making any stipulations for the ultimate emancipation of our slaves."[64]

Similarly, proslavery figures argued that the Southern institution of racial slavery was not retarding progress but, rather, was propelling it. Their version of the "human progress" argument was fourfold. First, the institution of slavery had been, in general, a civilizing force in history, elevating men from more primitive states of existence by permitting more labor-intensive modes of production. Second, the institution of racial slavery had meant, in particular, progress for Africans by exposing them to allegedly more advanced civilizations. Third, the institution had meant progress for everyone else by producing a higher standard of living and creating the background conditions for more personal freedom than would have been possible in its absence. Fourth, any stable, progressive society relied on the presence of protective institutions like slavery for its less fortunate members, so that broadly understood, slavery was not a dying institution but a universal one.[65] From this exalted perspective, Harper could proclaim that the defense of Southern slavery was "the defense of civilization," and Hammond could declare that the Southern slaveholders "stand in the broadest light of the knowledge, civilization, and improvement of the age."[66]

In placing slavery on the side of progress, the defenders of the institution adopted the mantle of progressive liberalism while relegating the abolitionists to the side of regress. Speaking in support of a series of proslavery resolutions he had introduced in the United States Senate, Calhoun warned:

> Experience had shown that the existing relation between them [the two races in the South] secured the peace and happiness of both. Each had improved; the inferior greatly; so much so, that it had attained a degree of civilization never before attained by the black race in any age or country. Under no other relation could they co-exist together. To destroy it was to involve a whole region in slaughter, carnage, and desolation; and, come what will, we must defend and preserve it.[67]

This warning suggests how the defenders of slavery rephrased the "house divided" argument. They maintained that the institution had not created a house divided; Northern agitation against the institution had. Remove the latter, they claimed, and the union could endure indefinitely half free and half slave. As Calhoun had predicted in an earlier Senate speech defending a gag rule on abolitionist petitions to Congress, "abolition and the Union cannot co-exist. As the friend of the Union I openly proclaim it,—and the sooner it is known the better."[68] In their incessant attacks on the abolitionists, Calhoun and other proslavery figures thus presented themselves not only as the true defenders of Southern slavery but also as the true defenders of the union who were especially vigilant against whatever threatened it.[69]

Proslavery figures also denied the "house divided" argument. If, as they contended, the North and the South merely solved their mutual problem of obtaining a sufficient supply of labor in different, but equally liberal, ways, then the union was not really a house divided against itself. As George Fitzhugh quipped in *Cannibals All*, "If, Mr. Garrison, this be the only difficulty to be adjusted between North and South, we are sure that your little pet, Disunion, 'living will linger, and lingering will die.'"[70]

The "house divided" argument was, however, asymmetrical. Even though the belief that the continued existence of racial slavery in the South was a necessary evil, or worse, was not universal in the antebellum United States, it was pervasive. The nation's liberal founding principles were *prima facie* antislavery. The abolitionists could well believe that the house would unite against slavery. The defenders of the institution could not muster the same confidence that the house would unite for the institution, although they might well believe that it would unite against abolitionism.[71] This asymmetry set in motion the course of events that led to disunion, civil war, and emancipation.

Conclusion

This course of events appears to have been a straightforward projection of the "house divided" argument or, rather, of two different versions of the argument. The majority in the North eventually accepted the antislavery version of the argument, a development signaled by Lincoln's use of the argument and his subsequent election as president of the United States on the strength of a highly sectional vote. Northern moderates came to believe that the Southern institution of racial slavery had created a house divided that could no longer stand and that the only alternative was to unite the house against the institution.[72] Conversely, the majority in the South accepted the proslavery version of the argument. Southern moderates came to believe that Northern agitation against the Southern institution of racial slavery had created a house divided that could no longer stand. They viewed Lincoln's election as the triumph of an incendiary spirit of abolitionism in the North and cited his use of the "house divided" argument as evidence for their point of view.[73] They thus were left with the unpalatable alternative of physically dividing the house. The people of the South supported this alternative very reluctantly because of their own nationalism, the same nationalism that induced the people of the North to resist Southern secession.[74]

In this dualistic way, the "house divided" argument became a self-fulfilling prophecy. The escalation of sectional rhetoric in the 1850s produced the very situation that this rhetoric predicted would occur if certain specified steps were not taken to prevent it. The "exit strategies" of the antislavery and proslavery movements were, however, unsuccessful because they were mutually antagonistic. Disunion followed. It was a direct result of the different ways that different groups of Americans had interpreted and concluded the "house divided" argument. Moreover, the fact that liberal ideas undergirded each of the various manifestations of the argument did not temper the sectional conflict over the fate of Southern slavery because those ideas themselves were subject to different interpretations and conclusions.

For the abolitionists, liberal ideas defined slavery as an unnecessary evil, an illiberal institution that created a house divided in the context of the nation's predominant liberal institutions. They argued that the institution could be abolished with overwhelmingly positive effects on the practical liberties of the vast majority of Americans. For the defenders of slavery, liberal ideas defined the institution as a positive good, an institution that did not create a house divided, since it—no less and perhaps more than the nation's other institutions—positively affected the practical liberties of the vast majority of Americans. They warned that the institution could not be abolished without serious negative effects on those liberties. For both groups, as well as for most other Americans at the time, liberal ideas inspired a missionary nationalism that strengthened their reluctance to physically divide the house and their resistance to accept that result once it occurred. In fact, the underlying dynamics of the antebellum debate over the fate of Southern slavery—the primacy of liberal arguments; the increasing use of such arguments over time; and the corresponding shift to contextualist arguments, especially to the "house divided" argument—are precisely the dynamics one would expect if a liberal consensus had existed in the antebellum United States.

The rest of this book traces these dynamics. Before returning to the question of civil-war causation in the final chapter of the book, I analyze the antislavery and proslavery arguments of six major participants in the antebellum debate over the continued existence of racial slavery in the American South to show how their arguments changed over time, either individually or in comparison to one another. The next four chapters further delineate two different forms of liberalism: an antislavery liberalism that envisioned the progressive extension of equal rights and liberties to all Americans and a proslavery liberalism that redefined such progress as a declension toward the social anarchy of a Lockean or, even more, Hobbesian state of nature.

Part II

3

Child, Douglass, and Antislavery Liberalism

The antislavery movement in the antebellum North attempted to launch a process of institutional change. The abolitionists worked to destroy one institution—Southern slavery—and to replace it with another set of institutions—universal male citizenship, equal liberty under law, and competitive labor markets. They viewed these identifiably liberal institutions as the prevailing institutions of their section of the country.[1]

The antislavery movement did lead to institutional change in the desired direction. But it did not lead to as much institutional change as the abolitionists desired, nor did the abolitionists themselves concentrate on the abolition of Southern slavery as a process of institutional change. Instead, they concentrated on the identifiably liberal principles of liberty, equality, and consent that, to them, clearly condemned Southern slavery and supported the alternative institutions of the North.

The abolitionists have been roundly criticized for not focusing on the abolition of Southern slavery as a process of institutional change and, in particular, for not focusing on that process as a process that required considerable public discussion of the precise nature of the transition from racial slavery to more racially egalitarian, liberal institutions in the South.[2] Instead, they spoke as if condemning racial slavery were sufficient to abolish the institution and as if the demise of the institution would automatically usher in the desired set of new institutions. This "failure" helps explain why it took a civil war to abolish racial slavery in the South. It also helps explain the abortive nature of Reconstruction.

The typical response to this critique is that for tactical reasons, the abolitionists avoided publicly discussing the abolition of Southern slavery as a process of institutional change.[3] For them to have openly debated all the practical barriers to abolishing racial slavery and introducing more racially egalitarian, liberal institutions in the South would have weakened their popular appeal, which was not very strong in the first place, precisely because most Americans considered those barriers to be insurmountable. The alternative strategy allowed the abolitionists to broaden their appeal. The growth of the antislavery appeal, in turn, helps explain both the very fact of civil war and its specific character. Furthermore, despite its abortive nature, Reconstruction did liberalize the South, as, lest we forget, it did the North with the passage of the Fourteenth and Fifteenth Amendments.

History supports both sides of this dispute. Southern slavery was abolished, but it did require a civil war to emancipate the Southern slaves; racial slavery was replaced by more racially egalitarian, liberal institutions in the South, but even today, that process of liberalization is still incomplete in both the South and North.[4]

This particular historiographical dispute, however, overlooks the way that the abolitionists' view of institutional change was rooted in both their reform strategy and their philosophy of history. They interpreted history as the progressive unfolding of liberal principles and as inevitable progress toward liberal institutions. This progressive-liberal philosophy discouraged concrete thinking about institutional change. Throughout the nation's history, Americans, and American reform movements, have tended to neglect the processes of institutional change because they subscribed to this same philosophy of history. But the abolitionists seemed to epitomize that tendency and philosophy. Their progressive liberalism emboldened them to attack publicly an extremely well entrenched institution as a fundamentally illiberal institution that stood in the way of liberal progress and yet would be swept aside by it. When the abolitionists attacked Southern slavery on such grounds, they went beyond merely condemning the institution on the basis of liberal principles. They also provided assurance of its eventual abolition and of the kind of institutions that would replace it. Over time, the abolitionists increasingly turned to antislavery arguments that highlighted their progressive liberalism.[5]

This tactic was part of a general shift from deontological and consequentialist antislavery arguments to contextualist ones. The "American exemplar," "human progress," and "house divided" arguments each were anchored in progressive liberalism, and each linked antislavery sentiments to consensual American values. They singled out the United States as the exemplary liberal society, as the harbinger of a more liberal future, and as a union dedicated to liberty. The continued existence of racial slavery in the South called all those values into question. By the late 1850s, the abolitionist crusade thus had redirected itself from "pure" antislavery arguments that stressed the intrinsic evils and most immediate harms of Southern slavery to "impure" antislavery arguments that traced the less obvious secondary and tertiary effects of the institution on, in particular, the preservation of the union.

This shift to contextualist arguments provided the abolitionists with a strategy for holding their movement together, gaining broader support, and quieting public skepticism about the feasibility of their ultimate goal. All abolitionists could agree with the contextualist arguments that both questioned the exemplariness and permanence of a nation divided between slavery and freedom and claimed that the future belonged to the latter, because those arguments directly appealed to their shared progressive liberalism. The abolitionists advanced the "American exemplar," "human progress," and "house divided" arguments as early as 1833, at the very beginning of their movement. As they divided and subdivided over such issues as women's rights, clerical opposition to their cause, the use of violent means to end slavery, disunion, and the efficacy of political party organization—issues that exposed serious tactical differences among them on deontological and consequentialist grounds—the abolitionists could always return to contextualist arguments to reestablish a measure of unity among themselves.[6] Relative to deontological and consequentialist arguments, contextualist arguments also more effectively curried public favor because they appealed to states of affairs that most Americans, at least in the North, seemed to care more about than they did about the fate of Southern slavery per se. The abolitionists finally found that they could use contextualist arguments to dispel public doubts about the feasibility of abolishing the institution without committing themselves to any contentious blueprint for institutional change. Since according to their versions of the "American exemplar," "human progress," and "house divided" arguments, change was inevitable and could occur in only one direction, they felt free to avoid discussing troublesome details about the transition from racial slavery to racial equality.[7] The growing threat of the physical division of the house in the 1850s and then its actual division during the secession winter of 1860–61 completed the shift to contextualist arguments.

In this and the next chapter, I analyze several important pieces of antislavery rhetoric dating from 1833 to 1861 to support the preceding interpretation of the abolitionists as progressive liberals.[8] The secondary literature on the antislavery movement is superior in quality to that on the proslavery movement. Ronald Walters's *Antislavery Appeal* is an excellent survey of abolitionist thought in the antebellum United States, and moving backward in time, David Brion Davis's *Problem of Slavery in Western Culture* expertly maps the relation between the Enlightenment and the rise of antislavery thought in early-modern Europe. Following Davis's lead, much of the secondary literature on the American antislavery movement assumes that the abolitionists were firmly committed to liberal institutions and principles.[9] Nevertheless, the case for antislavery liberalism has yet to be presented in depth or detail. While examining that case, I look at the antislavery arguments of three prominent abolitionists not to show that every argument they made was liberal but, rather, to show that their fundamental arguments were liberal. As discussed in chapter 1, I do not believe that either the antislavery or the proslavery movements were exclusively or explicitly liberal. Rather, the antislavery and proslavery liberalisms that I reveal in the following chapters were more a matter of rhetorical emphasis than of systematic philosophy and more a matter of historical interpretation than of conscious intent. That, however, does not make these liberalisms any less real, only less obvious.[10]

In this chapter, I start presenting the case for antislavery liberalism with Lydia Maria Child's *An Appeal in Favor of That Class of Americans Called Africans*. Child's *Appeal* was originally published in 1833, during the infancy of the abolitionist movement. The purpose of her book was to present all the antislavery arguments to a broader public in order to explain and justify the new Garrison abolitionism. Her book appeared before the abolitionists shifted their attention from converting the South to converting the North to their cause and before they splintered into various "circles." Child's *Appeal* was thus less concerned with questions of abolitionist unity and with targeting specific arguments to specific audiences than later antislavery works would be.[11] I next consider one of those later antislavery works, Frederick Douglass's "What to the Slave Is the Fourth of July?" This unusual Fourth of July oration was delivered in 1852 in Rochester, New York. By 1852, the abolitionist movement had experienced its initial failure to convert the South by means of moral suasion, such as in Child's *Appeal.* The movement also had undergone a number of divisions and subdivisions over the years. Douglass had become embroiled in this factionalization, and his speech reflects a profound concern for abolitionist unity. His antislavery arguments are less diffuse than Child's and targeted to a more specific, Northern audience.[12]

In chapter 4, I adopt a somewhat different methodology to trace the rhetorical dynamics of the abolitionist movement. I look at several of Wendell Phillips's major antislavery writings and speeches from 1837 to 1861 to demonstrate, on a personal level, how his antislavery arguments changed over time, specifically how they became more liberal as well as more contextualist and "impure." In contrast to Child and Douglass, Phillips remained a loyal member of the Garrison circle throughout this period, and as its chief strategist, he was at the center of its various disputes with other abolitionist factions.[13] But despite the many differences among these three prominent abolitionists—in timing, argument, and tactics as well as personal background—they each emerged as a powerful spokesperson for the progressive-liberal philosophy that united the antislavery crusade.[14]

Lydia Maria Child

Lydia Maria Child's *An Appeal in Favor of That Class of Americans Called Africans* is peculiar in that it takes an uncompromising deontological stance in favor of abolishing slavery, regardless of the consequences to American society or the abolitionists themselves, while remaining preoccupied with countering the consequentialist arguments opposing that course of action. The tone of Child's *Appeal* was strongly influenced by its timing, in both its antislavery "purity" and its concern with rebutting the antiabolitionist arguments. Child, however, also advances several contextualist arguments against the continued existence of the Southern institution of racial slavery that depict the institution as a cancer on the nation's liberal body politic.

The Wrong of Slavery

The basic premise of Child's *Appeal* is the equal humanity of the African American slaves (p. 148).[15] On the basis of that premise, the Southern institution of racial slavery can be seen to violate a number of deontological truths. Child combines religious and secular principles in her antislavery creed without any apparent inconsistency between them. She suggests that the Bible and the Declaration of Independence could be considered equally incendiary tracts in the South because of their antislavery teachings (p. 67). She also reproaches Northern whites for transgressing both the Golden Rule and republicanism in their discriminatory treatment of free blacks (pp. 200–1).[16]

In her most extended analysis of the wrong of slavery, Child reveals her underlying liberal philosophy. She claims that the institution is wrong because "the personal liberty of one man can never be the property of another" (p. 99). In true Lockean fashion, she goes on to explain that property rights are based on consent but that slavery, by definition, is based on force. She concludes this analysis by invoking religious sanction against the institution, although in a way perfectly consistent with the teachings of *The Second Treatise*: "Personal freedom is the birthright of every human being. God himself made it the first great law of creation; and no human enactment can render it null and void" (pp. 99–100; see also pp. 74–75, 138, 194, 209).

The most distinctive feature of Child's antislavery creed, however, is not its underlying liberal philosophy but its professed deontological purity. She continually advises her readers to act according to their conscience, regardless of the consequences to themselves or others. She even confesses to having placated her own doubts about publishing a book that she expects to displease "all classes" by telling herself that "worldly considerations should never stifle the voice of conscience" (p. 216). Most memorably, she declares: "'Duties are ours; events are God's'" (p. 213; see also pp. 99, 142, 207).[17]

But Child's advice is not pegged on any disjunction between deontological and consequentialist ethics. Quite the contrary; she believes that performing one's duty on deontological grounds always is useful on consequentialist grounds. Immediately after proclaiming that "duties are ours; events are God's," Child adds that "policy, with all her cunning, can devise no rule so safe, salutary, and effective, as this simple maxim" (p. 213). Then in the next paragraph, she observes that "to 'love our neighbor as ourselves,' is, after all, the shrewdest way of doing business" (p. 213; see also pp. 32, 83–84). The bulk of her *Appeal* is devoted to demonstrating that performing one's duty in personally opposing the continued existence of racial slavery in the South in whatever way one can is the safest and most expedient course of action for everyone concerned.[18] Child endorses the position of Garrison's (and her husband's) newly formed New England Anti-Slavery Society that "immediate emancipation is the only just course, and the only safe policy" (p. 138).

The Harm of Slavery

Almost every topic Child discusses in the *Appeal* touches on what the safest and most expedient policy is to pursue toward the Southern institution of racial slavery. For instance, her long defense in chapters 6 and 7 of African American slaves' intellectual and moral character rests on the argument that abolishing the institution is a safe policy because the freed slaves will become law-abiding citizens and not, as widely assumed, a source of political instability in the South. Similarly, her exposé of the influence of the institution on American politics in chapter 4 rests on the argument that *not* abolishing the institution is an unsafe policy because a corrupt Southern slavocracy will continue to be a source of political instability in the federal government. Finally, her comparison of the relative advantages of free labor and slave labor in chapter 3 rests on the argument that abolishing the latter is an expedient policy because the former is the more profitable economic system for the South, the North, and the nation as a whole.

Child's *Appeal* is, therefore, full of consequentialist arguments. These consequentialist arguments can be divided into three types: (1) arguments that discount the dangers of abolishing Southern slavery (anti-antiabolitionist); (2) arguments that highlight the dangers of not abolishing the institution (antislavery); and (3) arguments that indicate how abolishing the institution, in contrast to not abolishing it, will produce the greatest happiness for the greatest number of Americans (proabolitionist).

When Child explicitly discusses the possibility of a safe emancipation, she directly confronts the Southern "necessary evil" position that a general emancipation of the Southern slaves, while demanded by justice, would lead to racial violence.[19] Child turns to history to disprove this position. She chronicles how slave emancipations in other parts of the world have not led to racial violence and shows that in fact, the freed slaves have become, with few exceptions, law-abiding members of their new societies (pp. 84–95). She caps this discussion with the case of the American North, where the slaves "were manumitted without bloodshed, and there was no trouble in making free colored laborers obey the law" (p. 95).[20] She then acknowledges that abolishing slavery presents more formidable problems in the American South because of its much larger slave population (pp. 95–96). But she reminds Southern whites that because those problems are becoming more formidable every year as their slave population continues to grow, they should act now to free their slaves before their slave population becomes too large to be safely emancipated (p. 96).[21] She also reminds them that their slaves will be freed into an existing system of law and feigns disbelief at their apparent lack of confidence in the ability of their own legal system to maintain social order even if their slaves are as prone to violence as they seem to think they are (p. 96).[22] At this point, Child commends various schemes of gradual emancipation in which slaves work to earn their freedom, presumably as a safer policy than immediate emancipation (pp. 97–100). Later in the book, though, she endorses immediate emancipation as a safe (and presumably more just) policy precisely because it is less likely to cause racial unrest than are any of the other policy options (pp. 138–40). She also points out that drawing up concrete plans of emancipation is, in any case, the province of Southern legislators, not Northern abolitionists (pp. 144–45).[23]

Child strikes a more positive note in answering the objection that even if the Southern slaves could be safely freed, they still could not live together as equals with other Americans but would remain a black underclass to the white majority. Her answer to this objection takes two tracks. First, as we have seen, she states that blacks are not inherently inferior to whites. Second, she argues that white prejudices against blacks are not immutable. Child offers this second argument while attacking the American Colonization Society because she considers the contrary view the most generous reason for supporting efforts to colonize African Americans. In rebuttal, she emphasizes four points which, she believes, distinguish abolitionists from colonizationists: (1) a racially egalitarian society is possible (p. 132); (2) racial prejudices are tractable (p. 133); (3) white prejudices against blacks are rooted in racial slavery, and once the institution is abolished, those prejudices should wane (p. 134); and (4) it is the duty of all Americans to overcome whatever racial prejudices they may harbor (pp. 134–35), since it is unbecoming of Christians to "allow a prejudice so absurd to prevent the improvement of a large portion of the human race, and interfere with what all civilized nations consider the most common rights of mankind" (p. 135). These points suggest that a general emancipation of the Southern slaves is safe in the sense that it will not require a violent, geographic separation of the black and white races, either inside or outside the South.[24]

Child also inverts the objections to the safety of abolishing Southern slavery. However dangerous a general emancipation of the Southern slaves might be, the continued existence of the institution would be more so. In defending the New England Anti-Slavery Society's commitment to immediate emancipation, she remarks:

> That emancipation has in several instances been effected with safety has been already shown. But allowing that there is some danger in discontinuing slavery, is there not likewise danger in continuing it? In one case, the danger, if there were any, would soon be subdued; in the other, it is continually increasing. (P. 140)

The second type of consequentialist argument in Child's *Appeal* thus emphasizes the dangers of *not* abolishing Southern slavery. She argues that the continued existence of the institution is much more likely to create racial strife than abolishing the institution would be, because of the pent-up potential for slave insurrections under the status quo. She reports that the members of the New England Anti-Slavery Society support "universal emancipation, because they believe it is the only way to *prevent* insurrections" (p. 142; see also pp. 84, 138).[25] She also observes that the continued existence of Southern slavery is much more likely to fracture the union than abolishing the institution would be, because of the increasingly clashing interests of the free and slave states under the status quo. Near the end of the *Appeal*, Child voices this "house divided" argument in a particularly portentous form:

> If Southern politicians are determined to make a Siamese question of this also—if they insist that the Union shall not exist without slavery—it can only be said that they join two things, which have no affinity with each other, and which cannot permanently exist together. They chain the living and vigorous to the diseased and dying; and the former will assuredly

perish in the infected neighborhood. (P. 212; see also pp. 107–8, 111, 119, 146)

Child, however, contends not only that a general emancipation of the Southern slaves would be safe, and safer than the alternative, but also that it would be expedient, and more expedient than the alternative. Generally, this third type of consequentialist argument takes a negative thrust in her *Appeal.* Judged by its consequences, the continued existence of racial slavery in the South is *not* in the greatest happiness of the greatest number of Americans. Child's reasoning here is clearly utilitarian.[26] She insists that any fair-minded utilitarian calculus can, at best, prove that the continued existence of racial slavery in the South is in the interests of the few slaveholders, not the many nonslaveholders. She asks: "Must the country languish and die, that the slaveholder may flourish? Shall all interest be subservient to one?—all rights subordinate to those of the slaveholder? Has not the mechanic—have not the middle classes their rights?—rights incompatible with the existence of slavery?" (p. 81; see also pp. 31, 96).

According to Child, proslavery utilitarian calculuses ignore, in particular, the interests of the slaves. The members of the New England Anti-Slavery Society, however, believe that "it is unfair that all arguments on this subject should be founded on the convenience and safety of the master alone. They wish to see the white man's claims have their due weight; but they insist that the negro's rights ought not to be thrown out of the balance" (p. 143; see also pp. 108, 141). In Child's own utilitarian calculus, the Southern institution of racial slavery receives no positive marks. She believes that the institution "rests on the mere *appearance* of present expediency; while, in fact, all its tendencies, individual and national, present and remote, are highly injurious to the true interests of the country" (p. 31). She views the institution as unique among great evils in being "*all* evil"; "almost all [other great] evils" yield "*some* good results" (p. 9). She also attributes a variety of more concrete evils to the institution.

> The Southern states, according to their own evidence, are impoverished by it; a great amount of wretchedness and crime inevitably follows in its train; the prosperity of the North is continually checked by it; it promotes feelings of rivalry between the states; it separates our interests; makes our councils discordant; threatens the destruction of our government; and disgraces us in the eyes of the world. (P. 126)

In further specifying the evils of Southern slavery, Child hardly needs to describe its adverse effects on the Southern slaves. It is enough for her to ridicule the slaveholders' "happy slave" argument "that their benevolence is perfectly quixotic—that the negroes are happy and contented, and have no desire to change their lot" (p. 210; see also pp. 140–41, 210).[27] It is more important for her to describe its adverse effects on the slaveholders themselves because of the common assumption that they, at least, benefit from the institution. Her counterargument emphasizes the corrupting influences of the institution on the slaveholders, that "in the habit of slavery are concentrated the strongest evils of human nature—vanity, pride, love of power, licentiousness, and indolence" (p. 101). Child also discusses the corrupting influences of the institution on the slaveholders at some length in the first chapter of her book, arguing that the institution encourages the slaveholders to hold labor in contempt as fit only for black slaves (pp. 22–23), to prostitute their female slaves (pp. 23–24), and to become inured to physical cruelty through the brutalities they commit routinely on all their slaves (pp. 24–30).[28] In sum, the harmful moral effects of the institution on the slaveholders outweigh any economic benefits they might accrue from it.

But even those economic benefits appear illusory to Child. She believes not only that the aggregate economic effects of Southern slavery are detrimental to national (as well as regional) prosperity but also that the slaveholders themselves are economically disadvantaged by the institution. She offers this argument in the course of asserting the superiority of free labor to slave labor; a discussion that reveals her deep commitment to the central tenets of liberal economics and the North's emerging capitalist order.[29]

Child opens this discussion by invoking the authority of political economists who "found their systems on those broad and general principles, the application of which has been proved by reason and experience to produce the greatest possible happiness to the greatest number of people" (p. 76). She notes that they, "without exception, prefer free labor to slave labor" (p. 76). She herself is convinced that free labor is cheaper to the employer because of the higher fixed costs of slave labor and the lack of incentive it offers "employees" to work efficiently (pp. 76–77).[30] She contends that most Southern whites, at least those of the "necessary evil" persuasion, acknowledge the superiority of free labor to slave labor (pp. 77–80). She closes the discussion by claiming that the many advantages of free labor over slave labor are obvious to anyone who has traveled in both sections of the United States and compared "the happiness and contentment which prevails throughout the [Northern] country" to "the division, discontent, indolence, and poverty of the Southern country" (p. 80; see also pp. 111, 120, 212).[31]

Child offers two additional consequentialist arguments against the continued existence of racial slavery in the South that further reveal her underlying liberal, free-market ideology. The first refers to the negative consequences of the institution in promoting sectional discord. These consequences can be lumped under the "house divided" argument. Even if the continued existence of the institution is safe in the sense that it does not precipitate disunion or civil war, it still is expedient in diverting public attention and energy from promoting economic growth (pp. 107–8, 111, 114, 126). The second argument is that the continued existence of the institution undermines the nation's world-historic mission for liberty. These consequences fall under the "American exemplar" argument. Because of the continuing presence of racial slavery on its soil, the United States is setting an example of national hypocrisy to be shunned, not followed, by other nations around the world (pp. 200–1). Child finds it especially galling that the people of South America, who are "so much less enlightened than ourselves," have surpassed us in "liberality and consistent republicanism" because they, and not we, have abolished slavery (p. 208).[32]

The Impropriety of Slavery

In Child's hands, these final two consequentialist arguments against the continued existence of the Southern institution of racial slavery become contextualist arguments. Her "house divided" argument not only draws together the injurious effects of the institution on national security and economic prosperity, but it also suggests that the juxtaposition of slavery and freedom in the same society makes both worse. Within the context of a house divided, Child claims that slavery must assume unusually cruel forms in order to quarantine the slaves from the spirit of liberty at the same time as the spirit of slavery erodes popular support for liberal institutions. She cautions that slavery "is a disease as deadly as the cancer . . . and therefore it reverses all the rules which are applied to other human relations" (p. 146). Child's injunction to her fellow Americans is clear: we must abolish slavery in order to save our own liberal society (pp. 74–75, 95, 146, 212).[33]

Child also cites the juxtaposition of slavery and freedom in the modern world as the reason that modern slavery has assumed crueler forms than ancient slavery did (pp. 32, 38), generalizing that "the condition of slaves has always been worse just in proportion to the freedom enjoyed by their masters" (p. 38). This generalization establishes a definite pecking order among historical forms of slavery, with the Southern institution of racial slavery ranking at the bottom (pp. 38–39).[34] In the second chapter of her book, Child attempts to substantiate the unprecedented cruelty of the institution by quoting at great length from the Southern slave codes (pp. 41–71). Throughout, her premise is that excessive brutality is the only way of maintaining the institution of slavery in a liberal society. This premise does, however, call into question the extent to which the United States is a liberal society. At both the beginning and the end of the discussion, Child treats American claims to be the exemplary liberal society as more boast than reality, due to the continuing presence of racial slavery on American soil (pp. 39, 75). The injunction of her "American exemplar" argument is again clear: we must abolish slavery in order to refurbish our world-historic mission for liberty (pp. 72, 75, 126, 208).

Another way of looking at the jarring juxtaposition of slavery and freedom in the United States is through the perspective of the "human progress" argument. This perspective identifies slavery with the past and freedom with the future. It also casts the defenders of Southern slavery in a reactionary role. Child pointedly asks them whether they wish "to copy the evils of bad governments and benighted ages" (p. 32). She also warns them that they cannot stop progress, explicitly *liberal* progress. "The upholders of slavery will in vain contend with the liberal spirit of the age; it is too strong for them. They may as well try to bottle up the sunshine for their own exclusive use, as to attempt to keep knowledge and freedom to themselves" (p. 69; see also pp. 95, 104, 208). Child seems extremely confident that racial slavery will eventually be abolished throughout the United States. By resisting liberal progress, the defenders of the institution are ensuring only that a general emancipation of the Southern slaves will come later rather than sooner and violently rather than peacefully, for "it must come in some form or other" (p. 104). To Child, their position appears least defensible from this sweeping historical perspective.

Conclusion

Even though Child wended her way through a maze of deontological and, especially, consequentialist arguments against the continued existence of the Southern institution of racial slavery in the *Appeal*, she placed her ultimate faith in the contextualist argument that history has condemned the institution to a certain and deserving death. It was not biblical or liberal principles per se that gave her and other abolitionists the confidence they needed to speak out against racial slavery. Nor was it the social and economic liabilities of the institution. It was the belief in inevitable progress toward liberty and equality for all. The abolitionists were irrepressible because they firmly believed that history was on their side.[35]

Child was an early spokeswoman for the progressive liberalism that undergirded the abolitionist movement and buttressed its tendency to elide the difficulties of the process of institutional change that a general emancipation of the Southern slaves would initiate. Her primary antislavery arguments were liberal ones, invoking a natural right to labor, the superior economic efficiency of free labor, and the "liberalizing" tendencies of the age against the continued existence of Southern slavery. As an early abolitionist spokeswoman, Child was unsure, however, how much to stress these or any other antislavery arguments. Her typical antislavery arguments were "anti-antiabolitionist" ones that partially obscured her fundamental liberal values. Nineteen years later, Frederick Douglass seemed much more confident of which antislavery arguments to stress. His antislavery arguments were more explicitly liberal than Child's were, and they were also more contextualist and less consequentialist and deontologically "pure." Douglass's 1852 Fourth of July oration remains an extremely powerful statement of the abolitionists' progressive liberalism.

Frederick Douglass

In 1852, the Rochester Ladies' Anti-Slavery Society invited one of the city's most famous residents to deliver its Fourth of July oration. Frederick Douglass accepted the invitation and responded with perhaps the most memorable of all pieces of American antislavery rhetoric, "What to the Slave Is the Fourth of July?"[36] The speech is memorable stylistically for the way that it combines a "liberal" Fourth of July oration with a "Protestant" jeremiad. It also is memorable for the way that it attempts to synthesize the basic divisions within the abolitionist ranks through its combination of rhetorical genres as well as its underlying progressive-liberal philosophy. Finally, the speech is memorable for the way that it reflects both the strengths and weaknesses of the abolitionist crusade by projecting a vision of a racially egalitarian society that is providentially written into the nation's future. It was a prophetic speech but one where prophecy failed, or at least remains unfulfilled.

In attempting to synthesize the basic divisions within the abolitionist ranks, Douglass's speech differs from Child's *Appeal*, since those divisions did not emerge until several years after she had published her book. Many other events had buffeted the abolitionist crusade in the intervening years, but significantly, the abolitionists seemed no closer to success in 1852 than they did in 1833. Perhaps expressing his frustration over this fact, Douglass's speech is much darker in tone than Child's *Appeal*.

The difference in timing also distinguished the two works in other respects. Speaking two decades into the abolitionist crusade, Douglass could assume that his audience was more familiar with the antislavery arguments than Child could, writing at the beginning of the crusade. Douglass, therefore, was less concerned with presenting all the antislavery arguments and more concerned with offering those antislavery arguments that he thought, based on his own extensive lecturing experience as well as the experiences of other abolitionist orators, would be most effective.[37] This difference is compounded by the fact that Douglass's intended audience was narrower than Child's. Douglass spoke to a local Rochester audience that was largely antislavery in sentiment. Unlike Child, he did not attempt to address the nation as a whole.[38] The difference in timing, though, seems to have been the most important factor explaining why Douglass's antislavery arguments were more liberal as well as more contextualist and "impure" than Child's were. In these respects, Douglass's speech mirrored the rhetorical development of the broader movement of which he was a part.

Notwithstanding the many differences between their two works,

Douglass and Child shared an underlying progressive-liberal philosophy. In his speech, Douglass poignantly expresses this philosophy to demand an end to racial slavery in the United States and an extension of equal rights to members of his own race. This philosophy also dissipates the darkest moments of a speech that culminates with an unabashed millennialist vision of the future. In its progressive liberalism, Douglass's speech appeals to what unifies the abolitionists, over and above the more tactical concerns that divide them into evangelical and nonevangelical, political and nonpolitical, pacifist and nonpacifist, and unionist and disunionist camps.[39]

Rhetorically, Douglass's primary bridging device is his hybridization of a Fourth of July oration and a jeremiad. The characteristic trait of a Fourth of July oration is, of course, to celebrate the Declaration of Independence and its central, definitively liberal, claims to natural equality and unalienable rights. The jeremiad is, in contrast, a peculiarly Protestant rhetorical genre. By combining the two, Douglass is thus able to combine a Protestant millennialism with a more secular, liberal belief in progress. This combination not only epitomizes progressive liberalism, but it also invests Douglass's speech with great power as an indictment of the Southern institution of racial slavery.[40]

This reading of Douglass's speech is somewhat complicated by the fact that by the 1850s the Fourth of July oration itself had become something of a jeremiad.[41] The typical antebellum Fourth of July oration celebrated the nation's liberal founding principles and yet charged the present generation with more fully realizing those principles in practice. Even more significantly, by this time, the jeremiad had become "liberalized," one of the primary loci for the confluence of Protestant and liberal principles in American culture.[42] From this perspective, the major accomplishment of Douglass's speech was tightening that confluence by combining the two genres. Compared with the typical antebellum Fourth of July oration, he deepened the existing violations of the founding principles and extended the future realizations of those principles. Not surprisingly, as an escaped slave, a prominent abolitionist, and a powerful spokesman for his own race, Douglass fastened on Southern slavery as a massive violation of the founding principles and urged the current generation to assume the task of abolishing the institution and applying those principles equally to African Americans as to European Americans. His Fourth of July oration not only mimics the structure of a jeremiad; it becomes one.[43]

The First "Speech"

Douglass's speech is really two speeches in one. The first "speech" (II:359–66) is a fairly typical antebellum Fourth of July oration.[44] It celebrates the great deeds of the nation's revolutionary generation and seems fully engaged in the filiopiety appropriate to the occasion. The founding fathers "were great men" (II:364); they "loved their country better than their own private interests" (II:364); they "were peace men; but they preferred revolution to peaceful submission to bondage" (II:364–65); they "seized upon eternal principles, and set a glorious example in their defense" (II:365); and they "lay deep the corner-stone of the national superstructure" on "the great principles of justice and freedom" (II:365).[45] Throughout this first "speech," the relevant comparison is with the politicians of "these degenerate times" (II:365) who "hate all changes, but silver, gold and copper change" (II:362–63). Douglass's lesson is that the current generation cannot continue to prosper solely on its patrimony. Following the example of its "fathers," it must accomplish its own great deeds (II:366). In its celebration of "the great principles of justice and freedom" embedded in the American founding, Douglass's first "speech" shares the characteristic liberal traits of a typical antebellum Fourth of July oration. It could well have been delivered by any contemporary American orator, black or white, abolitionist or not. That is not true, however, of Douglass's second "speech."

The Second "Speech"

Douglass opens his much longer second "speech" (II:366–88) by emphasizing that his quarrel is with the present, not the past (II:366). He also leaves little doubt as to what the task of the present generation should be. Fitting the errand to the occasion, he bitterly asks: "Why am I called upon to speak here to-day? What have I, or those I represent, to do with your national independence? Are the great principles of political freedom and of natural justice, embodied in that Declaration of Independence, extended to us?" (II:367). They obviously are not: "The rich inheritance of justice, liberty, prosperity and independence, bequeathed by your fathers, is shared by you, not by me. . . . This Fourth [of] July is *yours*, not *mine*" (II:368).[46] Douglass then even more bitterly refers to his presence on such an occasion:

"Do you mean, citizens, to mock me, by asking me to speak to-day?" (II:368).[47] Up to this point, though, the speech still rather closely follows the traditional Fourth of July pattern. The nation's founding principles "of political freedom and of natural justice" are eternal; they only await further realization. The errand of the current generation is to extend those liberal principles to African Americans so that they, too, can celebrate this day. Douglass speaks as if that were the sole purpose of abolishing slavery.

At this point, the speech undergoes a violent shift in mood. Douglass abruptly declares that his theme is not really the Fourth of July but "AMERICAN SLAVERY," and he reiterates that he himself is not a typical Fourth of July orator, since he is "identified with the American bondsman" (II:368).[48] His second "speech" begins in earnest with this declaration. Douglass never quite leaves the Fourth of July genre—for his recurrent motif is the nation's "shameless hypocrisy" in supporting an institution that so blatantly violates its own liberal founding principles (II:371; see also II:369, 382–83)—but the genre cannot contain his indictment of slavery. However degenerate the times may look in other respects, with respect to slavery "the nation never looked blacker" (II:368). Douglass's speech now becomes a full-blown jeremiad as he goes on to condemn the institution "in the name of humanity which is outraged, in the name of liberty which is fettered, in name of the constitution and the Bible, which are disregarded and trampled upon" (II:369).

Following the jeremiad pattern, Douglass's second "speech" places hypocrisy at the center of American society, not at the periphery, and focuses on the evils of racial slavery, not on the blessings of the founding principles. It suggests that American hypocrisy is not confined to those principles insofar as the institution has evolved into "the great sin and shame of America" (II:369). Douglass's speech now assumes a more religious tone. He vows to condemn slavery "standing with God and the crushed and bleeding slave" (II:369), and his subsequent indictment of the institution blends Protestant and liberal principles. His language also becomes more apocalyptic and ultimately millennialist, laced with the Old Testament cadences of seventeenth-century Puritan jeremiads.[49]

Douglass indicts slavery on three counts. The first is deontological. Douglass defines the institution as a *prima facie* wrong. In contrast to the approach Child adopts in the *Appeal*, he claims that the antislavery creed is so "plain there is nothing to be argued" (II:369). Nonetheless, Douglass proceeds to specify the "plain" truths that define slavery as a *prima facie* wrong, blending Protestant and liberal principles in the process. If slaves are men, then slavery is wrong; if men enjoy a natural right to freedom, then slavery is wrong; if it is wrong to treat men like brutes, then slavery is wrong; and if the institution does not enjoy divine sanction, then slavery is wrong (II:369–70). Since according to Douglass, the premise of each of these propositions is plainly true, slavery must be plainly wrong.

If slavery is plainly wrong, then Americans who support the institution must not be supporting it out of ignorance because they (wrongly) believe that it is a just institution. They must be supporting it out of selfishness because they are willing to violate their own fundamental religious and secular principles when they see something to be gained from it. Douglass observes that "there is not a man beneath the canopy of heaven, that does not know that slavery is wrong *for him*" (II:370). He devotes the longest section of his speech to cataloguing the many hypocrisies that surround the institution (II:371–83), denouncing continued popular support for the domestic slave trade, which contains all the horrors of the justly outlawed international slave trade (II:372–74); for the new fugitive slave law, which transgresses time-honored notions of natural and common law (II:375–76); for the nation's churches, which venally uphold slavery as a divine institution for fear of losing Southern patronage (II:376–82); and for the two major political parties, both of which stand on the platform that "all men are created equal" but conspire to perpetuate the enslavement of 3 million Americans (II:382–83).[50]

The second count of Douglass's antislavery indictment takes a very different tack. After plumbing the depths of American hypocrisy concerning slavery, Douglass shows that the evil effects of the institution cannot be "sanitized" but threaten to engulf the entire polity. He warns Americans that the continued presence of slavery in their country

> destroys your moral power abroad; it corrupts your politicians at home. It saps the foundation of religion; it makes your name a hissing, and a by-word to a mocking earth. It is the antagonistic force in your government, the only thing that seriously disturbs and endangers your *Union*. It fetters your progress; it is the enemy of improvement, the deadly foe of education; it fosters pride; it breeds insolence; it promotes vice; it shelters crime; it is a curse to the earth that supports it. (II:383)

This second count is consequentialist. Douglass's attention has shifted from the intrinsic wrongs of racial slavery, which victimize African Americans, to the broader effects of the institution, which harm all Americans, even those who seem to derive the most profit from it. Again in contrast to the approach Child adopts in the *Appeal*, the argument also is elliptical. Douglass does not specify how the institution breeds these various social ills. The audience must flesh out the argument, as it surely could if it had heard him or other abolitionists speak on prior occasions or read Child's *Appeal.*[51]

Assuming we were such an audience, we would flesh out Douglass's argument in the following way: (1) slavery "destroys your moral power aboard" and "makes your name a hissing, and a by-word to a mocking earth" because the many hypocrisies that surround the institution weaken the force of the nation's liberal exemplar in other countries around the world; (2) slavery "corrupts your politicians at home" because it compels the nation's lawmakers to continually compromise with evil; (3) slavery "saps the foundation of religion" because it transforms the nation's churches into proslavery pulpits; (4) slavery "is the antagonistic force in your government, the only thing that seriously disturbs and endangers your union," because a nation half free and half slave is a house divided against itself that cannot long stand; (5) slavery "fetters your progress" because free labor is more conducive to national economic growth than slave labor is; (6) slavery "is the enemy of improvement, the deadly foe of education," because it requires an illiterate labor force; (7) slavery "fosters pride; it breeds insolence; it promotes vice; it shelters crime" because it encourages slaveholders to act like petty tyrants who physically abuse their slaves and, in particular, sexually abuse their female slaves; and (8) slavery "is a curse to the earth that supports it" because the plantation system exhausts the soil, and in this and the other specified ways, the institution impoverishes the South.[52]

Given that the end of slavery and the many evils associated with its continued existence does not seem imminent, Douglass's mood at this point in the speech can only be characterized as apocalyptic. True to the jeremiad form, he thunders: "Oh! be warned! be warned! a horrible reptile is coiled in your nation's bosom . . . *for the love of God, tear away*, and fling from you the hideous monster" (II:383–84). After a brief interlude to rebut the proslavery interpretation of the Constitution as a "slander" on the memory of its framers and their "GLORIOUS

LIBERTY DOCUMENT" (II:384–86),[53] the speech, however, undergoes another abrupt shift in mood. Douglass is able to find hope in the thought that history is indeed progressive. Even though the end of slavery is not imminent, it is inevitable. The peroration contains this third and final count of Douglass's antislavery indictment.

Douglass opens the peroration by calling attention to the dualistic nature of his speech.

> Allow me to say, in conclusion, notwithstanding the dark picture I have this day presented of the state of the nation, I do not despair of this country. There are forces in operation, which must inevitably work the downfall of slavery. "The arm of the Lord is not shortened," and the doom of slavery is certain. I, therefore, leave off where I began, with *hope*. (II:386–87)

As the peroration continues, Douglass draws "encouragement from the Declaration of Independence, the great principles it contains, and the genius of American institutions" in "the doom of slavery" (II:387). But he is ultimately "cheered by the obvious tendencies of the age" (II:387). Douglass defines those tendencies as tendencies toward universal enlightenment. He insists that the doom of slavery is "certain" because constantly improving means of communication and commerce increasingly expose national iniquities to the rebuke of world opinion, making it less and less likely that they will endure over time (II:387).[54]

If we link Douglass's shifting moods in this speech to his own conception of the relative power of the different counts of his antislavery indictment, then this third, contextualist count is the most powerful one. It dismisses slavery as an anachronistic institution. The institution may have been suitable to earlier, "darker" ages, but it is not compatible with this new age of enlightenment. From an international perspective, it is a dying institution.[55] It is condemned by the inexorable march of human progress, defined in terms of the "great principles" of the Declaration of Independence but fortified by the righteous God of the Old Testament.

The closing mood of Douglass's speech underscores its unity, since both the exordium and the peroration express confidence in the eventual end of slavery.[56] The peroration also returns the speech to its Fourth of July format. The past was glorious, but with the end of slavery, the future will be more glorious still. What comes in between—in the speech, in between the exordium and the peroration; in real time, in between the past and the future—does not appear so glorious, and one cannot help wondering how Douglass could remain so hopeful. At this point, though, the Fourth of July oration and jeremiad intersect once again. If the nation does change its evil ways and abolishes racial slavery, then the future will be glorious indeed.[57]

At the very end of the speech, Douglass recites a poem written by "the fervent aspirations of William Lloyd Garrison," that prays "God speed the year of jubilee" when "freedom's reign" restores "to man his plundered rights," when "the claims of human brotherhood" are universally recognized, and "when none on earth shall exercise a lordly power" and all men profit from "equal birth" (II:387–88).[58] Through this recitation, Douglass is clearly reaching out to his former associates among the Garrison abolitionists and especially to Garrison himself. But he also is combining, one final time, Protestant and liberal principles in a powerful expression of the progressive-liberal philosophy shared by all the abolitionists and earlier expressed—albeit less powerfully and less prominently—by Child in her *Appeal*.

Conclusion

For Garrison, Douglass, Child, and many other American abolitionists, the abolition of the Southern institution of racial slavery may have portended an apocalypse, but they envisioned it as a major step toward a millennium of liberty and equality for all. They believed that liberal progress would cease only with the end of history. Their progressive liberalism ensured not only the eventual end of racial slavery in the United States but also the subsequent extension of equal rights to African Americans. In a speech welcoming the Emancipation Proclamation as one of "those stately steps of mankind . . . from abject serfdom to absolute citizenship," Douglass confessed: "I believe in the millennium—the final perfection of the race, and hail the Proclamation, though wrung out under the goading lash of a stern military necessity, as one reason of the hope that is in me" (III:551–52).[59]

This same progressive liberalism had initially emboldened the abolitionists to undertake their campaign against Southern slavery, and in their own minds, it justified brushing aside all the practical barriers standing in the way of a general emancipation of the Southern slaves. Over the years, however, this attitude moved more toward the center of antislavery rhetoric. The "human progress" argument, which perfectly captured the abolitionists' progressive liberalism, was one of the many, apparently coequal, antislavery arguments in Child's *Appeal*, but it was the climactic antislavery argument in Douglass's Fourth of July oration. In the intervening years, even as the end of racial slavery in the United States seemed ever distant, the abolitionists increasingly emphasized the "human progress" and other contextualist antislavery arguments. While these antislavery arguments were less "pure" or "immediate" than were the deontological and consequentialist antislavery arguments that Child had emphasized, they were more explicitly liberal. They also were more evocative of the abolitionists' sanguinity about the future. Accordingly, Douglass's Fourth of July oration, in striking contrast to Child's *Appeal*, does not contain any "anti-antiabolitionist" arguments aimed at countering public fears of a postemancipation apocalypse, as if uttering such arguments would dispel all his hopes for the future.[60]

A comparison of Douglass's Fourth of July oration and Child's *Appeal* reveals a number of significant rhetorical developments within the abolitionist movement toward more liberal, contextualist, and "impure" antislavery arguments. An analysis of the changing nature of Wendell Phillips's antislavery rhetoric provides further evidence of those developments.

4

Wendell Phillips

Liberty and Union

Wendell Phillips voiced the "house divided" argument as early as 1837 in his very first speech as an abolitionist.

> Our fate is bound up with that of the South, so that they cannot be corrupt and we sound; they cannot fall, and we stand. Disunion is coming, *unless* we discuss this subject; for the spirit of freedom and the spirit of slavery are contending here for mastery. . . . *We* must prosper, and a sound public opinion root out slavery from the land, or there must grow up a mighty slaveholding State to overshadow and mildew our free institutions. (P. 5)[1]

In his later antislavery writings and speeches, Phillips elaborated on the "house divided" argument and the various options it left open. When he first used this argument, the Garrison abolitionists, with whom he was long associated, were still unionists. They hoped to appeal to what they saw as the latent antislavery sentiments of the people of the South in order to unite the house against slavery. By the time of Phillips's controversial 1844 American Anti-Slavery Society pamphlet, *The Constitution, a Pro-Slavery Compact*, the Garrisonians had shifted to disunionism for fear that the house was uniting (or already had united) for slavery. They now sought to unite the people of the North against slavery. The Garrisonians remained disunionists until the eve of the Civil War, which almost overnight transformed the abolitionist movement, as it did so many other aspects of American society. Then they again hoped to unite the house against slavery by remaking a rebellious South in the North's image.

The bulk of Phillips's antislavery writings and speeches were explicitly disunionist. Instead of focusing on the evils of the Southern institution of racial slavery per se, he concentrated on the evils of the institution in a union divided into free states and slave states. In this context, he believed not only that Southern slavery might require Northern disunion but also that Northern disunion might spell the end of Southern slavery. Phillips used three standard disunionist arguments: one deontological, one consequentialist, and one contextualist. He argued that disunion was a way for the people of the North to (1) dissociate themselves from an evil institution (deontological), (2) induce the people of the South to dismantle that evil institution and thereby expand the rights and liberties of the African American slaves (consequentialist), and (3) protect their own rights and liberties from the encroachments of an imperious Southern slavocracy (contextualist).

Over time, Phillips's emphasis shifted from the first type of disunionist argument to the second and especially the third type. This shift toward more contextualist arguments meant an increasing emphasis on how disunion could be justified on liberal grounds as protecting the rights and liberties of Northern whites. As we saw in the comparison of Douglass's Fourth of July oration with Child's *Appeal*, Phillips's shift toward more contextualist arguments entailed a shift toward more liberal antislavery arguments as well as less "pure" antislavery arguments that focused on the way that the fate of Southern slavery was tightly joined to the fate of the union rather than on the intrinsic evils of the institution.

Phillips's antislavery rhetoric also was structured by a second dynamic. This dynamic involved his oscillations between unionism and disunionism: the initial shift from unionism to disunionism and then, much later, the shift back to unionism. But from Phillips's own perspective, his antislavery rhetoric formed a seamless web; earlier positions were carried forward in later ones. He always combined deontological, consequentialist, and contextualist arguments in opposition to slavery as well as in favor of disunion. He never was as disunionist as he seemed, because of his nationalistic belief in the "naturalness" of the union, nor as pessimistic about the prospects of uniting the house against slavery as he seemed, because of his progressive-liberal faith in inevitable progress toward liberty and equality for all.

Historical events certainly influenced these two dynamics. The Garrisonians' shift to contextualism and disunionism mirrored the more general developments that were dividing the house and eventually led to civil war. Their shift back to unionism on the eve of that war was part of a more general wave of patriotism that swept the

North in response to Southern secession. All but a few of the most radical Garrisonians recoiled from the reality of what previously had been "merely" rhetorical and quickly identified the war as their best hope for abolishing Southern slavery.[2]

These two dynamics also mirrored their own experiences as social reformers.[3] When the South resisted their antislavery appeals and the North spawned antiabolitionist mobs, the Garrisonians began to concentrate on converting the North, not the South, to their antislavery creed. They started exploring the ways that union with the South was endangering the North's exemplary liberal society as well as the ways that the North could prosper independently of the South. When disunion resulted from Southern, not Northern, secession and antiabolitionist mobs reappeared in the North, specifically targeting their disunionism, the Garrisonians moved to embrace the cause of union. Not coincidentally, they now defined the cause of union as the cause of freedom.

The dynamics toward contextualism and unionism were part of a concerted effort by the Garrisonians to broaden their popular base in the North. This effort was moderately successful. They started the period as a small, despised minority in the North, and by the end of the period, a sizable Northern majority had elected a Republican president committed to uniting the house against slavery. While the Garrisonians and Republicans were not in perfect accord in their views on slavery, they did concur on the need to unite the house against the institution.[4]

The Garrisonians' shift to contextualism was a move toward broader popular support because antislavery contextualist arguments directly connected the fate of Southern slavery to the fate of Northern liberty.[5] That type of argument also tended to bring Northern antislavery radicals and moderates closer together by focusing on what they could agree on—the undesirability of slavery—rather than on what they could not agree on—the desirability of immediate abolition and racial equality. Southern secession, civil war, and the Garrisonians' shift back to unionism cemented this confluence.[6]

By the same token, the Garrisonians' shift back to unionism was a move toward broader popular support because it realigned them with the powerful nationalist sentiments of the Northern public. The people of the North valued the union so highly because they thought it exemplified universal liberty and progress. Through the "American exemplar" and "human progress" arguments, the Garrisonians portrayed

Southern slavery as a threat to the things that made the union seem so valuable. The "house divided" argument introduced an additional dimension by portraying the institution as a threat to the very existence of the union. Even when the Garrisonians tacked an unpopular disunionist conclusion onto the argument—insisting on the urgency of disunion in order to salvage the things that made the union seem so valuable—they did not necessarily undercut their effort to broaden their popular base, at least not in the long run. For if the people of the North could not accept the Garrisonians' disunionist conclusion to the "house divided" argument, they equally could not accept the proslavery conclusion of uniting the house *for* slavery. They then were left with the alternative of uniting the house *against* slavery.[7] Ironically, even as disunionists—and it was never clear to what extent they were disunionists—the Garrisonians evoked the powerful nationalist sentiments of their audiences in such a way as to advance the antislavery cause, despite the fact that it did not redound to their own immediate political advantage.[8]

In order to suggest the underlying rhetorical dynamics of the abolitionist crusade, I analyze how Phillips's antislavery rhetoric changed over time. This analysis substantiates the dynamics toward contextualism and unionism in the dominant Garrisonian wing of the abolitionist movement.[9] I concentrate on five of Phillips's most important antislavery writings and speeches: *The Constitution, a Proslavery Compact* (1844), "Welcome to George Thompson" (November 26, 1850), "Speech at the Worcester Disunion Convention" (January 15, 1857), "Progress" (February 17, 1861), and "Under the Flag" (April 21, 1861).

"No Union with Slaveholders"

The 1844 pamphlet, *The Constitution, a Pro-Slavery Compact*, marked the Garrisonians' shift to disunionism. Phillips assembled the pamphlet for the American Anti-Slavery Society to justify publicly its new disunionist philosophy.[10] The pamphlet includes a variety of historical documents directed toward proving that the Constitution is "a covenant with death and an agreement with hell" for its compromises with slavery and that, even if it were not, the experiences of the last fifty years under the Constitution confirm that "no union with slaveholders" is possible without involving the North "in the guilt and responsible [*sic*] for the sin of slavery" (p. 7). As a whole, the import of the pamphlet is that the proper response to a house divided between freedom and slavery is to divide it physically.

Phillips packed the pamphlet with documents ranging from extracts from the original debates in the Continental Congress over what later became the three-fifths clause of the United States Constitution to extracts from a recent speech by John Quincy Adams claiming that the three-fifths clause placed the federal government in the hands of a corrupt Southern slavocracy.[11] Each of the documents was intended to build the case for the proslavery nature of the Constitution and the proslavery practices of the federal government under it. Besides the introduction, Phillips was personally responsible for the executive address of the American Anti-Slavery Society, which summarizes the evidence and presents the argument for disunion based on it. The address presses the argument for disunion in three specific directions: (1) as a way of maintaining personal and sectional purity (deontological), (2) as a way of ending Southern slavery (consequentialist), and (3) as a way of protecting Northern liberty (contextualist). The address stresses the first type of argument. The primary audience was undoubtedly other abolitionists, in particular, the non-Garrison, political abolitionists who interpreted the Constitution quite differently, as an antislavery compact. The whole pamphlet seems structured for internecine warfare, not necessarily to appeal to members of the broader public who, one surmises, were much less concerned with ethical casuistry in relation to the Constitution or the union, or even to racial slavery.[12]

The executive address begins by declaring that secession from the present government is "a religious and political duty" (p. 93). It goes on to paraphrase the Declaration of Independence, insisting that if "secession" from the British government was justified in 1776, then secession from the United States government certainly is justified in 1844 (pp. 93–94; see also p. 109). In view of the Lockean language of the Declaration of Independence, Phillips sees no need to demonstrate that slavery is wrong or that revolution is lawful with respect to a government that is "the prop and safeguard of American slavery" (p. 94).[13] At this point, the address takes an explicitly anticonsequentialist tack, denouncing the argument that the Constitution's compromises with slavery were necessary to preserve the union as "the jesuitical doctrine, that the end sanctifies the means" (p. 95). Phillips quotes the Bible to oppose that doctrine and pronounces "a partnership between right and wrong . . . wholly wrong" (p. 95).

Phillips continues in this deontological vein, mixing religious and secular arguments against compromising with slavery, when he turns to examining the precise nature of the Constitution's compromises with the institution.[14] He launches his assault on the Constitution by calling it "anti-republican and anti-Christian" (p. 96) and contends that no fewer than five constitutional clauses are "at war with the law of God and the rights of man" (p. 101). Closely examining those clauses, one by one, he finds that (1) the slave trade clause (article I, section 9) alone renders the Constitution "incompatible with the duties which men owe to their Creator, and to each other" for not immediately abolishing the practice (p. 100); (2) the three-fifths clause (article I, section 2) is clearly antirepublican in granting the Southern states unequal representation in Congress, thus providing for "the safety, perpetuity and augmentation of the slaveholding power" and "the complete subjugation of the non-slaveholding States" (p. 101); (3) the fugitive slave clause (article IV, section 2) transforms slavery into a "national crime" and violates the Old Testament teaching against returning fugitive slaves (p. 104); and (4) the domestic insurrection (article I, section 8) and (5) the domestic violence (article IV, section 4) clauses both hold the federal government responsible for suppressing, and consequently deterring, slave rebellions, thereby capping a system of "national barbarity" that "stains with human blood the garments of all the people" (p. 107).[15]

The address concludes by reasserting the anticonsequentialist theme. Phillips appeals to all those who "believe it is right to obey God rather than man" to enlist under the banner of disunion (p. 108). He variously describes that banner as the banner of liberty, of equal rights, and of universal peace (p. 108) and urges his readers to support disunion in order to secure these great goods, disregarding the potential consequences to themselves (pp. 110–11) and trusting in "the God of justice" (p. 112).

Despite its explicit anticonsequentialist theme, the address contains several consequentialist and contextualist arguments in favor of disunion. These arguments show that the banner of disunion is also the banner of liberty, of equal rights, and of universal peace. They also show that maintaining personal and sectional purity is not the only goal Phillips has in mind, and that accordingly, he hopes to address a broader audience than his fellow abolitionists.

In a consequentialist vein, Phillips contends that the people of the North should secede from the present government both in order "to obey God and vindicate the gospel of his Son" and "to hasten the downfall of slavery in America, and throughout the world" (p. 110). Earlier in the address, he suggested that Southern slavery might be destroyed by a successful slave revolt, which the Southern states would not be able to quell without the practical support of the Northern states in enforcing the constitutional guarantees against domestic insurrection and violence (p. 107).[16] In the conclusion, he suggests that by uniting the North against Southern slavery, an abolitionist-inspired disunionist movement might convince the South "that her only alternative is, to abolish slavery, or be abandoned by that power on which she now relies for safety" (p. 111). The consequences of such a movement then would not necessarily be violence or anarchy or, for that matter, disunion. Phillips also notes that the consequences of *not* abolishing Southern slavery would be the continued suffering of 3 million African Americans (p. 110; see also pp. 93, 95) and accuses the founding fathers of not taking that suffering into account in their willingness "to enslave others, that they might secure their own freedom" (p. 100; see also p. 97).[17] He seems fairly confident that Northern disunion, or even the serious threat thereof, would be the death knell of Southern slavery. In this address, Phillips thus defends disunion on consequentialist grounds by associating it with the liberal, though still controversial (to Northern whites), goal of maximizing the rights and liberties of African Americans.

Phillips also presents in the address several contextualist arguments in favor of disunion. These arguments associate disunion with the far less controversial (to Northern whites) and still liberal goal of maximizing the rights and liberties of the people of the North. In rebutting the argument that the Constitution's compromises with slavery were necessary to preserve the union, Phillips claims not only that it was wrong to compromise freedom with slavery but also that such a compromise was impractical anyway (pp. 93, 95).[18] The Constitution could not be sustained over time as an equal compromise, nor could it create a true union. It instead had created a house divided against itself that could not long endure and that by 1844 was clearly leaning in the direction of slavery. For a union that was a house divided between slavery and freedom, the continued existence of the institution of racial slavery in the South threatened the rights and liberties of all Americans, except perhaps those of the slaveholders themselves. According to Phillips, the best antidote to a house divided was disunion, which at least would insulate Northern liberty from the contagion of Southern slavery (pp. 106, 108).[19]

The address, therefore, insists that "the American Union is and always has been a sham" because it has inaugurated "the absolute reign of the slaveholding power over the whole country, to the prostration of Northern rights" (p. 95). Phillips later quotes John Quincy Adams at some length, on exactly how the union inaugurated the absolute reign of the slaveholding power (pp. 102–3), and he observes that Northern abolitionists, in particular, cannot freely exercise their constitutional rights of movement, speech, petition, press, and assembly joined in a union with Southern slaveholders (pp. 109–10).[20] When Phillips declares that it would have been "better that the American union had never been formed, than that it should have been obtained at such a frightful cost" (p. 95), his reference seems to be the cost to nonslaveholding whites as much as to black slaves. In his hands, the "house divided" argument becomes a powerful argument in favor of disunion, because of the way that it discounts the possibilities of continued union and heightens the dangers of that state of affairs.

The disunionism of the executive address is ambiguous, however.[21] Phillips does not abandon all hopes of appealing to a staunchly unionist Northern public. He implies that a serious Northern threat of disunion would be sufficient to persuade the Southern states to free their slaves. And none of the four advantages of a Northern disunionist moment that he lists at the end of the address entails an actual separation of the states (pp. 111–12). Indeed, the four advantages point to a disunionist movement that is more a moral stance on the part of the Garrison abolitionists than a broad-scale political movement.[22] Furthermore, if it were ever to become a broad-scale political movement that resulted in Northern secession and Southern emancipation, disunion would need to be only a temporary condition, and reunion could occur on the basis of liberty and equality for all. Phillips himself would support the union once it was "purged from its corruption" (p. 95).

None of this is to deny that the tone of Phillips's pamphlet is stridently disunionist, that it mainly defends disunion on deontological grounds, and that its primary audience is his fellow abolitionists. Disunion is a way for the abolitionists, individually or collectively, to purge themselves of their guilt and responsibility for the continued existence of racial slavery in the South. Phillips correctly predicts that at least in the short run, disunionism will make the Garrisonians more, not less, unpopular (p. 110). The pamphlet, nevertheless, does anticipate Phillips's later contextualism and unionism as well as the Garrisonians' quest for broader public support.

Measures of Progress

The year 1850 witnessed the passage of a tougher federal fugitive slave law as part of the infamous (for the Garrison abolitionists) Compromise of 1850 and another visit from the prominent British abolitionist George Thompson. Thompson's 1835 American tour had served as a lightning rod for antiabolitionist mobs, and his 1850 visit did so as well.[23] The Garrisonians had planned a public reception for Thompson in Boston's Faneuil Hall on November 15 only to have the mayor cancel the event because of the threat of mob violence. The Garrisonians then reconvened in several cities outside Boston. Phillips was the featured speaker at the November 26 meeting in Lynn, Massachusetts. Obviously, these events reintroduced the collateral issue of the abolitionists' ability to exercise their own constitutional rights. Phillips reintroduces the issue as an indication of a house divided. He also measured progress from 1835 (and from 1844) as progress toward disunion but more as progress toward freedom.

After commenting on the year's momentous events (pp. 24–28), Phillips's "Welcome to George Thompson" places them in a broader context (pp. 28–30).[24] Phillips measures progress as progress toward the end of Southern slavery, invoking the "human progress" argument as guaranteeing the abolitionists' ultimate success. He not surprisingly highlights British colonial emancipation, which Thompson symbolizes, as a critical step in human progress.[25] Accordingly, the question of a general emancipation of the Southern slaves "is now only one of time" (p. 29). Phillips also universalizes the American antislavery struggle, insisting that the cause of freedom is one around the world, just as is the cause of tyranny (pp. 29–30). This perspective allows him not only to defend Thompson's presence in the United States but also to claim that "every true word spoken for suffering man, is so much done for the negro beneath the weight of American bondage" (p. 30). At this point in the speech, his progressive liberalism is palpable. Phillips seems supremely confident that history favors the cause of freedom over the cause of tyranny and that the end of Southern slavery is therefore inevitable. Phillips has much to tell Thompson about "our success and marvellous progress" over the fifteen years since he last visited the United States (p. 30).

At least initially, Phillips points to the growing possibility of disunion in 1850, not of the end of Southern slavery, as evidence of the abolitionists' progress (p. 31). He does not argue how disunion or, for that matter, antislavery agitation may lead to the end of Southern slavery but, rather, how antislavery agitation may lead to disunion. Here Phillips seems to adopt the perspective of the antiabolitionists, North and South, who identify antislavery agitation as the greatest threat to continued union, even though he more positively evaluates that state of affairs.

The first antiabolitionist that Phillips targets in the speech is Benjamin Curtis. Curtis, a leading Massachusetts "Cotton Whig" and future Supreme Court justice, had spoken in favor of the compromise measures, including the new fugitive slave law, at a prounion rally in Faneuil Hall that was held in lieu of the canceled abolitionist event.[26] According to Phillips, Curtis appealed for public support of the compromise measures on the grounds that they were the price of continued union (pp. 31–32). Phillips scoffs at Curtis's plea of necessity not because he does not believe that the union is in danger but because he does not believe that it is sufficiently important. Once more assuming an explicitly anticonsequentialist stance, Phillips contends that other values, such as justice and humanity, are more important than continued union (pp. 32–33). Then after denouncing the new fugitive slave law for violating the dictates of justice and humanity (pp. 34–35),[27] Phillips targets Henry Clay, the national Whig leader and chief architect of the Compromise of 1850. He challenges Clay's claim that the nation must choose between preserving the union and silencing antislavery agitation, a claim that Clay made in an open letter to a recent prounion rally in Philadelphia (p. 35).

While Phillips accepts the basic terms of Clay's "house divided" argument, he takes the argument one step further. He contends that it is impossible to silence antislavery agitation and that attempting to do so will only result in disunion (pp. 36–38). This reasoning places Clay and other antiabolitionists in an awkward position. Disunion may result either from attempting to silence antislavery agitation or from not attempting to do so. From Phillips's perspective, though, the crucial point is that any attempt to silence antislavery agitation is futile because history favors the cause of freedom. Significantly, he now defines progress toward freedom in terms of ending Southern slavery *and* protecting Northern liberty and not necessarily as progress toward disunion. In fact, the choice between silencing antislavery agitation and preserving the union now appears to be a false choice. Antislavery agitation cannot really be silenced, nor can disunion really accomplish anything, since with or without it, the end of Southern slavery is inevitable.

In responding to Clay's "house divided" argument, Phillips suggests, as he had earlier in the speech, that Southern slavery stands condemned by the inexorable march of history. He reminds his audience that if Clay has his way, "it is the fetter and the chain, the unspeakable blessings of slavery, for whose sake reason is to be hoodwinked, and eloquence to be gagged" (p. 36). Phillips also reminds his audience that slavery is a dying institution. "The fetter and the chain" already have been worn away on the other side of the Atlantic by "the beneficent action" of trade and the "indignant rebuke" of Christianity (p. 36). The demise of slavery on this side of the Atlantic is only a matter of time, owing to both the general course of history and America's special mission in it.

> To the anointed eye, the planting of this continent is the exodus of the race out of the bondage of old and corrupt institutions. The serene and beautiful spirit that leads it, laughs with pitying scorn at the efforts of the mightiest Pharaoh to stay this constant and gradual advance of humanity. (P. 36)

At this point in the speech, Phillips's progressive liberalism is again palpable. Given both the general and the special processes of history, any disunionist movement either to preserve Southern slavery or to abolish it seems as futile as the efforts to silence antislavery agitation.

After responding to Clay's "house divided" argument, Phillips reiterates his belief that other values are more important than continued union. However, he does not, as one might expect at this point, refer to abolishing Southern slavery as more important than continued union and suggest that the people of the South might disrupt the union in order to protect their institution of racial slavery. Instead, he refers to free speech as more important than continued union and suggests that the people of the North might disrupt the union in order to protect their own constitutional rights (pp. 36–37). But he again undercuts this very possibility by speaking of free speech in the same terms he had spoken of the demise of Southern slavery, as part of an inexorable stream of human progress that cannot be diverted and of a national destiny to which the South, too, cannot fail to be committed (pp. 37–38).[28] Any Northern effort to protect free speech through disunion seems as futile as a Southern effort to protect racial slavery through disunion. Phillips himself observes that "no man of full age and sound mind really believes that any thing can be maintained in this country which requires for its existence the stifling of free discussion" (p. 36).

Of course, protecting free speech and abolishing racial slavery are not necessarily the same thing. If protecting free speech is the more important goal, then maximizing the rights and liberties of white citizens seems paramount; if abolishing racial slavery is the more important goal, then maximizing the rights and liberties of black slaves seems paramount. For Phillips, though, these two identifiably liberal goals form a seamless web. He contends that protecting racial slavery currently provides the only rationale for stifling free speech (p. 36) and rejoices that the antiabolitionists have wedded "the cause of the slave with the cause of free speech" because their attempts to stifle the abolitionists' free speech promise to expand the antislavery appeal (p. 37).[29]

In the peroration, he returns to the inevitability of abolition, once more connecting it to the collateral issue of free speech and portraying it as part of a "manifest destiny" that precludes (permanent) disunion.

> Perpetuate slavery amid such a race as ours! Impossible! Re-annex the rest of the continent, if you will; pile fugitive slave bills till they rival the Andes; dissolve, were it possible, the union God has made between well-doing and well-being,—even then you could not keep slavery in peace till you got a new race to people these shores. The blood which has cleared the forest, tortured the earth of its secrets, made the ocean its vassal, and subjected every other race it has met, will never volunteer its own industry to forge gags for its own lips. (Pp. 38–39)[30]

Phillips appears much more optimistic about the prospects of abolition in 1850 than he did in 1844. His progressive liberalism is much more apparent in his "Welcome to George Thompson" speech than in his 1844 American Anti-Slavery Society pamphlet. By 1850, Phillips seems to believe that the Garrison abolitionists have started to reach a wider audience. He also seems to believe that the events surrounding the passage of the Compromise of 1850 favor their cause and that, in any case, broader historical trends guarantee their eventual success. The contextualist "human progress" and "American exemplar" arguments he invokes in "Welcome to George Thompson" offer hope of a satisfactory conclusion to the "house divided" argument: uniting the house for freedom and against slavery without disunion. Phillips's disunionist rhetoric is certainly temperate compared with his earlier pamphlet, evidence of his own efforts to reach a wider audience. Even the extent to which the union is a house divided appears attenuated in "Welcome to George Thompson."

Phillips clearly has not abandoned disunionism, however. He recognizes and even welcomes the increased threat of disunion in 1850 as one measure of progress toward the end of Southern slavery. His own disunionism could be reenergized if, in the future, he were to become more pessimistic about the course of liberal progress and the imminence of a successful conclusion to the antislavery crusade.

The Idolatry of Union

By 1857, Phillips seems to have become much more pessimistic about the future, at least about the short-term future. Perhaps the recent events in "Bleeding Kansas" and the congressional reaction to those events have discouraged him. Or perhaps the fact that his twenty-year struggle against the slave power seems likely to continue into the indefinite future is the source of his frustration. But for whatever reason, he considers the union more of a house divided in 1857 than he had in 1850. He also advocates disunion in the form of Northern secession from the union more explicitly than he did in either 1850 or 1844.

As he did in *The Constitution, a Pro-Slavery Compact*, Phillips argues for the desirability of disunion on several different grounds. His emphasis, though, has shifted from deontological to consequentialist and contextualist arguments. He sees the desirability of disunion less as a way of maintaining personal and sectional purity and more as a way of ending Southern slavery and protecting Northern liberty. Especially through the latter argument, he is appealing to the emerging Republican majority in the North for whom disunionism is a, if not the, major barrier to supporting Garrison abolitionism. Phillips is trying to assure

Northern whites that disunion is the best policy for them and that it is the best policy for them on identifiably liberal grounds. His bold claim is that disunion will maximize their own rights and liberties as well as those of the African American slaves. Rather than hedging his disunionism to the Northern public, as he did in "Welcome to George Thompson," Phillips now is trying to convince it that disunion advances its dearest interests.[31]

Phillips's presence and speech at the Worcester (Massachusetts) Disunion Convention of January 15, 1857, reveal this new strategy.[32] He opens his speech to the convention by declaring that "we are assembled to consider the expediency of seeking a dissolution of the Union." He himself favors disunion "first and primarily, to protect the slave" because it is "an Anti-Slavery measure" (p. 1; see also pp. 6, 10). He then begins to critique a recent public letter written by Henry Wilson, one of the state's two Republican senators, which impugns Garrison disunionism as treasonous. In reply, Phillips argues that if the union or any other institution must be sacrificed to destroy Southern slavery, so be it, since "slavery is so monstrous an evil, that in its presence all others pale away" (p. 2).[33] His theme for the speech is the expediency of disunion as against the idolatry of union.

Near the end of his "Worcester Disunion" speech, Phillips presents two consequentialist arguments for how disunion will promote a general emancipation of the Southern slaves. The first is that disunion will compel an independent South to emancipate its slaves because it will need a free, educated labor force to tax in order to raise sufficient revenues to support its own federal government (pp. 12–13).[34] The second argument is the same one that he offered in *The Constitution, a Pro-Slavery Compact*: an independent South will be compelled to emancipate its slaves or else face the prospect of slave insurrections (pp. 15–16).[35] In addition, Phillips states that disunion will end Southern slavery much sooner than will a policy of divorcing the federal government from any support of the institution, a policy he expects the Republican Party to pursue if it ever gains power (pp. 9–10). He also argues that disunion will end Southern slavery much sooner than will a policy of simply appealing to religious morality against the institution. Obliquely criticizing the evangelical wing of the abolitionist movement as well as suggesting the limits of any purely deontological antislavery stance, Phillips claims that he does not "doubt the power of the Sermon on the Mount in the long run" but adds that in the meantime, self-interest—the "two thousand million of dollars, invested in slaves"—supports the continued existence of Southern slavery (p. 14). Without disunion, self-interest could sustain the institution for centuries to come. Conversely, disunion rechannels self-interest in the direction of the abolition of Southern slavery. It allows "God's laws of political economy" that "villainy should always be loss" to assert themselves (p. 13). Phillips therefore believes that disunion is the best policy for the African American slaves because it transmutes abolition from a policy that seems highly antagonistic to the interests of Southern whites into one that seems highly conducive to the interests of Southern whites, slaveholders and nonslaveholders alike.

Before discussing the advantages of disunion for the African American slaves, Phillips describes the advantages of disunion for Northern whites, despite claiming that his "second motive" for favoring disunion is "to protect the white race" (p. 1; see also pp. 5–6). He bridges his two motives for favoring disunion by insisting that "the fate of four millions of slaves" is linked "with the welfare of the white race" (p. 2). In linking the fate of the African American slaves with the welfare of Northern whites, Phillips refers to an impressive list of Protestant and liberal values: "the purity of religion," "freedom of conscience and thought," "civil liberty," "an impartial judiciary," "personal character," and "all civil rights." He contends that the importance of the union also pales before all these other values (p. 2). Indeed, he believes that the continued existence of the union actually endangers all these other values. According to Phillips, the union is "pregnant with momentously bad results. It has prostituted the pulpit,—it has made the people cowards,—it has made slavery triumphant,—it has made literature vassal and corrupt,—it has transformed twenty millions of people into slave catchers" (p. 4).

Phillips devotes the bulk of his speech to assailing "this idolatry of the juggle of a Union" among the people of the North (p. 6). As he sees it, this idolatry consists of continuing to support the union and opposing disunion, without any regard to the relative utility of those two courses of action. Here the people of the North imitate their leading politicians, such as Wilson, who "undertakes to sacrifice every possibility of the slave question" to the union but "has yet to find the first good thing that it had done for twenty millions of people" (p. 4). To disabuse Northern whites of their idolatry of union, Phillips attempts to demonstrate why disunion is the more beneficial policy for them.

This demonstration abstracts from the probable consequences for the Southern slaves of either disunion or continued union and, correspondingly, the question of whether disunion or continued union is more likely to lead to the end of Southern slavery.

The demonstration opens with Phillips's rebuttal of the argument that disunion will devastate Northern commerce. To the contrary, "the genius and energy of the Yankee race," not the union, is responsible for Northern commerce (p. 3).[36] Phillips next points out that even if the union has manufactured great wealth, it has not manufactured great men, which is "the highest test of government" (p. 3). He cites Daniel Webster, Caleb Cushing, and Franklin Pierce as examples of "the knaves" the union has produced and later contends that "the South has bought up our great men faster than nature can make them" (p. 13).[37] Phillips also charges the union with stifling the free speech of the few Northern politicians who have not prostituted themselves to the South, referring to Preston Brooks's recent caning of Charles Sumner on the floor of the Senate (p. 5).[38] Most broadly, though, he argues that the union fosters the continued dominance of the slave power over national counsels (pp. 7–8) and the continued exposure of Northern whites to the corrupting influences of Southern slavery (pp. 9–10). The real problem with any policy of divorcing the federal government from slavery without disunion is that it would mean "the slow, faltering, diseased, gradual dying out of slavery, constantly poisoning us with the festering remains of this corrupt political, social and literary state" so that "all this timid servility of the press,—all this lack of virtue and manhood,—all this corruption of the pulpit,—all this fossil hunkerism,—all this selling of the soul for a mess of pottage,—is to linger" for as many as sixty years (p. 10). Disunion, in contrast, would leave both the North and the South free "from a very large share of the corrupt influence of each other" (p. 11).[39] The demonstration closes with Phillips's confession that "if the slaveholder loves the Union," then he, Phillips, must "hate it" (p. 13).

These various consequentialist arguments for disunion, however, form one sweeping contextualist argument for that state of affairs. Just as Phillips claims that the union itself is not responsible for all the beneficial results that its idolaters attribute to it, he also does not claim that the union itself is responsible for all the harmful results that he, conversely, attributes to it. Yet those harmful results would not occur, or they would not be so "momentously bad," if the North and the

South were separate nations. Disunion stops the contagion of Southern slavery on Northern liberty. Now fearing that the house is uniting for slavery rather than against it, Phillips is boldly advocating Northern secession from the union as the most satisfactory conclusion to the "house divided" argument. And he believes that it is the best conclusion on liberal grounds, in terms of maximizing the rights and liberties of the people of the North.

Phillips frames his "Worcester Disunion" speech to attract support for disunion among Northern whites, especially among Northern Republicans such as Wilson, who are opposed to Southern slavery or at least to a Southern slavocracy, but are also suspicious of abolitionism and hostile to disunionism. He places his primary emphasis on the consequentialist arguments that disunion serves the immediate interests of a moderately antislavery, Northern audience. Nonetheless, he also observes that disunion serves the interests of the African American slaves by encouraging the Southern states to dismantle their institution of racial slavery and, on contextualist grounds, that disunion serves the interests of all Americans by short-circuiting sectional conflict over the ultimate fate of the institution. He even maintains, on deontological grounds, that disunion is "a question of personal honor and duty" by ridding him and other Northern whites of their complicity in the evils of Southern slavery (pp. 7–8). Phillips might have expected each of these arguments, but especially the first type, to achieve some resonance with the Northern public.

In this speech, Phillips offers the deontological, consequentialist, and contextualist arguments for disunion that he had offered in his 1844 American Anti-Slavery Society pamphlet but with different priorities among them. Overall, he presents disunion as the ideal geopolitical solution to the "maximum liberty" problem central to liberal thought. Progress toward disunion is, now more than ever, progress toward freedom.

Although Phillips's disunionism is much more strident in this speech than it was in "Welcome to George Thompson" and perhaps even in his 1844 American Anti-Slavery Society pamphlet, it remains ambiguous. Phillips does not appear to "hate" the union as much as he claims he does, nor is he as pessimistic about its long-term prospects as he seems to be. He admits that disunion is an evil, even if a lesser one than the continued existence of Southern slavery (p. 10). He also suggests that disunion will be only a temporary state of affairs—allowing Americans to "begin again" to "create a great nation" (pp. 11–12)—which would seem both probable and desirable if it did lead to the end of Southern slavery. But regardless of how the Garrison abolitionists intended disunionism and how seriously they intended it, they did not broaden the antislavery appeal through that philosophy. Just the opposite happened.

Southern Secession as Progress

When disunion did come, it of course came through Southern, rather than Northern, secession. Initially, Phillips acted as if it made no difference. He welcomed Southern secession for all the reasons he had advocated Northern secession. He adopted a "let the South go in peace" attitude toward Southern secession and treated it as the fulfillment of all the Garrisonians' dreams. In fact, the speech he delivered in Boston on February 17, 1861, in defense of disunion is entitled "Progress."[40]

Phillips does not even seem concerned that the speech occasioned another antiabolitionist mob in anticipation of its defense of disunion.[41] Despite this contrary evidence, he considers Northern public opinion closer in sentiment to the Garrison abolitionists than it ever has been before. In contrast to the audiences of the first three of Phillips's works that we have examined, the intended audience of the "Progress" speech was a general one. Phillips therefore must attempt to bridge more directly than he has before any gaps that still might exist between Northern public opinion and the Garrisonians, with respect to both disunionism and abolitionism.

Now that disunion has come, Phillips is optimistic about the future. The exordium of his speech is an unequivocal expression of the abolitionists' progressive liberalism. Unlike "most men," Phillips does not believe that "the golden age is one long past" (p. 371) but that it is in the future. He goes on to measure progress on many different fronts, from scientific discovery to penal reform to women's rights (pp. 371–72). Phillips concludes this section of the speech with a hymn of unbounded confidence in the workings of history in the direction of liberty and equality for all. "Popes and kings no longer mark the ages; but Luther and Raphael, Fulton and Faust, Howard and Rousseau. A Massachusetts mechanic, Eli Whitney, made cotton king; a Massachusetts printer, William Lloyd Garrison, has undermined its throne. Thus civilization insures equality. Types are the fathers of democrats" (p. 373).[42] As he did in "Welcome to George Thompson," Phillips highlights disunion as a measure of progress. He insists that disunion is not the end of the golden age of the United States, as many Americans fear, but the beginning. "Disunion is gain, disunion is *peace*, disunion is virtue" (p. 374; see also pp. 376, 386, 387).[43]

Phillips does not explain why disunion is peace, gain, and virtue until the penultimate section of the speech, where he again combines deontological, consequentialist, and contextualist arguments to show that disunion would particularly benefit the people of the North. He argues that disunion is peace because even if it were so inclined, the South will be too weak to fight a war with the North (pp. 387–90); that disunion is gain because the union is a financial drain on the North to the profit of the South (pp. 390–92); and that disunion is virtue because it will end the degrading concessions to the spirit of slavery that the union forces the North to offer to the South (pp. 392–95).[44]

In the final section of the speech, Phillips attacks the disposition of Northern politicians to offer further concessions to the South in order to patch the union together again. Ironically, he does not choose to target a prominent Northern politician but instead Richard Dana, a distinguished member of the Massachusetts bar and author of *Two Years before the Mast*, who in a recent speech in Boston had publicly expressed his support for intersectional compromise to resolve the current crisis of union. Phillips claims that the fact that ordinary citizens who are "above the temptations of politics" are making such speeches exposes precisely "how wide the gangrene of the Union spreads" (p. 395).[45] He concludes his own speech by demanding that the people of the North, in the spirit of the Revolutionary heroes Josiah Warren and James Otis, "scorn to be slaves" to the union (p. 395). Besides peace, gain, and virtue, disunion also apparently means freedom for the people of the North.

For the most part, though, Phillips's "Progress" speech attacks the disposition of Northern politicians to offer further concessions to the South and the various efforts being undertaken in that direction as an alternative to letting it go in peace.[46] Phillips views intersectional compromise as a more probable and less desirable alternative to disunion than war between the states. If disunion is progress, then reunion, at least at this time, must be regress.

In criticizing the efforts of Northern politicians to offer further concessions to the South, Phillips begins with the North's "original sin": the United States Constitution (p. 377).[47] He believes that the Constitution was just the first in a series of "barren concessions" the North offered to the South that have simply augmented the slave power and perpetuated Southern slavery (p. 378).[48] Even if another intersectional compromise were now cobbled together, it would save the union only temporarily. The people of the North, unlike their politicians, seem content to "let the Union go to pieces, rather than yield an inch" (p. 379). They, again unlike their politicians, also seem committed to "freedom to the slave" and "justice to the negro" (p. 380).[49] Because of the irreversible progress of antislavery sentiments among the people of the North (pp. 380–81), Phillips believes that no lasting compromise between the two sections is possible without ending Southern slavery (pp. 381–82). He then explains why compromise at this time is not expedient, once more combining deontological, consequentialist, and contextualist arguments in this discussion.

Phillips's first "argument" against compromise is deontological. He simply claims that compromise "is wrong" (p. 382), presumably because slavery is wrong, and as he argued in his 1844 American Anti-Slavery Society pamphlet, one should not compromise with wrong. Four consequentialist arguments against compromise follow, two of which focus on ending Southern slavery and two on protecting Northern liberty. According to Phillips, compromise "is suicidal" to the North because it only will invite further demands from the South; "it delays emancipation" because with disunion Great Britain will search for other, more dependable cotton markets and "South Carolina will be starved into virtue"; it "demoralizes both parties" because it merely will postpone the inevitable and portend a retreat, especially in Northern antislavery sentiments; and it "risks [slave] insurrection, the worst door at which freedom can enter" (pp. 382–83).[50] All four arguments hinge on the contextualist "house divided" argument. Phillips's point is precisely that a union that chains a free North to a slave South will produce these illiberal results. Compromise will prolong those results, whereas disunion will obviate them.

At this point in the speech, Phillips's attention shifts from the evils of compromise to the evils of slavery. After arguing that a slave insurrection would be the worst way of ending Southern slavery, he asserts that it still would be preferable to the continued existence of the institution

(p. 383).[51] Whatever horrors that a race war may hold for both Southern whites and blacks, they could not be worse than the horrors that slavery holds for black slaves.[52]

> Take the broken hearts; the bereaved mothers; the infant, wrung from the hands of its parents; the husband and wife torn asunder; every right trodden under foot; the blighted hopes, the imbruted souls, the darkened and degraded millions, sunk below the level of intellectual life, melted in sensuality, herded with beast, who have walked over the burning marl of Southern slavery to their graves; and where is the battle-field, however ghastly, that is not white,—white as an angel's wings,—compared with the blackness of that darkness which has brooded over the Carolinas for two hundred years? (P. 384)

In stating this preference, Phillips notes that he never has been committed to nonviolence.[53] He claims that he opposed slave revolts in the past on grounds of policy, not principle, hinting that they now have a much better chance of succeeding (p. 385). Then, reinforcing the strong deontological stance he has just taken against racial slavery, he promises that if it ever does come to a race war, he will side with "right" and not his own race (pp. 385–86).[54]

Of course, Phillips does not believe that it ever will come to a race war. As long as the North makes clear to the South that it will "welcome the black race to liberty" if a slave insurrection ever occurs, "there will never be an insurrection" because the Southern states will choose instead to free their slaves. The Northern states only need stand firm for "Liberty and Justice" (p. 386).[55] This point leads Phillips away from the evils of slavery to a final argument against compromise. "Compromise degrades us, and puts back freedom in Europe" (p. 386). Here he appeals to the American sense of mission to counter the temptations faced by Northern politicians to offer further concessions to the South. The argument is again contextualist and even more identifiably liberal in nature. It is a union of free institutions and racial slavery that has transformed free institutions into "breeders of men" (p. 386). For Phillips, the "American exemplar" argument becomes yet another argument for why a house divided against itself cannot stand and why it should be reunited only on the basis of "Liberty and Equality" (p. 387).[56]

Phillips's arguments for disunion seem relatively unaffected by the change from a hypothetical Northern secession to an actual Southern secession. His primary emphasis remains on the evils of continued union, not on the evils of racial slavery per se; on how continued union adversely affects the people of the North, not the Southern slaves; and on how those deleterious consequences arise from a house divided, not on a decontextualized analysis of the likely impact of the continued existence of Southern slavery. Still he also, as before, presents several deontological appeals to personal and sectional purity against continued union as well as several scenarios as to how, on consequentialist grounds, continued union would adversely affect the Southern slaves by postponing the end of Southern slavery. This remarkable continuity in rhetoric persists even though the house has now physically divided; the South, not the North, has divided it; and Phillips's arguments for disunion have become arguments against "premature" reunion.

In the "Progress" speech, Phillips presents one new argument for disunion. He now explicitly argues that it can only be a temporary condition. Sounding as unapologetically nationalistic as Richard Dana or Daniel Webster or any other antiabolitionist, Phillips declares that

> the people of the States between the Gulf and the great Lakes, yes, between the Gulf and the Pole, are essentially one. We are one in blood, trade, thought, religion, history; nothing can long divide us. If we had let our Constitution grow, as the English did, as oaks do, we had never passed through such scenes as the present. The only thing that divides us now, is the artificial attempt, in 1787, to force us into an unripe union. (P. 375; see also pp. 387–88)[57]

While Phillips, in striking contrast to the antiabolitionists, denounces the Constitution as an artificial attempt "to force us into an unripe union," he assumes that notwithstanding the current situation, the union has grown together over time and that it eventually will reassert itself (pp. 375-76). As he explains, "The heat of sixty years' agitation has severed the heterogeneous mass; wait awhile, it will fuse together all that is really one" (p. 376). The implication of this passage is that Southern slavery is the source of this "heterogeneous mass," that the abolition of the institution will render the mass homogeneous, that any effort to fuse it together before then will be "unripe," but that at that time such an effort will not be problematic.[58] Phillips's argument for temporary disunion was bound to be received more favorably by the staunchly nationalistic Northern public of 1861 than an argument for permanent disunion would have been.

Temporary disunion, however, has been for many years the unstated logic of Phillips's "house divided" argument. Phillips, furthermore, remains a disunionist, albeit a provisional one.[59] Only the actual outbreak of hostilities finally dislodged him from that position. Yet his subsequent shift from disunionism to unionism was not as abrupt or as arbitrary as it seemed. In view of his earlier antislavery writings and speeches, it was a predictable reaction to developing events. In this case, developing events made a mockery of his optimism about the prospects for a peaceful disunion and a peaceful abolition of Southern slavery and reunion on that basis. His shift from disunionism to unionism thus turned on him, conceptually relocating progress toward freedom from progress toward disunion to progress toward reunion on the basis of the North's forcing the South back into the union and destroying its institution of racial slavery in the process. Not coincidentally, this shift became the sine qua non of popular support for Garrison abolitionism.

A War to Save the Union

In another widely attended speech in Boston, only two months after the "Progress" speech, Phillips publicly announced his shift from a "let the South go in peace" attitude toward disunion to his support of a war to force the South back into the union. What intervened between his earlier speech and this "Under the Flag" speech of April 21, 1861, was the firing on Fort Sumter, which made civil war seem inevitable, whether or not Phillips supported it.[60] Not surprisingly, he framed his support of the impending war as support for a war not simply to save the union but also to destroy Southern slavery. He predicted that the institution would inevitably be one of the causalities of the war (p. 408). His speech occasioned a *pro*abolitionist mob in Boston.[61] The Garrison abolitionists finally seemed to be aligning themselves with Northern public opinion in their attitudes toward the Constitution and union.

Phillips opens his "Under the Flag" speech with a defense of his own personal consistency. He refuses to retract any of his prior public statements in favor of disunion (p. 396). According to Phillips, what has changed is not his own stance toward the union but the stance of the union toward slavery. He now can conscientiously place himself "under the flag" because "to-day it represents sovereignty and justice" (pp. 396–97).

During the speech, Phillips suggests a scenario that supports his claim to personal consistency. In this scenario, he previously had welcomed Southern secession from the union under the assumption that disunion would be peaceful and that it would be temporary (pp. 406–7; see also p. 413).[62] But the firing on Fort Sumter has dashed his hopes for a peaceful disunion and subsequent reunion on that basis. As he interprets the event, it demonstrates that a bellicose South is determined to wage war, forcing a conciliatory North to prepare for hostilities (p. 407).

Phillips's views, however, have changed in more dramatic ways than this scenario suggests. The North did, in fact, have a choice. It could have been even more conciliatory toward the South, as Phillips himself had originally advocated. It could have recognized Southern independence, which, among other things, would have meant abandoning Fort Sumter.[63] Phillips's attitude toward Southern secession has also changed in other ways. He acknowledges that President Lincoln could not have legally recognized Southern independence because secession is a revolutionary, not a constitutional, right (p. 402).[64] Although Phillips does recognize secession as a revolutionary right (pp. 403–4), he now insists that the South cannot legitimately exercise that right without emancipating its slaves (pp. 404–5). Again appealing to the Declaration of Independence's Lockean guidelines for legitimate revolutions, Phillips contends that no people can claim "the right of revolution to set up or preserve a system which the common conscience of mankind stamps as wicked and infamous" (p. 405). He believes that the North now is determined to see justice done to the Southern slaves before it accepts Southern independence (p. 407) and therefore suggests that it is really the North's determination to destroy Southern slavery, not the South's determination to wage war, that has made civil war inevitable.[65]

This last point calls attention to a second, more dramatic shift in attitude. Previously, Phillips argued that an independent South *was* likely to abolish slavery without the necessity of war. But now he is claiming that war has historically been the only way of abolishing slavery (pp. 410–11) and that this particular war will mean the end of Southern slavery with or, probably, without the South's acquiescence (p. 408).[66]

Finally, Phillips's views of the Constitution and union have changed. He remarks, in a classic understatement, that before the current crisis, "we Abolitionists have doubted whether this Union really meant justice and liberty" (p. 407). In this crisis, he, however, believes that the people of the North have silenced those doubts. "They have said, in answer to our criticism: 'We believe that the Fathers meant to establish justice. We believe that there are hidden in the armory of the Constitution weapons strong enough to secure it'" (pp. 407–8). He also characterizes the present struggle as one "to show that [17]89 meant justice" (p. 409) and goes on to paraphrase John Quincy Adams on the war powers as the weapon "hidden in the armory of the Constitution" that can be wielded to establish justice and liberty by destroying Southern slavery (pp. 409–10). He even filiopietistically challenges the people of the North to prove in the impending war that they are the true heirs of the founding fathers (p. 412), now that they no longer need to read the Constitution any further than the preamble's "establish *Justice* and secure *Liberty*" (p. 413). At least rhetorically, Phillips has traveled quite a distance from vitriolically denouncing the Constitution as "a covenant with death and an agreement with hell" and righteously vowing to support "no union with slaveholders."[67]

But Phillips's claim to personal consistency contains a large measure of truth. As we have seen, his earlier antislavery writings and speeches were never as disunionist as they seemed. The logic (stated and unstated) of his disunionist position entailed temporary disunion and reunion on the basis of a general emancipation of the Southern slaves. He has always believed "in the certainty of union" (p. 414). Since 1837, Phillips has used the "house divided" argument to stress the incompatibility of the Southern institution of racial slavery and the nation's predominant liberal institutions and to predict the ultimate triumph of the latter over the former. The rush of events has "merely" shortened the timetable.[68] A union with slaveholders no longer exists and, according to Phillips, never will again. The Constitution and union have been purged of the corrupting influences of Southern slavery, justifying more favorable attitudes toward each.[69] Whereas previously the "house divided" argument had counseled disunion to save Northern liberty, the argument now counsels a war to save the union. Because Phillips is convinced that a war to save the union is a war to destroy Southern slavery, the alternatives are now either "Emancipation or Disunion," not, as before, emancipation or union (p. 412).

Near the beginning of the speech, Phillips indicates that the abolitionists' greatest mistake was their failure to appreciate just how divided or heterogeneous the union really was (p. 399).[70] This heterogeneity explains why their tactic of moral suasion succeeded only in converting the North, and not the South, to the antislavery creed. The partial nature of the abolitionists' success, in turn, has brought the two sections of the country to the brink of civil war as well as required the abolitionists themselves to change many of their long-held attitudes in the face of such a war (pp. 398–99).[71] At this point in the speech, Phillips describes the vast differences he sees between the two sections of the country, clearly aligning the North with progress and the South with regress.

> The North *thinks*,—can appreciate argument,—it is the nineteenth century,—hardly any struggle left in it but that between the working class and the money-kings. The South *dreams*,—it is the thirteenth and fourteenth century,—baron and serf,—noble and slave. . . . Our struggle, therefore, is between barbarism and civilization. Such can only be settled by arms. (P. 399)[72]

In the peroration, Phillips returns to this hyperbolic comparison between the North and the South as a house divided between civilization and barbarism. The outcome of their irrepressible conflict no longer appears doubtful.

> But really the war is one of opinions: it is Civilization against Barbarism: it is Freedom against Slavery. The cannon-shot against Fort Sumter was the yell of pirates against the DECLARATION OF INDEPENDENCE; the war-cry of the North is the echo of that sublime pledge. The South, defying Christianity, clutches its victim. The North offers its wealth and blood in glad atonement for the selfishness of seventy years. The result is as sure as the throne of God. I believe in the possibility of justice, in the certainty of union. Years hence, when the smoke of this conflict clears away, the world will see under our banner all tongues, all creeds, all races,—one brotherhood,—and on the banks of the Potomac, the Genius of Liberty, robed in light, four and thirty stars for her diadem, broken chains under feet, and an olive-branch in her right hand. (P. 414)

This passage is a strong testament to the progressive liberalism that Phillips shared with Douglass, Child, and other Garrisonian and non-Garrisonian abolitionists and that he articulated in his earlier antislavery works.[73] He believes in the progressive expansion of "the Genius of

Liberty" to "all tongues, all creeds, all races." Southern slavery is wrong because it stands in the way of that expansion, but the institution will be swept aside by it. Phillips is confident that the North will conquer the South in the coming war because the North embodies liberal progress. It is built on such institutions as "free speech, free toil, school-houses, and ballot-boxes," whereas the South is built on an institution that is incompatible with those liberal institutions (p. 411). Indeed, in order for "a New England man" to perfect his liberal society, he need only "wipe away the stain which hangs about the toleration of human bondage" (p. 412). Phillips firmly believes that both the North's victory in the coming war and its exemplary role in liberal progress depend on its determination to destroy Southern slavery and remake the South in its own liberal image (pp. 411–12).[74]

Obviously, Phillips does not believe that liberal progress is the only thing that condemns Southern slavery. In this speech, as in his earlier antislavery works, he also advances several deontological and consequentialist arguments against the institution. The peroration, for instance, asserts a number of deontological claims against it, of the mixed religious and secular character typical of the abolitionists. Phillips accuses the South of defying both the Declaration of Independence and Christianity in holding onto the institution (p. 414). He also defends civil war on the consequentialist grounds that it portends the end of Southern slavery. Whatever tragedies civil war may contain, he believes that it cannot possibly be as tragic as the continuing existence of such a pernicious institution (pp. 400, 411). In sum, Phillips contends that the North has both "right" and "might" on its side in its irrepressible conflict with the South (pp. 411–12).

These deontological and consequentialist arguments, however, are embedded in a broader contextualist argument that defines Southern slavery as an anachronistic institution doomed by inevitable progress toward liberty and equality for all. In this speech, the "human progress" argument becomes Phillips's climactic argument in reinforcing Northern antislavery sentiments and in rallying Northern war efforts and, for that matter, in attempting to fuse the two together. The argument tells him the house cannot long remain divided and also that the house can reunite only on the basis of freedom for the Southern slaves. With the storms of war gathering, it is Phillips's hopes for the future that are truly irrepressible.

For Phillips, the "human progress" argument has long fueled an unshakable faith in the future, at least in the long-term future, and provided the "house divided" argument with its "proper" conclusion. Recent events, though, have accentuated those tendencies. Now that the house has actually divided, Phillips fully expects the emergent Republican majority in the North to conclude, with him, that the house can reunite only on the basis of freedom for the Southern slaves, not merely on the basis of free soil or the other moderate antislavery measures initially contemplated by the Lincoln administration. The purpose of his "Under the Flag" speech is precisely to ensure that the Republican majority reaches no other conclusion. This rhetorical purpose explains Phillips's newly invigorated unionism; its anticipated success explains his exuberant progressive liberalism.

Conclusion

Unfortunately, a war to end slavery lasted much longer than Phillips or anyone else expected, and the result was not a perfect liberal society of liberty and equality for all. When in late 1862, the Lincoln administration finally abolished the institution of racial slavery in the South as a means of restoring the union, the abolitionists cheered on the action, but it obscured the differences between them and their more moderate Republican allies regarding racial equality.[75] Although those differences quickly reemerged once the union was restored, the abolitionists themselves had helped obscure them. During the antebellum period, they increasingly emphasized the ways that Southern slavery adversely affected the rights and liberties of the people of the North, and not just the rights and liberties of the African American slaves. They also increasingly emphasized the ways that the continued existence of the institution adversely affected the long-term stability of the union. Such tactics could not fail to marginalize the freed slaves in the postbellum South.

The abolitionists certainly bear some responsibility for the failure of Reconstruction.[76] Yet more than the choices they made, the public intransigence they encountered in both the North and the South was responsible for those failures. The abolitionists were absolutely correct about one thing: it was not that the institutional barriers to abolishing racial slavery and achieving racial equality were so high; it was that the racial prejudices and economic anxieties of Northern and Southern whites ran so deep. As Douglass stated repeatedly in his Fourth of July oration, American hypocrisy was at the core of the problem of slavery. The slavery issue in the antebellum United States was defined centrally by the failure of a people to bear witness to its own liberal principles. However, as we shall see in the next two chapters, the defenders of slavery at the time were unwilling to concede that definition of the issue to the abolitionists.

Part III

5

Dew, Fitzhugh, and Proslavery Liberalism

The proslavery movement in the antebellum South attempted to forestall a process of institutional change. The defenders of slavery were ultimately not successful in preventing the abolition of the Southern institution of racial slavery, an event that unleashed a process of institutional change that at least partially remade the South in the North's image.[1] This failure, however, seems to have been less a failure of the proslavery movement on a political or rhetorical level than it was a failure of Southern power. By all accounts, the defenders of slavery were successful within their own milieu.[2]

That milieu was liberal. Despite the way that they usually have been interpreted, the defenders of slavery did offer predominantly liberal proslavery arguments, as they were the arguments most likely to appeal to their predominantly liberal audiences in the South. Hence, they did not rely solely, or even primarily, on racist proslavery arguments, instead preferring to continually, even if never completely, recast the racist beliefs they shared with their audiences as liberal proslavery arguments. As I intend to demonstrate further in this and the next chapter, the public face of the proslavery movement was more liberal than it was racist or ascriptive.[3]

The defenders of slavery paid obeisance to both mainstream progressive and liberal beliefs.[4] They argued that slavery was not a dying but a universal institution and that it possessed all the progressive features that the abolitionists attributed to free-labor, and not slave-labor, institutions. Furthermore, they contended, also in opposition to the abolitionists, that the continued existence of racial slavery in the South did not belie the nation's special mission in history but, rather, advanced that mission. Like the abolitionists, they thus sought to portray themselves as progressive liberals and not as the reactionary racists that scholars commonly depict them as being or that we might think they really were in their heart of hearts.[5]

In short, many of the same rhetorical dynamics that affected the proslavery movement also affected the antislavery movement.[6] The movement became more liberal and "positive good" over time as the proslavery arguments shifted from antiabolitionist to proslavery. It also became more "impure" or contextualist over time as the proslavery arguments shifted from defending slavery to defending slavery and union. Proslavery figures insisted that the continued existence of racial slavery in the South did not create a "house divided" but that continued Northern agitation over the existence of the institution did. During the antebellum period, they refined these unionist proslavery arguments in an attempt to solicit more moderate Southern opinion. Ironically, the success of this tactic became the precondition of disunion during the secession winter of 1860–61.[7]

In this and the next chapter, I analyze several important pieces of proslavery rhetoric, dating from 1832 to 1860, to support the preceding interpretation of the defenders of slavery as progressive liberals equal to, though perhaps not as straightforward as, the abolitionists. In comparison to the secondary literature on the antislavery movement, the literature on the proslavery movement is inferior in quality. Also in comparison to the literature on the antislavery movement, the literature on the proslavery movement generally assumes that the movement was illiberal, not liberal, in nature. Louis Hartz's *Liberal Tradition in America* propounded this view, and Rogers Smith's *Civic Ideals* recently restated it.[8]

A related strain in the literature, running from Eugene Genovese's *Political Economy of Slavery* to John Ashworth's *Slavery and Capitalism*, interprets the proslavery movement as illiberal in the sense of being precapitalistic rather than racist or ascriptive.[9] James Oakes's *Slavery and Freedom* contests this view, as does Kenneth Greenberg's *Masters and Statesmen*, although from a republican instead of a liberal perspective.[10] Neither study, then, presents a systematic case for proslavery liberalism. In presenting that case, as I did in presenting the case for antislavery liberalism, I either significantly go beyond the existing secondary literature or depart from it. Also as I did in presenting the case for antislavery liberalism, I analyze the arguments of three prominent participants in the antebellum debate over the fate of Southern slavery, not to show that all their arguments were liberal ones, much less explicitly or self-consciously so. Liberal principles were more implicit in the proslavery arguments than in the antislavery arguments, which is one of the points of departure for the literature on the proslavery movement. But that literature generally overlooks the way that liberal principles were nonetheless fundamental to the proslavery arguments, just as they were to the antislavery arguments.

I start presenting the case for proslavery liberalism with Thomas R. Dew's *Review of the Debate in the Virginia Legislature, 1831–32.* Dew's *Review* was written and originally published in 1832.[11] The thrust of this early proslavery pamphlet was antiabolitionist, to repudiate the various schemes proposed during a recent debate in the Virginia legislature to rid the state of slavery (and blacks).[12] It clearly was intended for an internal Virginia audience, to (re)unify the state behind racial slavery in the wake of an unprecedented, and very divisive, debate over the future of the institution in the state.[13] Next, I analyze George Fitzhugh's *Cannibals All! or Slaves without Masters.* Fitzhugh's *Cannibals All* was published in 1857, a quarter century after Dew's *Review.*[14] Fitzhugh clearly had broader intentions and audiences in mind. The thrust of *Cannibals All* was unapologetically proslavery. In contrast to Dew's earlier work, its defense of racial slavery was more liberal and contextualist as well as more "positive good." Fitzhugh sought to defend the institution as a liberal institution within the context of the existing union, instead of the state of Virginia, and his rhetorical foils were not fellow Virginians of a more antislavery bent but radical Northern abolitionists.[15]

In chapter 6, I shift from an interpersonal to an intrapersonal comparison. I analyze several of James Henry Hammond's major proslavery works to show how his proslavery arguments changed over time. In contrast to both Dew and Fitzhugh, Hammond was a native of South Carolina and a prominent slaveholder and politician. Yet despite these and other differences among these three men, each emerged as a powerful spokesman for progressive liberalism on the proslavery side.[16] Together, they argue for the "liberal consensus" thesis in the face of its toughest case.

Thomas R. Dew

The Antiabolitionist Argument

Thomas R. Dew seemed to gleefully accept the role of the antiabolitionist. The intention of his review of the 1831–32 debate in the Virginia legislature over the fate of slavery in the state was negative. It did not so much defend the institution as attack the various emancipation schemes that had been proposed during the recent legislative debate. Dew's focus seems perfectly consistent with the "necessary evil" school of proslavery thought.[17]

But Dew actually straddled the "necessary evil" and "positive good" schools. He framed his "necessary evil" attack on abolition with a "positive good" defense of slavery. While the central section of the essay details the many potential harms of abolition, the first and last sections praise the many alleged benefits of slavery.[18] Given the timing of his essay, it is not surprising that Dew straddled the two schools of proslavery thought. The essay reflects the shift in emphasis from antiabolitionist "necessary evil" arguments to proslavery "positive good" arguments that had emerged in the American South by the 1830s. It also, however, indicates the lack of demarcation between the two schools.[19]

Necessary Evil

Reviewing the various emancipation schemes proposed or contemplated in the second section of his essay, Dew rejects each of them on consequentialist grounds. He divides the schemes into two categories: emancipation with removals and emancipation without removals. He initially targets emancipation with removals as the general scheme favored by his state's antislavery legislators. Dew seems to take them at face value. At least for the sake of argument, he considers their plans for colonizing Africa with freed Virginia slaves as *bona fide* efforts to gradually abolish slavery in the state. Here Dew assumes that everyone—he, they, and the broader public in Virginia and elsewhere—opposes emancipation without removals.[20]

As a plan of emancipation, Dew insists that colonization is totally impractical. To rid Virginia of slavery (and blacks), colonization would have to be carried out on such a grandiose scale that it would be economically unfeasible. It would bankrupt the state because it could never bear the costs of compensating the slaveholders for their slaves and transporting the freed slaves to Africa (pp. 357–66). On the other hand, if colonization were carried out on an economically feasible scale, it never would come close to ridding Virginia of slavery (or blacks). At best, it would merely slow the rate of increase of the state's slave (black) population (pp. 366–79). Therefore, as a plan of emancipation, Dew contends that colonization inevitably would fall far short of its goal.[21]

Dew next criticizes three variations on colonization that seek to shift the costs from the state of Virginia to individual slaveholders or to the slaves themselves: (1) the slaveholders voluntarily emancipate their slaves and pay the costs of transporting them to Africa (pp. 379–81);[22] (2) the slaves work to purchase their own freedom and pay their own transportation costs to Africa (pp. 381–84);[23] and (3) the state compels (without compensation) the slaveholders to free their slaves and pay the costs of transporting them to Africa (pp. 384–91).[24] According to Dew, these cost-shifting schemes only seem to make colonization more economically feasible. The insurmountable barrier to any plan of emancipation with removals is the $100 million that Virginians have invested in their slaves. Dew warns that "Virginia will be a desert" if a serious colonization effort is ever undertaken in the state (p. 384; see also p. 380).

Even if hundreds of thousands of slaves could be miraculously freed and transported to Africa without costing anyone anything, Dew still would consider colonization an ill-advised policy. He claims that the costs to the freed slaves—in terms of the high mortality rates they would suffer as they adjusted to their new environment (pp. 394–400)—and to Virginians—in terms of the large sums of money they would have to contribute to the new colony as it struggled to become self-sufficient (pp. 400–4, 411–12)—would be prohibitive.[25] He also believes that any serious colonization effort would not, as its proponents contend, result in the freed slaves' "civilizing" Africans but, rather, in wars of extermination between the two now-separate races (pp. 409–10). From every angle he looks at colonization, Dew considers it a disastrous policy.

At this point in the essay, Dew turns his attention to the second category of emancipation schemes: emancipation without removals. He insists that if Virginia's antislavery legislators are really serious about abolishing slavery in the state, they will be forced to move in this direction because of the impracticability of any scheme of emancipation with removals (pp. 420–21). Whereas Dew's critique of emancipation with removals emphasizes its impracticability, his critique of emancipation without removals emphasizes its undesirability.

According to Dew, the reason that everyone opposes emancipation without removals is because everyone agrees that it is impossible for people of two different races to live together as equals in peace, harmony, and prosperity (p. 444). He presents this impossibility as a historical truth, confirmed by the recent experiences of other nations such as Haiti (pp. 440–41) and Guatemala (p. 445–46) with emancipation without removals. Nor, he argues, is the American North a counterexample because of its paucity of blacks (p. 446); besides, as he points out, free blacks do not live exactly as equals to whites there (p. 436). In view of its large black population, Dew anticipates a dramatic increase in black-on-white violence in Virginia if emancipation does not include a physical separation of the two races. "But one limited massacre is recorded in Virginia history; let her liberate her slaves, and every year you would hear of insurrections and plots, and every day would perhaps record a murder; the melancholy tale of Southampton would not alone blacken the page of our history" (p. 444).[26]

Dew considers the slaves' lack of preparedness for freedom as the source of the other undesirable consequences of emancipation without removals (pp. 437, 442). He believes that blacks will not prosper as free laborers because they fancy that freedom means freedom from work (pp. 428–30). He thus predicts that the freed slaves will become the drones of society, as, he alleges, has occurred in the American North and Latin America (pp. 422–24). He also believes that free black labor will depress free white labor to its own inefficient level (p. 443) and therefore that emancipation without removals will precipitate a general famine in Virginia (p. 433).[27] He finally believes that the freed slaves also will hurt society (as well as themselves) with their high rates of lawlessness (pp. 433–35), drunkenness (p. 439), and indebtedness (p. 440). As a result, Dew is "almost certain" that emancipation without removals will "bring down ruin and degradation both on the whites and the blacks" (p. 446; see also p. 451).

Even when viewing emancipation without removals solely from an African American perspective, Dew sees it as an undesirable policy. He claims that the freed slaves "would still be virtually slaves; talent, habit, and wealth, would make the white the master still, and the emancipation would only have the tendency to deprive" them of the "sympathies and kind feelings" of Southern whites (p. 437). He predicts that Virginia would be forced to impose a compulsory labor system, "more intolerable" than slavery, on the freed slaves in order to prevent a general famine in the state (pp. 441–42).[28] And he suggests that blacks will never be truly free and equal to whites in the United States, since they always will face the same racial prejudices they currently face in slavery (pp. 435–36, 447–48).[29] In part because the promise of freedom would remain unfulfilled, Dew insists that blacks are happier now as slaves than they would be as free persons (pp. 437, 442).[30] He asks rhetorically why "the happiest of the human race are constantly invited to sigh for such freedom, and to sacrifice all their happiness in the vain wish" (p. 442)? He also laments the fact that emancipation would prematurely stop the process of improvement blacks are undergoing in slavery (pp. 429, 443). As Dew interprets the historical record, it confirms that "liberty has been the heaviest curse to the slave, when given too soon" (p. 437).

Dew's own racial prejudices facilely place African Americans in the category of peoples unprepared to meet the requirements of self-government, but it is important to note that those requirements are liberal.[31] They include a proper definition of "rational liberty" as industriousness and not idleness or licentiousness. They also include certain behavioral components such as productive labor and an ability to govern oneself without falling prey to the temptations of crime, alcohol, or debt. In insisting that the slaves do not meet these requirements, Dew is in effect arguing that a liberal society cannot afford to emancipate them because it would mean no more freedom for them and less freedom for everyone else.[32]

After Dew has finished attacking these various emancipation schemes, his readers must have wondered whether he thought the time ever would come when the slaves would be prepared for freedom and their emancipation would not be "too soon." Later in the essay, he does propose his own emancipation scheme. His plan is to transform Virginia into a more economically progressive state by crisscrossing it with internal improvements (pp. 477–81). His hope is that this policy would make the state more attractive to free labor, thereby decreasing its dependence on slave labor and the proportion of blacks in its population to the point that the state's slaveholders would no longer feel any need to keep slaves or any danger in freeing them. Dew expects that "in due time the abolitionists will find this most lucrative system working to their heart's content, increasing the prosperity of Virginia, and diminishing the evils of slavery, without those impoverishing effects which all other schemes must necessarily have" (p. 479).[33]

Besides the fact that Dew's plan of emancipation is open to many of the same objections that he himself has leveled against other such plans, his plan places the end of slavery in Virginia in such an indeterminate future that it seems gratuitous for him to offer it as a plan of emancipation. Appropriately, in the penultimate paragraph of his essay, Dew states that he now has proved "by reasoning almost as conclusive as the demonstrations of the mathematician . . . that the time for emancipation has not yet arrived, and perhaps it never will" (p. 489).

If Dew adhered to the "necessary evil" school on Southern slavery, he also adhered to the "necessary evil" school that believed that the institution might always be necessary. He offers no suggestions for preparing the slaves for freedom, despite his insistence that they need to be so prepared. Indeed, he strongly implies that they never will be ready to be free persons because as members of an allegedly inferior race, they are naturally unsuited to that status (pp. 421–22, 428–30, 433, 449–50).[34] Dew's "necessary evil" defense of slavery merges into a "positive good" defense of the institution. The more positive aspects of his defense of the institution emerge in the first and third sections of the essay.

Positive Good

Dew presents a "positive good" ideology most explicitly in the third and final section of his essay, in which he answers five objections to the "injustice and evils of slavery": (1) "slavery is wrong, in the *abstract* at least, and contrary to the spirit of Christianity" (pp. 451–54); (2) "the moral effects of slavery are of the most deleterions [*sic*] and hurtful kind" (pp. 454–61); (3) "slavery is unfavorable to a republican spirit" (pp. 461–62); (4) "insecurity of the whites, arising from plots, insurrections, and c., among the blacks" (pp. 462–82); and (5) "slave labor is unproductive, and the distressed condition of Virginia and the whole South is owing to this cause" (pp. 482–89).

In answering the first, deontological, objection, Dew develops a biblical defense of slavery. This defense turns on the claim that in the abstract, Judeo-Christian principles may condemn the institution, but in practice, they actually justify it.

Dew's initial response to the objection is that "any question must be determined by its circumstances, and if, as really is the case, we cannot get rid of slavery without producing a greater injury to both the masters and slaves, there is no rule of conscience or revealed law of God which *can* condemn us" (p. 451). He has already argued the point that abolishing slavery in Virginia would produce a greater injury to both the masters and slaves than the continued existence of the institution would. He also has already noted that the British government, not the people of Virginia, was responsible for the original injustice of introducing the institution into the state; a point he repeats here (p. 451).[35] He then admits the truth of the objection, but with a serious qualification.

> With regard to the assertion that slavery is against the spirit of Christianity, we are ready to admit the general assertion, but deny most positively, that there is any thing in the Old or New Testament, which would go to show that slavery, when once introduced, ought at all events to be abrogated, or that the master commits any offence in holding slaves. (P. 451)

At this point, Dew launches into his biblical defense of slavery. He observes that the ancient Hebrews themselves were slaveholders and were justified in the Old Testament for being so (pp. 451–52). He also observes that the New Testament justifies slaveholding. Even though Jesus "was born in the Roman world—a world in which the most galling slavery existed, a thousand times more cruel than the slavery in our own country . . . he no where encourages insurrection; he no where fosters discontent; but exhorts *always* to implicit obedience and fidelity" (p. 452). Dew concludes his biblical defense of slavery by quoting the scriptural exhortations to servants to obey their masters, which prove that "slavery in the Roman world was no where charged as a fault or crime upon the holder" (p. 453). By this point, Dew's admission of the truth of this first objection seems to be an admission without any substance.

Dew's responses to the four remaining objections are more strictly consequentialist. He takes the second objection from Jefferson's *Notes on the State of Virginia*, citing the passage that describes how the children of slaveholders learn to act like petty tyrants by watching how their fathers treat their slaves (pp. 454–55).[36] Dew claims that on the contrary, the children of most slaveholders learn the most elevated habits by watching how their fathers treat their slaves. "Instead of being reared a selfish contracted being, with nought but self to look to," the child of the typical slaveholder "acquires a more exalted benevolence, a greater generosity and elevation of soul, and embraces for the sphere of his generous actions a much wider field" (p. 455). Not surprisingly then, Dew contends that the slaveholding population of the American South has been conspicuous not for its despotic habits but for its "humane and virtuous" ones, as shown by its record of disinterested statesmanship in the national councils (pp. 455–56).[37]

In rebutting the third objection, Dew's attention shifts from the beneficial effects of slavery on those most intimately involved in the institution to its beneficial effects on the broader public. He first cites the ancient Greek and Roman republics as counterexamples to the claim that the institution undermines a republican spirit (p. 461). He goes on to suggest that as a rule, slave societies are freer than free societies.[38] For evidence, he quotes his favorite source, Edmund Burke, to the effect that the people of the South were more zealous partisans of liberty at the time of the American Revolution than the people of the North were. He concurs with Burke's reasoning that the former entertained "a higher and more stubborn" spirit of liberty than the latter did, because they regarded freedom as "a kind of rank and privilege" in comparison to their slaves (p. 461).[39] He adds that in the South, the institution of racial slavery has had a leveling effect on whites, making them more equal to one another than in the North, by reserving all menial employment for blacks (pp. 461–62). Dew views "this spirit of equality" as "the generator and preserver of the genuine spirit of liberty" (p. 462).[40]

Dew's reply to the fourth objection continues to portray Southern slave society as superior to Northern free society. He counters the claim that black slavery fosters a psychology of fear among Southern whites by pointing out that their fears of racial violence would only increase with emancipation (without removals) (p. 462). He also denies the premise of the objection, contending that Southern fears of racial violence are not very great now, nor should they be, given how infrequently slave revolts have occurred in the South in the past (p. 471).[41]

He acknowledges that those fears have increased recently because of the Nat Turner rebellion, but he expects that increase to be a temporary aberration (p. 481). Dew insists that the South "enjoys as much or more conscious security, than any other people on the face of the globe," more so than the North and other free societies whose lower classes are not safely tucked away in slavery (pp. 481–82; see also pp. 465–66).[42]

In answer to the last objection, Dew considers the real cause of the depressed economic conditions in Virginia and the rest of the South to be the unjust policies of the federal government, not slavery (pp. 486–87).[43] He argues that slave labor, while generally inferior to free labor, is the superior form of labor under Southern conditions of a predominantly African American workforce, a semitropical climate, and large-scale crop production (pp. 483–85).[44] Under these conditions, Dew believes that slavery significantly boosts regional economic performance.

In this final section of his *Review*, Dew constructs a "positive good" ideology for the antebellum South, associating its institution of racial slavery with such widely shared values as Christian charity, public service, political equality, collective security, economic prosperity, and, above all, the definitive liberal value of personal freedom. In the first section of the essay, Dew states the case for slavery as a positive good on an even grander scale, chronicling "its effects on the progress of civilization" (pp. 294–324), the "advantages which have resulted to the world from the institution of slavery" (pp. 324–36), and the positive "influence of slavery on the condition of the female sex" (pp. 336–42). Here, he attempts to align slavery with human progress. This effort focuses on possible Judeo-Christian and liberal justifications of the institution.[45]

The first section of the essay contains the first of several discussions of the ancient Hebraic institution of slavery. Dew uncovers two justifications of the institution. First, it was a substitute for killing captives of war: during their conquest of Canaan, the ancient Hebrews at least partially departed from the then-prevalent practice of killing captives of war by instead enslaving some of them (pp. 306–7). Second, it was a substitute for starvation: along with other ancient peoples, the Hebrews sold themselves into slavery as a way of paying off their debts or in other cases of extreme poverty (pp. 317–18).[46] Under those circumstances, the institution appears to have been a pragmatic exchange of liberty for life, justified by Judeo-Christian principles on that basis and less barbaric than the alternative.

Viewed from a liberal perspective, slavery seems similar. Dew cites a number of natural-law theorists, including the quintessential liberal theorist, John Locke, on the justice of enslaving captives of war, at least under certain circumstances (pp. 308–10).[47] He then considers William Blackstone's rebuttal of this "just war" justification of slavery. Blackstone argued that because conquering armies do not need to kill their captives, enslaving them instead is unjust. Dew finds Blackstone's reasoning fallacious because Blackstone wrongly assumed that slavery exists "in its pure, unmitigated form, 'whereby an unlimited power is given to the master over the life and fortune of the slave,'" when in reality the institution has never existed in that form (p. 310). To the degree that it is a genuine and legally regulated exchange of liberty for life, Dew thinks that liberal principles do justify enslaving captives of war and justify the captives' accepting the implicit bargain.

For Dew, Judeo-Christian and liberal principles also coincide in justifying slavery in those cases in which people sell themselves into slavery in order to preserve their lives. He again criticizes Blackstone for failing to recognize that slavery in its existing, "impure" forms is sometimes a good bargain for the slave (p. 321). It is a good bargain on liberal grounds because according to Dew, the slave receives more than subsistence in exchange. Dew insists that "in most parts of the world," the slave is not only guaranteed "nourishment and subsistence" but is also "carefully protected in life, limb, and even in a moderate share of liberty, by the policy of the laws" (p. 321). Dew, therefore, is not content to place the slave's "bargain" solely on the basis of trading liberty for life.

In regard to the liberal goals of life, happiness, *and* liberty, Dew believes that many people around the world would be better off as slaves than they currently are as free persons. His example is a Chinese laborer who lives on the brink of starvation (pp. 321–22). Dew contends that this person is clearly worse off than a slave, for "he is subjected to all the hardships and degradation of the slave, and derives none of the advantages" (p. 322). When he sells himself into slavery, Dew believes that such a person is making a good bargain. Dew speculates that more people around the world would sell themselves into slavery if the laws of their countries did not prevent them from doing so. He even contends that the supply would exceed the demand. The British capitalist, for one, "could not afford to purchase the operative, and treat him as we do the slave" (p. 322; see also p. 319).

Still, his readers might well have asked, what is the relation between these two Judeo-Christian and liberal justifications of slavery and the Southern institution of racial slavery? After all, Dew admits that American laborers, who unlike Chinese laborers live in a relatively prosperous and sparsely populated country, do not need to sell themselves into slavery in order to survive (p. 321). Nor does he offer any "just war" justification of Southern slavery.[48]

Dew, however, is making a broader point through these two justifications of slavery, and that broader point does apply to Southern slavery. It is that some people enjoy more practical liberty as slaves than they would as free persons. Dew's racial prejudices again facilely place African Americans in the category of people who enjoy more practical liberty as slaves than they would (or do) as free persons. But his point is not strictly a racial one. It is that all societies are structured around different statuses; that the precise status leading to the most practical liberty for any one person depends on the capacities of that person and the conditions of the society in which he or she lives; and that the abstract distinction between the status of free persons and slaves confounds the more finely tuned analysis necessary to determine how much practical liberty people actually enjoy in any particular status. On the basis of such an analysis, Dew argues not only that the Southern institution of racial slavery is relatively benevolent but also that the status of slaves and statuses analogous to it are extremely prevalent. He finds that "looking to the whole world, we may, even now, with confidence assert, that slaves, or those whose condition is infinitely worse, form by far the largest portion of the human race" (p. 296).[49]

After establishing a universalistic basis for the institution, Dew tightens the linkage between slavery and progress. He opens this discussion by stating that "slavery has been, perhaps, the principal means for impelling forward the civilization of mankind. Without its agency, society must have remained sunk into that deplorable state of barbarism and wretchedness which characterized the inhabitants of the Western World, when first discovered by Columbus" (p. 325). He initially stresses the fact that slavery has made wars more humane because historically, as he argued earlier, it was instituted as a substitute for killing captives of war (pp. 325–26). Once instituted, though, he claims that it instigated further progress by elevating men from the hunting stage of civilization to the agricultural stage (pp. 326–29). Dew contends that this advance is especially evident among the African American slaves. He, indeed, contends that "there is not, in the annals of history, an instance of such rapid improvement in civilization, as that undergone by the negro slaves in our country, since the time they were first brought among us" (p. 334). Finally, he claims that slavery also has elevated the status of women by creating a stable family structure (pp. 338–39, 341). According to Dew, the institution has fueled such widespread progress that "even the slave, in the agricultural, is happier than the free man [and woman] in the hunting state" (p. 339; see also pp. 337–38).[50]

In this first section of the *Review*, Dew thus dissents from the antislavery version of the "human progress" argument, which characterizes slavery as a regressive rather than a progressive institution. Much later, he also dissents from the antislavery version of the "house divided" argument. In the final paragraph of his essay, Dew notes that the ancient Greek and Roman republics were houses divided against themselves that did stand. He also observes that the Polish people have maintained a strong spirit of liberty despite their continuing feudal relations.[51] Dew then draws the parallel with Virginia.

> We must recollect, in fine, that our own country [Virginia] has waded through two dangerous wars—that the thrilling eloquence of the Demosthenes of our land [Patrick Henry] has been heard with rapture, exhorting to death, rather than slavery,—that the most liberal principles have even been promulgated and sustained, in our deliberate bodies, and before our judicial tribunals—and the whole has passed by without breaking or tearing asunder the elements of our social fabric. (P. 490)

In this final paragraph, Dew draws together two of his major "positive good" arguments: (1) some of the freest societies in history have been slave societies, and (2) once Americans properly situate the status of slaves within a more general set of dependent statuses, they can better appreciate its universality as well as its necessity. But most important for our purposes, Dew explicitly asserts that the nation's liberal founding principles and the Southern institution of racial slavery are not incompatible with each other.

Dew's main goal in the *Review* is not to neutralize the antislavery versions of the contextualist "human progress" and "house divided" arguments. Rather, it is to criticize his state's antislavery legislators on consequentialist grounds, for failing to assess realistically the probable effects of their pet projects. Accordingly, Dew closes his essay by reminding them that "the relations of society, generated by the *lapse of ages*, cannot be altered in a *day*" (p. 490). This theme of legislative irresponsibility recurs throughout the essay (see also pp. 288, 293–94, 354–55, 443, 450–51, 482).[52] In particular, Dew accuses his adversaries of failing to adjust the nation's liberal founding principles to existing conditions. In a key passage, he scolds them for "pompously and ostentatiously" proclaiming that "all men are born equal" and "the slave has a natural right to regain his liberty." Again citing Burke with approval, he retorts that "no set of legislators ever have, or ever can, legislate upon purely abstract principles, entirely independent of circumstances, without the ruin of the body politic" (pp. 354–55). Although Dew straddles the "necessary evil" and "positive good" schools on Southern slavery, his primary arguments remain antiabolitionist. He uses liberal principles mostly implicitly and negatively to denounce his adversaries for recklessly misusing those principles to attack the continued existence of racial slavery in Virginia and the rest of the South.

Twenty-five years later, by the time of Fitzhugh's *Cannibals All*, the priorities of the proslavery movement had changed. The immediatist philosophy of the Garrison abolitionists had replaced the colonizationist philosophy of Virginia's dissident legislators as the principal antislavery vehicle in the United States. Although Fitzhugh certainly offers both antiabolitionist and proslavery consequentialist arguments in *Cannibals All*, his focus is elsewhere. Compared with Dew, he develops a more "positive good" defense of racial slavery that does not even admit the institution was wrong on deontological grounds. He also defends the institution more explicitly and positively on liberal grounds. Given the increased sectional tensions of the 1850s, Fitzhugh's work, moreover, reveals a greater contextualist emphasis on how the union (as opposed to Virginia) was, or was not, a house divided.

George Fitzhugh

The Proslavery Argument

In *Cannibals All*, George Fitzhugh develops a two-pronged defense of Southern slavery. On the first prong, he defends the institution as part of a broader family of protective institutions, as a universally based institution akin to the institutions of the American North and other parts of the world. On the second prong, he defends the institution as a peculiarly Southern institution, as an institution of racial slavery specially fitted for the members of an allegedly inferior race. Fitzhugh hopes the first, more liberal prong will carry the second, more racist prong along with it. He, however, cannot completely neglect the second prong because the Southern institution of racial slavery is the institution he has chosen to defend to the world. Together, the two prongs of his defense of Southern slavery have the advantage of allowing him to appeal to both the liberal and the racist sentiments of his audience and of blurring the distinction between them.

This approach can be confusing, and purposely so. Corresponding to the two prongs of his defense of Southern slavery, Fitzhugh uses the words *slaves*, *government*, and *slave society* in both a narrow and a broad sense so that to follow his argument, the reader must know which prong Fitzhugh is "on." *Slaves*, for instance, can refer to slaves per se or to anyone he regards as having a more or less equivalent status, that is, to almost anyone. Similarly, *government* can refer to government per se or to any protective institution, even to public opinion and other, more informal forms of social regulation, that is, to almost anything. Accordingly, *slave society* is the opposite of *free society* in the sense that it is a society with the specific institution of slavery or a society with a very imprecise "more of government."[53] Conflating the two prongs can lead to some fairly perverse results, that Fitzhugh favors enslaving the whole working class instead of merely establishing a stronger network of protective institutions for free (white) laborers or that he favors a substantial increase in governmental powers instead of merely advocating more public responsibility for the "weaker" (white) members of society. All this confusion of language, however, serves his polemical purposes because it portrays the Southern institution of racial slavery as part of a family of institutions that few people would reject and obfuscates the way that it may differ from those other institutions. By taking his readers' focus off slavery and specifically racial slavery, Fitzhugh can better defend the institution on liberal grounds.[54]

Who Is Really Free?

In *Cannibals All*, Fitzhugh insists on defending slavery as a positive good (p. 199). He even credits his first book, *Sociology for the South*, with moving the South from a "necessary evil" to a "positive good" position (p. 7).[55] What a "positive good" defense of slavery means to Fitzhugh is a defense of the institution as a universally necessary institution. It is part of a more general set of institutions that promote the benevolent purpose of protecting the "weak" from the "strong." Such institutions are necessary because according to Fitzhugh's Hobbesian social vision, all people are "cannibals" who strive to live off the labor of others (pp. 16–18, 38–39, 87). All societies have an obligation, and heretofore have fulfilled that obligation, to prevent the most powerful cannibals from devouring their victims, or, less metaphorically stated, to prevent the "strong" from (unduly) exploiting the "weak" by establishing an adequate network of protective institutions (pp. 28, 187, 236).[56]

Fitzhugh considers slavery the most efficient of these protective institutions because it joins the interests of those in the dominant status ("masters") most tightly with the interests of those in the dependent status ("slaves") (pp. 25, 31, 84, 205, 246). Feudal serfdom is a closely related institution (pp. 73, 79–80, 107–9, 184–85), but so are, though less closely, other forms of compulsory labor (pp. 28, 109–10, 187–88, 232–33), families (pp. 28, 80, 187, 235), churches (pp. 99–101), charitable institutions (pp. 28, 109–10, 187–88, 236), and even governments (pp. 65–66, 94, 247, 254–55). At some point in his book, Fitzhugh compares wives (pp. 80, 99, 187, 235), children (pp. 28, 80, 187, 235), wards (p. 80), apprentices (p. 80), prisoners (p. 80), soldiers (pp. 80, 236), sailors (pp. 80, 236), the poor under the English poor laws (pp. 109–10, 187–88), imported Chinese laborers in the British colonies (pp. 232–33), as well as the remaining serfs of eastern Europe and central Asia (pp. 79–80, 200) with slaves. Thus broadly understood, the status of slaves is a very widespread status indeed, and every society seems to be a slave society.

According to Fitzhugh, contemporary free societies in the American North, Great Britain, and western Europe are unique in attempting to destroy, or at least dilute, all these protective institutions and dependent statuses (pp. 66, 94, 247, 253–54). He cautions that the attempt will not rid these societies of "masters" and "slaves" but only make their interests more antagonistic (pp. 25, 31–32, 34). Free laborers, for example, remain dependent on their capitalist employers, though no longer personally. They therefore are now "miscalled" free laborers or, really, "slaves without masters" (pp. 17, 32, 72–73, 78, 221, 258).[57]

Fitzhugh claims that "slavery is the natural and normal condition of society. The situation of the North is abnormal and anomalous" (p. 40). Later, he notes that "free society is a recent and small experiment" (p. 118; see also pp. 72, 102, 106). He believes that free societies, unlike slave societies, fail to adequately protect the "weak" from the "strong," for they place no legal or moral obligations on "masters" (capitalists) to protect their "slaves" (free laborers) (pp. 15–18, 31–32, 73, 84, 184–85). Fitzhugh also believes that neither the interests nor the sentiments of the capitalist encourage him to protect his employees, in sharp contrast to the master-slave relations of the South (pp. 17, 32, 72–73, 78, 258). In fact, Fitzhugh contends that the pecuniary interests of the capitalist encourage him to exploit his employees. "It is the interest of the capitalist . . . to allow free laborers the least possible portion of the fruits of their own labor; for all capital is created by labor, and the smaller the allowance of the free laborer, the greater the gains of his employer" (p. 25). Fitzhugh adds that public opinion reinforces this message: "That same public opinion which shields and protects the slaves encourages the oppression of free laborers—for it is considered more honorable and praiseworthy . . . to make good bargains than bad ones" (p. 25). He concludes that the actual enslavement of the working classes of free societies would be resisted not by the workers but by the capitalists, "for the gain would be all on the laborer's side, and the loss all on that of the capitalist" (p. 223).[58]

For Fitzhugh, the comparison between slave societies and free societies is a comparison not only between societies with the institution of slavery and societies without that specific institution but also between societies with strong protective institutions and societies without such institutions. As a result, the choice between the South and the North is a choice not only between slave labor and free labor but also "between more of government and no government" (p. 94; see also pp. 65–66, 247, 253–55). Fitzhugh considers this choice unproblematic. He believes that the North is a society on the verge of institutional collapse, a society on the road "to no private property, no church, no law, no government" (pp. 253–54). Conversely, he believes that those institutions are in good repair in the South, so much so that "Southern institutions are far the best now existing in the world" (p. 246; see also pp. 66, 97, 106, 191–92).[59]

Fitzhugh describes the free North as a society rife with crime, violence, vice, poverty, underemployment, and civil unrest (pp. 65, 231–

34, 245, 247, 259)—all because of its relative lack of protective institutions and its underlying laissez-faire philosophy. He observes that many admit the failure of free society but few agree on a cure (pp. 9, 85–106, 191, 209–12, 225–27). Consequently, the North is also a society rife with "isms": "Bloomer's and Women's Right's men, and strong-minded women, and Mormons, and anti-renters, and 'vote myself a farm' men, Millerites, and Spiritual Rappers, and Shakers, and Widow Wakemanites, and Agrarians, and Grahamites, and a thousand other superstitious and infidel Isms" (p. 103; see also pp. 9, 93, 96, 228–29, 234). Fitzhugh insists that the slave South suffers from neither those social ills nor these pretended cures (pp. 9, 97, 228–29, 234, 259). He reminds abolitionists, socialists, and other would-be social reformers that it is free society, not slave society, that has failed (p. 106).

Paralleling his attack on free society, Fitzhugh attacks its abolitionist champions. Ironically, he claims that the abolitionists are the champions of free society not in thinking free society is healthy but in thinking the remedy for its ills is still less government.[60] He accuses them of wanting to abolish "slavery in every form" (p. 218). Abolishing racial slavery is only their immediate goal and not their real motive, for "they would not spend so much time and money for the mere sake of the negro" (p. 253; see also p. 201).[61] Eventually they mean to abolish all protective institutions, "to disregard the natural relations of mankind, and profanely to build up states, like Fourierite Phalansteries, or Mormon and Oneida villages, where religion shall be banished, and in which property, wife and children shall be held somewhat in common" (p. 72; see also pp. 85, 98–99, 190, 198, 214). Fitzhugh is convinced that all the popular "isms" of the day share this goal. He contends that "the great movement in society, known under various names, as Communism, Socialism, Abolitionism, Red Republicanism and Black Republicanism, has one common object: the breaking up of all law and government, and the inauguration of anarchy" (p. 194; see also p. 254). But rather than achieving a utopia of liberty and equality for all, Fitzhugh predicts that the abolitionists will achieve a dystopia conspicuously lacking liberty and equality: "Abolition ultimates in 'Consent Government'; Consent Government in Anarchy, . . . and 'Self-elected Despotism winds up the play'" (p. 244; see also pp. 245, 254).

Fitzhugh's strategy here is clear. He associates attacks on slavery, which few Americans would strongly defend, with attacks on the family and other institutions that most Americans would strongly defend. In pursuing this strategy, he offers a "slippery slope" argument to the effect that abolishing slavery would result in the demise of all those other institutions.[62] Fitzhugh's own defense of slavery then becomes a defense of all those other institutions and a seemingly well intentioned effort to prevent the total collapse of American society. What is not clear is how such a defense of slavery could be liberal.

In this connection, it is important to note that Fitzhugh argues that protective institutions provide the "weak" with other benefits beside protection. Accordingly, he claims that under slavery, workers are less exploited than they are under a free-labor system because they retain a greater share of what they produce in the form of food, shelter, and even personal property (pp. 15–18, 31–32, 73, 84, 184–85). Fitzhugh even goes so far as to suggest that under slavery, workers actually enjoy more practical liberty than they do under a free-labor system because they are less burdened by their daily toils (pp. 12–13, 17, 21, 32, 223–24).

A major portion of Fitzhugh's argument on this point involves a comparison of the condition of the British working class before and after the end of serfdom, an institution that he, again, considers closely related to slavery.[63] To Fitzhugh, such a comparison shows that the condition of the British working class has deteriorated substantially since its "emancipation" (pp. 12, 73, 107–9, 184–85, 258). British workers not only led a more secure and comfortable existence as serfs than they do now as free laborers but also enjoyed a greater degree of freedom. "The laborers of England are not half so free now as before their pretended emancipation. They have lost all their rights, half their liberty . . . and live in a state of continued destitution, hunger, and excessive labor, from generation to generation—from infancy to old age" (p. 185; see also pp. 12, 21, 73, 78, 107–9). Following the same line of argument, Fitzhugh also claims that as free laborers, British workers are less free than Southern slaves.

> Free laborers have less liberty than slaves, are worse paid and provided for, and have no valuable rights. Slaves, with more of actual practical liberty, with ampler allowance, and constant protection, are secure in the enjoyment of all the rights which provide for their physical comfort at all times and under all circumstances. (P. 32; see also pp. 12, 15–16, 19, 185, 222–24)[64]

Fitzhugh even suggests that Southern slaves are freer than British (and American) capitalists.

> But the reader may think that he and other capitalists and employers are freer than negro slaves. Your capital would soon vanish, if you dared indulge in the liberty and abandon of negroes. You hold your wealth and position by the tenure of constant watchfulness, care, and circumspection. You never labor; but you are never free. (P. 19)[65]

Fitzhugh seems to delight in the paradox that slaves really are free and free persons really are not. Yet, polemically, the suggestion that slavery is not really slavery and freedom is not really freedom was a suggestion that the dynamics of a liberal consensus almost forced him to make.[66]

In the end, Fitzhugh wants to defend slavery on the grounds that in a certain sense no one, including the wealthiest capitalist, is *really* free and in a certain sense every one, including the poorest slave, *is* really free. More precisely, he analyzes the question of who is really free into the following propositions: (1) every one in every society is constrained in one way or another; (2) no one in any society is constrained in every way; (3) there are many different ways of gauging how constrained people are; (4) overall, some people are more constrained than others are; (5) a person's legal or social status is not always a very accurate gauge of how constrained he or she is; and (6) the ways that people are constrained are, or should be, calculated to increase either their own practical liberty or the aggregate practical liberty of the members of the society in which they live. This analysis is liberal, not only because of the goal it is intended to serve, but also because of the question it is intended to answer.

Fitzhugh imagines that slaves have traded liberty for security but that they have not traded away all their liberty and also have gained a certain amount of liberty through the greater security they now enjoy. He, therefore, imagines that slaves have made a trade similar to the one that classical liberal theorists imagine every one makes when entering civil society. Finally, Fitzhugh assumes that slaves are better off for having made an "additional" trade of liberty for security than are free laborers who have not. Alternatively, he insists that free societies verge on states of nature, as if the proponents of such societies and their underlying laissez-faire philosophies had not learned the valuable liberal lesson that governments and other protective institutions can actually increase the aggregate practical liberty of the members of a given society.

Interestingly, Fitzhugh criticizes Locke himself for this "oversight." In particular, he repudiates Locke's social-contract theory for overlooking the fact that "man is naturally a social and gregarious animal" and that "there is no such thing as *natural human* liberty" (p. 71; see also pp. 13, 36, 52). But while Fitzhugh clearly rejects both the historicity and the abstract nature of social-contract theory, he does not reject its underlying liberal logic. Indeed, the intention behind his critique of social-contract theory is not to renounce Lockean principles but to criticize those who are misusing them to attack slavery. This intention becomes clear when he goes on to criticize William Paley, Montesquieu, and Blackstone for their "vain" (p. 71) and "perilous" (p. 81) attempts to distinguish liberty and slavery on definitional grounds (see pp. 73–77). Fitzhugh ridicules those attempts as really showing, contrary to these philosophers' own intentions, that "liberty is a mere modification of slavery" (p. 77). Their unintended conflation of liberty and slavery, however, becomes the linchpin of Fitzhugh's own defense of the institution in *Cannibals All*.[67]

Racial Slavery

At any one of a number of points in *Cannibals All*, Fitzhugh seems primed to recommend slavery as the optimal condition for the laboring classes across racial and sectional lines. He does not, however, ever make that recommendation. Instead, he advocates continued racial slavery in the South and "more of government" in the North. He attributes the impending collapse of free society in the North to its failure to distance itself from laissez-faire philosophy and not to its failure to enslave its laboring classes.

> We must, in all sections, act upon the principle that the world is "too little governed." You of the North need not institute negro slavery, far less reduce white men to the state of negro slavery. But the masses require more of protection, and the masses and philosophers equally require more of control. Leave it to time and circumstances to suggest the necessary legislation; but rely upon it, "Anarchy, plus the street constable" won't answer any longer. (P. 247)[68]

The key chapter in Fitzhugh's "retreat" from "white slavery" is, not surprisingly, the chapter entitled "Negro Slavery." He opens the chapter by announcing his "new" strategy to "vindicate that institution in the abstract" (p. 199). Such a defense of slavery must include the possibility of white slavery because "to insist on less, is to yield our case, and to give up our religion; for if white slavery be morally wrong, be a violation of natural rights, the Bible cannot be true" in view of the non-racial character of the ancient Hebraic institution of slavery (p. 200).[69]

Fitzhugh then begins his retreat. He acknowledges that "human and divine authority do seem in the general to concur, in establishing the expediency of having masters and slaves of different races" (p. 200). He contends that the ancient Hebraic institution of slavery did not violate this generalization because native-born slaves were treated more like wards and apprentices than like slaves. As for the other slaves of Judea and the other nations of antiquity, he observes that in most cases, they at least belonged to different nationalities than those of their masters. He ascribes the present-day animus against racial slavery to the fact that world opinion has latched onto the undeniable cruelties of the African slave trade and West Indian slavery (pp. 200–1).[70] Southern slavery, though, has progressed far beyond West Indian slavery, for it has developed into "a benign and protective institution, and our negroes are confessedly better off than any free laboring population in the world" (p. 201).

At this point, Fitzhugh briefly returns to the possibility of white slavery, asking, "How can we contend that white slavery is wrong, whilst all the great body of free laborers are starving; and slaves, white or black, throughout the world, are enjoying comfort?" (p. 201).[71] He soon answers his own query and completes his retreat from white slavery by invoking racial inequality to justify the wholesale enslavement of the black, as opposed to the white, race. Fitzhugh asserts that

> as a general and abstract question, negro slavery has no other claims over other forms of slavery, except that from inferiority, or rather peculiarity, of race, almost all negroes require masters, whilst only the children, the women, the very weak, poor, and ignorant, and c., among the whites, need some protective and governing relation of this kind. (P. 201)[72]

According to Fitzhugh, the "protective and governing relation" suitable for "weak" white Americans is not slavery; it is not even the dependent statuses suitable for many Europeans; it is merely "more of government." Only for most blacks is slavery the best fit. Fitzhugh's defense of the specific Southern institution of racial slavery is less abstract or universalistic than it is circumstantial. Whether the status of slaves or some other status is best suited to any one individual depends on the state of the society in which he or she lives as well as on his or her own moral and intellectual development. Fitzhugh's analysis of these different statuses is fairly complex, but in the Southern case, it settles on two basic statuses: slaves for blacks and free persons for whites.[73]

Because Fitzhugh wants to take his readers' focus off *racial* slavery, he does not defend, at any length, his belief that blacks are best suited to the status of slaves. He does, however, offer a few remarks on the point, and like Dew, he moves back and forth between natural and environmental explanations of racial inequality (pp. 18–19, 77, 185, 187, 199–201). In his most extended statement on race in *Cannibals All*, he claims that

> the blacks in America are both positively and relatively weak. Positively so, because they are too improvident to lay up for the exigencies of sickness, of the seasons, or of old age. Relatively so, because they are wholly unequal to the whites among whom they live, in the war of the wits and free competition, which universal liberty begets, and political economy encourages. (P. 187)

Fitzhugh also insists, again like Dew, that the enslavement of blacks to whites is helping the former ascend the scale of civilization (pp. 29, 79–80, 185, 200). It then may be only the mixing of relatively "weaker" and "stronger" races that temporarily makes racial slavery a necessary institution in the American South. Yet even as Fitzhugh holds out this "necessary evil" possibility, he never suggests that black Americans will ever attain moral or intellectual equality with white Americans nor that the two races will ever live together as equals in the same society.

While Fitzhugh echoes Dew's views on racial inequality, his defense of the Southern institution of racial slavery surpasses Dew's in two significant respects. Only once does he even refer to the possibility of abolishing the institution, and he never refers to it as an evil institution on deontological or any other grounds. His defense of Southern slavery is clearly more "positive good" than Dew's.[74]

But if Fitzhugh does not follow Dew into the polemics of antiabolitionist consequentialism, he does follow him into the polemics of proslavery consequentialism. Here Fitzhugh surpasses Dew in his focus on the benefits of Southern slavery for the nonslaveholding whites of the South.[75] These benefits are clearly those of racial, specifically black, slavery, not of slavery per se or, obviously, of white slavery.

Fitzhugh explicitly targets the abolitionist charge that the institution of racial slavery especially disadvantages lower-class whites in the South by subordinating them to an ever-encroaching slavocracy.[76] To the contrary, he argues that the institution "elevates those whites; for it makes them not the bottom of society, as at the North . . . but privileged citizens, like Greek and Roman citizens, with a numerous class far beneath them." He then points out that "one white man does not lord it over another" in the South, "for all are equal in privilege, if not in wealth" (p. 220). Fitzhugh later expands this "Herrenvolk democracy" argument by claiming that the institution of racial slavery allows voting rights to be safely extended to nonpropertied whites in the South more than in the North, because the institution unites their interests with those of propertied whites as part of a privileged class (pp. 245–46; see also pp. 133, 136). According to Fitzhugh, the conservative tendencies of the institution allow the South to support both a more democratic and a more liberal society than the North does. He insists that "the slaveholding South is the only country on the globe that can safely tolerate" the general extension of such rights as freedom of the press, speech, and religion because it is the only "country" on the globe where the majority can be trusted not to abuse those rights so as to "disturb the peace of society, threaten the security of property, offend public decency, assail religion, and invoke anarchy" (pp. 131, 135).

Consequently, Fitzhugh's point is not that free white laborers should be enslaved but that they gain greater freedoms from the enslavement of African American laborers. Of course, any recommendation Fitzhugh might have made for enslaving white Americans would have been politically untenable, and perhaps that is the reason he did not make such a recommendation. The relevant question, however, is not why he actually did not recommend white slavery but why he constructed such a massive intellectual scaffolding to justify a recommendation he never made.

Fitzhugh's professed reason for this tactic is that the South must seize the offensive on the slavery issue and, accordingly, defend its institution of racial slavery as a universal and not as a racial and peculiarly Southern institution. What Fitzhugh gains through this type of defense of Southern slavery is precisely a liberal defense of the institution. By stating his defense of the institution in universalistic terms, he shows that it is logically one among many types of exchanges of liberty for security, exchanges that are not necessarily racial in character and that, for most people, actually increase their practical liberty. Government is the paradigmatic case of such an exchange. Yet Fitzhugh believes that government is only quantitatively, not qualitatively, different from such exchanges as slavery, serfdom, and marriage. He also gains the important point of showing that slavery is not a dying institution because it does belong to a more general pattern of exchanges of liberty for security. In defending the institution, he thus sees himself as advancing, not retarding, the cause of liberal progress.[77] Finally, Fitzhugh gains the important point of showing that the union is not a house divided. He suggests that the North and the South differ merely in their general patterns of exchanges of liberty for security (p. 188). He also indicates that to the extent the union is a house divided, it is divided over different philosophies of government and not slavery per se (pp. 106, 254). This conflict is one that he is confident will be resolved in the South's favor because "every good citizen" has begun to realize that "'the world is too little governed'" (p. 255; see also pp. 6, 52).[78] In defending Southern slavery, Fitzhugh also sees himself as advancing, not retarding, the cause of union.[79]

In his efforts to defend Southern slavery to the world, Fitzhugh faces a rhetorical dilemma. On the one hand, he must specifically defend racial slavery in order to defend Southern slavery. In developing this more circumstantial, more "necessary evil" defense of the institution, he not surprisingly uses race as a critical determinant of status. On the other hand, he develops a more universalistic, more "positive good" defense of the institution that diverts his readers' attention from racial slavery. By appearing to be open to the possibility of white slavery, his defense of black slavery seems more liberal. The scaffolding he constructs to justify white slavery—which, politically, he need not and cannot defend—is in the service of justifying black slavery—which, politically, he does need and is better able to defend. Together, the two prongs of Fitzhugh's defense of Southern slavery make his use of race as a critical determinant of status seem relatively benign, as one among many ways of deciding in which status any one individual may enjoy the most practical liberty. They also make the differences between a free North and a slave South appear relatively minor, as hardly the fodder for disunion and civil war. Although Fitzhugh's two-pronged defense of Southern slavery is rather tortured, it does serve his polemical purposes.

Conclusion

The comparison of Fitzhugh and Dew reflects the rhetorical development of the proslavery movement in more liberal as well as more "positive good" and contextualist directions. Over time, Southern proslavery figures extolled the positive aspects of the continued existence of racial slavery in their region of the country at the expense of the negative aspects of its abolition. They argued that the institution was congruent, not incongruent, with the uniquely liberal and progressive qualities that antebellum Americans attributed to their own national experience, thereby denying that the "American exemplar" and "human progress" arguments were necessarily antislavery in scope. Proslavery figures devoted even more attention to denying a third contextualist argument, the "house divided" argument. As disunion neared, they focused their polemics more on the increasingly intertwined fates of Southern slavery and the union than on the fate of Southern slavery alone. In making this shift, their intention was not to encourage disunion but to forestall it. Parallel developments in the North, however, obviated this intention, working instead to sectionally polarize public opinion in the nation and to produce the very result that most antislavery *and* proslavery figures dreaded.

James Henry Hammond perfectly embodies the politics of brinkmanship that characterized the proslavery movement.[80] He seemed, alternately, adept and inept at juggling disunionism and unionism. He also reflects the internal dynamics of the proslavery movement in other ways, in many of the same ways that the differences between Dew's "early" and Fitzhugh's "late" defenses of the Southern institution of racial slavery did. Hammond's defense of the institution became more liberal, "positive good," and contextualist over time. In the next chapter, I look at the rhetorical development of the proslavery movement on an intrapersonal level, by comparing several of Hammond's major proslavery works.

6 James H. Hammond
Slavery and Union

The multiple meanings of the "house divided" argument structured James Henry Hammond's political career. At various times in his career as governor of South Carolina, United States representative and senator, and local statesman-in-waiting, Hammond took four different positions on the argument. Early in his career, he professed to see the union as a house divided ideologically between a South committed to slavery and a North committed to freedom. In the middle years of his career, he insisted that the union was not a house divided because Southern slavery was not really slavery nor was Northern freedom really freedom. Later in his career, he portrayed the union as a house in the process of dividing physically over the fate of slavery. Finally, on the eve of the Civil War, he viewed the union as a house divided but now contended that this condition need not be fatal to it. His apparent shift from disunionism to unionism in the late 1850s seemed as dramatic and sudden as the Garrisonians' parallel shift from disunionism to unionism.[1] But neither the Garrisonians nor Hammond would have taken the positions they did if their earlier positions had not been carried forward in their later ones. In Hammond's case, he would not have taken the position late in his career that the union could remain indefinitely a house divided if he had thought the union was as divided as he sometimes claimed it to be early in his career.

Scholars have attempted to track Hammond's career on the unionism-disunionism dimension.[2] This effort has proved very difficult. At each stage of his career, Hammond seemed to combine unionism with disunionism, fluctuating not on the question of whether the union was, *ceteris paribus*, a mutually beneficial arrangement but on the question of whether it could survive its divisions over slavery. Because Hammond never did advocate disunion, it is probably best to call him a conditional unionist and to track his political movements in terms of how he stood on the "house divided" argument rather than on the union per se.[3]

Relating Hammond's political movements to his own political prospects or to the current state of sectional controversy provides two more ways of tracking those movements. These alternatives, however, also are problematic. Hammond's professed antipathy to political expediency stands in the way of the first alternative, as does the fact that his late-1850s shift from disunionism to unionism clearly hurt his political prospects. That shift also does not comport with the heated state of sectional controversy at the time. These considerations are not conclusive.[4] But they do suggest that Hammond's increasing focus on the "house divided" argument and what he understood to be its changing practical implications played an independent and important role in influencing his political movements.

We thus can identify in Hammond's writings and speeches a rhetorical shift from deontological and consequentialist arguments in defense of slavery to contextualist arguments joining the fate of the institution to the fate of the union.[5] Although Hammond did not completely eschew deontological and consequentialist arguments in his later works, or contextualist arguments in his earlier ones, he did increasingly focus on the relation between slavery and union rather than on slavery per se. By the late 1850s, the "house divided" argument was the one argument that antislavery and proslavery figures had, in particular, to affirm, deny, or reinterpret in such a way as to justify their position on the ultimate fate of the Southern institution of racial slavery. At least on the proslavery side, the tendency was toward affirming the argument and attaching a disunionist conclusion to it, a tendency that made the "house divided" argument even more central to proslavery figures, like Hammond, who did not favor physically dividing the house. These proslavery figures were compelled to deny the argument by either discounting the depth of the union's ideological divisions or showing how it could survive them. Hammond, at various times, pursued both rhetorical strategies.

This focus on the "house divided" argument did not mean that the defenders of slavery abandoned their attempt to defend slavery as a positive good and a liberal institution. Far from it. They continued to argue again increasingly over time, that the institution maximized the practical liberty of the members of Southern society, in spite of, or sometimes because of, its effects on the slaves themselves. For the defenders of slavery, this "maximum liberty" argument bridged the ideological divisions between Southern slave society and Northern free society and directed attention to Northern antislavery agitation as the anomaly that created a house divided. The perceived size of that anomaly became another key variable in how Hammond and other proslavery figures concluded the "house divided" argument at any one time.[6]

In the rest of this chapter, I map Hammond's changing positions on the "house divided" argument over the course of his political career: first, as he burst into national prominence in 1836 by taking a leading role in "gagging" the abolitionist petitions to Congress during his brief tenure in the House of Representatives;[7] second, in the mid-1840s, at the close of his term of office as governor of South Carolina; third, during his semiforced retirement from politics in the late 1840s through his unexpected elevation to the United States Senate in 1858;[8] and, fourth, in the critical pre-Secession years of 1858–1860 while he served in the Senate. These four stages of Hammond's career were united by his unapologetic defense of slavery and his conditional unionism. Although he always thought the South could adequately protect its interests in the union—interests he considered intimately connected to its institution of racial slavery—he was never quite sure that it could, and his level of confidence that it could wavered over time. This variable probably best explains his changing positions on the "house divided" argument.

Asserting the "House Divided" Argument

Hammond's controversial House speech of February 1, 1836, opposing the reception of the abolitionist petitions to Congress was a strident defense of slavery.[9] The purpose of the speech, however, was not only to defend slavery but also to warn the North of disunion. Hammond believed that the reason the South now had to break its silence on the future of its institution of racial slavery was not because the rapid growth of the abolitionist movement in the North threatened the continued existence of the institution but because it threatened the continued existence of the union (p. 46). Already in 1836, he viewed the abolitionist movement as a clear indication that the union was a house divided and, at least at this time, he held out little hope that it would survive its division.

According to Hammond, the principal argument against Congress's receiving the abolitionist petitions is that the petitions ask it to do something that it constitutionally cannot do: abolish slavery in the District of Columbia (pp. 17–18).[10] Hammond, though, soon introduces the broader issue of abolishing slavery in the Southern states, which he correctly identifies as the abolitionists' ultimate objective (p. 19).[11] He argues that abolishing Southern slavery is both an unconstitutional and an unattainable goal. He discusses three possible agents of abolishing the institution and claims none of the three will be willing or able to accomplish the task. The slaveholders never will voluntarily free their slaves without adequate compensation (p. 31); the federal government cannot afford to adequately compensate the slaveholders for freeing their slaves, nor can it, constitutionally or otherwise, compel them to do so (p. 35); and the slaves never will be able to forcibly free themselves (p. 37). In the process of arguing that abolishing Southern slavery is an unattainable goal, Hammond also argues that it is an undesirable one. The institution is not merely a necessary evil; it is a positive good that the slaveholders, the federal government, the slaves, and other interested parties should not even want to abolish.

Hammond pronounces slavery "the greatest of all the great blessings which a kind Providence has bestowed upon our favored region" (p. 34). More specifically, he portrays the institution as a great blessing to the slaveholders, the slaves, and the South as a whole. It is a great blessing to the slaveholders because they have "less fear of danger from their operatives" than employers in any other part of the world (p. 32).[12] It is also a great blessing to the slaveholders because slave labor is an extremely profitable system of labor, especially suited to the staple production and warm climate of the American South (pp. 33–34). Hammond insists that "it is not in the interest of the planters of the South to emancipate their slaves, and it never can be shown to be so" (p. 34).[13]

According to Hammond, abolishing Southern slavery also can never be shown to be in the interest of the slaves, for "there is not a happier, more contented race upon the face of the earth than our slaves" (p. 36). They, furthermore, "have every reason to be happy" because they are "lightly tasked, well clothed, well fed—far better than the free laborers of any country in the world" (p. 36)[14] and because "their lives and persons [are] protected by law, all their sufferings alleviated by the kindest and most interested care, and their domestic affections cherished and maintained" (p. 36).[15] Hammond concludes this idyllic picture of Southern slavery by asserting that "our slaves" are "satisfied with their lot, happy in their comforts, and devoted to their masters" (pp. 36–37).[16]

If Southern slavery ever were abolished, Hammond believes that the freed slaves clearly would be worse off than they were before. He quotes a *Cincinnati Gazette* report on the squalid conditions in two free-black settlements in southern Ohio as evidence of the probable consequences of emancipation for the Southern slaves (pp. 38–39). He insists that black Americans never can be made equal to white Americans, and even if they could, white Americans never would accept them as equals (pp. 39–40). He pointedly asks:

> Are the people of the north prepared to restore to them two-fifths of their rights of voters, and place their political power on an equality with their own? Are *we* prepared to see them mingling in our legislation? Is any portion of the country prepared to see them enter these halls and take their seats by our sides in perfect equality with the white representatives of the Anglo-Saxon race? (P. 40)[17]

Hammond goes on to predict that the first step toward a general emancipation of the Southern slaves would precipitate race wars in the South, with the result that the freed slaves would be either annihilated or resubjugated (p. 40).

Hammond contends not only that abolishing Southern slavery would adversely affect the Southern slaveholders and their slaves but also that it would impoverish the whole South, because he is convinced that members of the African American race cannot form an efficient free-labor force (pp. 19, 39). Conversely, he believes that the continued existence of racial slavery in the South would greatly benefit the region. The South, thanks to its institution of racial slavery, is a much more stable society than the free societies of the American North and western Europe.[18] Near the end of the speech, Hammond excoriates the leveling spirit that would abolish racial slavery and attempt to render all men equal (pp. 43–46).[19] This leveling spirit will fail to achieve its ultimate objectives, but the effort may well prove very costly to society because inequality is the order of nature (p. 45).

He considers racial slavery part of this natural order and only one of many legitimate forms of social inequality. In this respect, the comparative advantages of the slave South to existing free societies appear threefold. First, racial slavery enslaves the lower classes, making them less likely to generate a leveling spirit (pp. 32, 36). Second, it creates a true natural aristocracy "of talents, of virtue, and of generosity and courage" (p. 45).[20] Third, it joins racial and class lines, making every white man a free man and every free man "an aristocrat" (p. 45). Hammond triumphantly declares that "domestic slavery regulated as ours is produces the highest toned, the purest, best organization of society that has ever existed on the face of the earth" (p. 45).

Hammond's defense of Southern slavery in this speech is heavily consequentialist. Hammond introduces deontology only to attack it. He criticizes the abolitionist banner of the "equality of all mankind" as a "visionary and disastrous sentiment," claiming that not even in heaven are all men equal (p. 45). He also accuses the abolitionists of being committed to abolishing slavery at any cost, neglecting all the consequentialist considerations that speak against their position (pp. 29–30). Accordingly, he complains of the abolitionists that even if slavery is "an evil, it is one to us alone, and we are contented with it—why should others interfere?" (p. 34). Hammond, however, is not content merely to offer such antiabolitionist consequentialist arguments, as in a traditional "necessary evil" defense of the institution. For, he goes on to claim that slavery "is no evil" but, rather, a great blessing that "has rendered our Southern country proverbial for its wealth, its genius, and its manners" (p. 34). He builds his case for slavery in this speech primarily on the basis of a proslavery consequentialism that blurs the line between "necessary evil" and "positive good" defenses of the institution. His defense of slavery in the speech also is implicitly liberal. The abolitionists' liberal deontology of the "equality of all mankind" may point toward abolishing the institution, but Hammond's own liberal consequentialism indicates that the members of Southern society—at least the white members of Southern society—enjoy more practical equality and liberty with racial slavery than they would without it.

But the theme of the "gag rule" speech is the union as much as it is slavery, and in this sense, the primary logic of the speech is neither consequentialist nor deontological but contextualist. In its main outlines, the speech shows that the union is a house divided between a South committed to slavery and a North committed to freedom, that the resulting mix is an extremely volatile one, and that neither section is likely to abandon its fundamental commitment in order to preserve the union. Hammond's 1836 version of the "house divided" argument projects disunion as its probable conclusion, although not its inevitable conclusion or the one he necessarily prefers.

Hammond's index of a house divided is the rapid rise of abolitionism in the North. This phenomenon means the increasing risk of disunion and civil war—of dissolving "in blood the bonds of the confederacy" (p. 19)—because the South never will voluntarily abandon racial slavery (pp. 31, 49).[21] Hammond is very impressed with the abolitionists' organizing efforts, estimating that they already have made at least 100,000 converts to their cause (pp. 19–21).[22] Furthermore, he believes that the roots of abolitionism are planted deep in Northern soil and are growing deeper every year.

> It is indeed natural that people not owning slaves should entertain a strong aversion to domestic servitude. It is natural that the descendants of the Puritans, without any deep investigation of the subject, should have an instinctive hostility to slavery in every shape. It is natural that foreigners, with whom the North is crowded—just released themselves from bondage—extravagant in their notions of the freedom of our institutions, and profoundly ignorant of the principles on which society and government are organized—should view with horror the condition of the Southern operatives. (P. 41)[23]

The "natural" antislavery sentiments of the North represent the fault lines of a house divided, "which, if pushed much further, will inevitably separate us into two nations" (p. 41).

Disunion, nevertheless, is not Hammond's preferred outcome. Referring to the widely held belief in the nation's world-historic mission to advance the cause of human freedom, Hammond claims that he would regard disunion "as a calamity to the whole human race" (p. 41). At this point in the speech, he also denies that the North entertains "any peculiar feelings of hostility" toward the South (p. 41). Then near the end of the speech, he proposes that the Northern states demonstrate this lack of hostility and solve the immediate crisis by passing laws restricting the publication of abolitionist tracts (pp. 46–47). He supports this proposal by observing that both the North and the South are "devoted to the same principles of constitutional liberty," principles that, he argues, do not prohibit proscribing such "libelous" publications (p. 47).[24] As for himself and other Southern whites, he vows that "we of the South will endeavor to avert [disunion] by every means save the sacrifice of our liberties, or the subversion of our domestic institutions" (p. 41). Hammond's intention here is clear. He seeks to (re)unite a house divided by appealing to shared principles. He presents both sections of the country, notwithstanding their differences over slavery, as being committed to the same liberal principles and as being part of the same liberal mission. He also assumes that the union is important to all the parties involved in the current dispute, except for the abolitionists "out-of-doors." The implication is that if it were not for them, the house would not be divided, or at least, it would be in no danger of falling.

Hammond's vow also reveals the conditional nature of his and, in his mind, other Southern whites' unionism. In the peroration of the speech, Hammond reiterates this conditional unionism by insisting that the South will "dissolve this Union" before it will surrender its institutions (p. 49). Earlier, he threatened to resign his seat in Congress "to practise disunion and civil war" if it ever passes legislation on the subject of slavery (p. 35).[25] Hammond realizes that the result might well be disunion because it would be (almost) as difficult for the people of the North to muzzle the abolitionists (and their own antislavery sentiments) as it would be for the people of the South to abandon racial slavery (p. 47).[26] Despite his attempt in this speech to repair rhetorically the rents in the fabric of union, it still appears as a house divided and as a house divided between a South committed to slavery and a North committed to freedom. During the next stage of his career, Hammond undertakes a more concerted effort to span this sectional divide by more explicitly defending Southern slavery on liberal grounds, thus calling into question the "house divided" argument he has just asserted.

Tempering the "House Divided" Argument

In early 1845, after completing a two-year term in office as governor of South Carolina, Hammond wrote two public letters addressed to the British abolitionist Thomas Clarkson. These letters were written ostensibly in response to an antislavery circular that Clarkson had sent to the "professing Christians in our Northern States."[27] In them,

Hammond develops a more explicitly liberal defense of Southern slavery than he had in the "gag rule" speech. They present an American South to the world that is as committed to human freedom as Great Britain or the American North is, and by the same token, they present a union to the world that is united behind the cause of human freedom. The two letters, however, were not written primarily for foreign consumption.[28] In the face of the strong, antislavery-inspired opposition among Northern politicians to the annexation of Texas, Hammond appears to have seen a new need to defend to a liberal America the idea of Southern slavery as a liberal institution and to temper to a nationalistic America the image of the union as a house divided.[29] It is difficult to determine which need, or commitment, was foremost in his own mind.

Hammond's two letters to Clarkson present his most extensive defense of slavery. Given the addressee of the letters, it seems natural that the fate of the union would take a back seat to the fate of slavery. The addressee, though, does provide an "excuse" to reintroduce the fate of the union as a way of defending national pride.[30] After all, the primary audience of the letters was the people of South Carolina, not Thomas Clarkson. Hammond seems intent on convincing his fellow citizens that the union is not really a house divided, and his defense of slavery in the letters conspicuously de-emphasizes the North-South divisions over the fate of the institution.

The initial defense of slavery Hammond offers in these letters is a biblical one. Based on his refusal to defend slavery "in the abstract" (p. 119), his biblical defense of the institution may be construed narrowly as a "necessary evil" defense of an ongoing institution, not as a "positive good" defense of the institution itself or of its origins. In this vein, Hammond claims that neither Christ nor his apostles attacked the "most revolting" and "cruel" Roman institution of slavery because they regarded it "as an *established* as well as *inevitable condition of human society*" (p. 123). Hammond, however, finds more positive defenses of slavery in the Old Testament (pp. 121–23; see also pp. 177–82), which he marshals to insist that "American slavery is not only not a sin, but especially commanded by God through Moses, and approved by Christ through His Apostles" (p. 124). Hammond later adds that Christ did not attack Roman slavery not only because he thought the institution was "established and inevitable" but also because he thought it was "sound and wholesome" (p. 180).[31]

According to Hammond, the abolitionists have been forced to pervert the meaning of the Bible in order to use it to attack slavery (pp. 125, 180–81). They even have gone so far as to state publicly that they would abandon the Bible rather than their antislavery crusade if they ever were convinced that it justified slavery (p. 182).[32] Hammond contends that the abolitionists will be remembered, at best, as relatively benign religious fanatics and, at worst, as self-deluded sowers of civil discord in launching a futile, though potentially destructive, campaign to create heaven on earth (pp. 120–21, 198).[33]

But Hammond does not rely solely on religion to tell him that slavery is a just institution. The institution is also defensible as the system of labor best suited for "an inferior Race, [which] never will effect, as it never has effected, as much in any other condition as in that of Slavery" (p. 165). For members of this "inferior" race, Hammond argues that freedom is not conducive to reason and order but to idleness and improvidence (p. 168).[34] As a result, "the enthusiastic love of liberty" fostered by the American Revolution was wrongly applied to African Americans during public deliberations over the fate of slavery in the post-Revolutionary period (pp. 193–94), as was Jefferson's "specious" doctrine that "all men are born [*sic*] equal" (p. 126). All societies, in fact, are divided into "a natural variety of classes" (p. 126). Hammond claims that racial slavery is merely one of many manifestations of the duty of the more fortunate classes to provide the less fortunate classes with a measure of self-protection (pp. 153–54).[35] While he admits that the institution is ultimately based on "the law of force" (p. 182), he maintains that all institutions are ultimately based on the same "law" and then goes on to portray the institution in highly paternalistic terms (pp. 183–86).

According to Hammond, the abolitionists' tendency toward "reasoning in the abstract" precludes them from lending credence to these practical justifications of slavery (p. 194). This tendency has also caused them to treat the fate of the institution as if it were a matter for "mere moral or metaphysical speculation" (p. 194) and to accept "the most fatal of all fallacies": that members of the black and white races "can exist together, after any length of time or any process of preparation, in terms at all approaching to equality" (pp. 169–70). In their paroxysms over "abstract rights," they are the heirs of the French more than the American Revolution (pp. 171, 194). The abolitionists' abstract reasoning or, equally, their religious millennialism also is evident in their insistence that human institutions can be ultimately based on "the law of love" (p. 182). Overall, Hammond is convinced that their "radical and revolutionary doctrines" are calculated "to overthrow all government, disorganize society, and reduce man to a state of nature—red with blood, and shrouded once more in barbaric ignorance" (p. 182; see also pp. 193–94).[36]

Despite its strong religious and racist overtones, Hammond's defense of slavery in the Clarkson letters is, nonetheless, predominantly liberal.[37] His invocation of a state of nature supports this conclusion. Hammond fears that the abolitionists would return men to a state of nature because they fail to adjust the abstract principles of Lockean liberalism to real-life conditions. When such principles as consent, liberty, and equality are adjusted to real-life conditions, he is confident that they will legitimize, not de-legitimize, Southern slavery.

Hammond suggests that Southern slavery is based on a type of consent: the slaves' contentment with their own conditions. One index of this contentment is the lack of slave revolts (pp. 128–29). Another is the slaves' apparent happiness (pp. 184–86). Hammond claims that Southern slaves are, indeed, "the happiest three millions of human beings on whom the sun shines" (p. 152). Again rejecting "all abstract reasoning on the matter," he also suggests that the master-slave relationship is based on mutual affection as much as it is on force (pp. 183–84).[38] As a practical matter, Hammond believes that slaves enjoy many comparative advantages over free laborers. The Southern slaves are clearly better off than the free laborers of Great Britain (pp. 154–60, 184–85), and if it were not for the way that Southern slavery props up its economy, they would be better off than the free laborers of the American North (p. 155). Hammond adds, in a now-familiar refrain, that the laboring classes of free societies are not really free anyway. In such societies, "nominal Free Labor prevails, with its ostensive privileges and its dismal servitude" (p. 128; see also pp. 149, 159, 185).[39]

Hammond's point is not that the laboring classes of free societies should be (re)enslaved. Rather, it is that the (free) laboring classes of slave societies also enjoy many comparative advantages over the laboring classes of free societies. Hammond substitutes McDuffie's "slavery is the corner stone of our Republican edifice" for Jefferson's "all men are born [*sic*] equal" (p. 126). He interprets McDuffie to mean that in order to ensure their own long-term stability, republican societies must withhold the franchise from their lower classes, something they can sustain over time only when the lower classes are generally members of a different race than the upper classes and especially when the one group is enslaved to the other. In his version of the "Herrenvolk democracy" argument, Hammond asserts that racial slavery elevates all the members of the dominant race, allowing the franchise to be safely extended to every one of them. He insists that even the least privileged Southern whites are "elevated far above the mass, are higher toned and more deeply interested in preserving a stable and well ordered Government, than the same class in any other country" (p. 127). He therefore contends that the institution of racial slavery maximizes the practical liberty and equality of Southern society as a whole, regardless of any adverse effects it may have on the practical liberty and equality of the slaves themselves. In the Clarkson letters, Hammond aggressively appeals to race but in such a way as to support racial slavery on the basis of liberal, not illiberal, principles.

Hammond's defense of Southern slavery in these letters is not only predominantly liberal, and more so than in his "gag rule" speech, but it is also predominantly positive good, and more so than in his "gag rule" speech. He opens his defense of slavery in the first letter by vowing to defend the institution as "not only an inexorable necessity for the present, but a moral and humane institution, productive of the greatest political and social advantages" (p. 115). He closes his defense of slavery in the second letter by thanking the abolitionists for goading the South into undertaking the shift from "necessary evil" to "positive good" defenses of the institution.

> And before the commencement of the Abolition agitation here, it was the common sentiment that it was desirable to get rid of Slavery. Many thought it our duty to do so. When that agitation arose, we were driven to a close examination of the subject in all its bearings, and the result has been an *universal conviction* that in holding Slaves we violate no law of God—inflict no injustice on any of his creatures—while the terrible consequences of emancipation to all parties and the world at large, clearly revealed to us, make us shudder at the bare thought of it. The slaveholders are therefore indebted to the Abolitionists for perfect ease of conscience, and the satisfaction of a settled and unanimous determination in reference to this matter. (Pp. 193–94)[40]

To be sure, Hammond offers "necessary evil" (antiabolitionist) arguments in his Clarkson letters that highlight "the terrible consequences of emancipation to all parties." He accuses the abolitionists of contemplating a violent end to Southern slavery, since they know that their tactic of moral suasion will never succeed in convincing the Southern slaveholders to free their slaves (pp. 161–62, 170, 182). He doubts, however, that the institution will ever be abolished by violent means (p. 162), but even if it were, he predicts that such an emancipation would be short-lived, as Southern whites would either exterminate the freed slaves or force them back into slavery (p. 169).[41] The best-case scenario for the abolitionists is for Southern slavery to wither away, like serfdom, and even then, it is likely to assume new forms (pp. 165, 168, 185). For instance, in Antigua, which Hammond considers the abolitionists' most plausible counterexample, slavery was not really abolished, since according to his accounts, the freed slaves remain slaves in everything but name (pp. 164–67).[42] The abolitionists, again, "conveniently" forget that members of the black and white races cannot live together as equals in the same society because "they differ essentially, in all the leading traits which characterize the varieties of the human species, and color draws an indelible and inseparable line of separation between them" (p. 170).[43] For Hammond, slavery seems to be "an inexorable necessity" for the present and all future times. Nevertheless, his primary arguments in these letters are "positive good" (proslavery) arguments that Southern slavery is not merely an inexorable necessity but "productive of the greatest political and social advantages."

As we have seen, Hammond argues that Southern slavery has produced only beneficial effects for the slaves themselves,[44] and even marshals two pieces of statistical evidence of those beneficial effects: the relatively high fertility rates of the Southern slaves and their relatively low suicide and insanity rates (pp. 150–51).[45] Hammond also details the beneficial effects of Southern slavery for the slaves by refuting the antislavery arguments that the institution has subjected them to high levels of sexual abuse (pp. 136–37) and physical cruelty (pp. 142–46) as well as denied them the advantages of a stable family structure (pp. 151–52) and religious instruction (pp. 152–53).[46]

Hammond, however, seems much more anxious to refute the antislavery arguments that racial slavery adversely affects Southern whites. As already noted, his general response to those arguments is that the institution elevates, rather than degrades, the nonslaveholding "mass" of the South. With specific reference to the effects of the institution on the slaveholding class, Hammond does not find it to be an incentive to personal violence (pp. 130–31) or sexual immorality (pp. 134–37), or a disincentive to formal education (pp. 132–33) or religious piety (pp. 133–34).[47] Far from being the intellectual and moral morass the abolitionists insist that it is, he asserts that the South is a society "whose men are proverbially brave, intellectual and hospitable, and whose women are unaffectedly chaste, devoted to domestic life and happy in it," a result largely due to "our system of Slavery" (p. 138). Hammond, finally, praises the institution for cultivating "the tenderest and purest sentiments of the human heart" among the Southern slaveholders (p. 183).

Given its beneficial effects on both black slaves and free whites, the blessings of racial slavery to the whole community should be evident. To Hammond, they are. In creating the conditions for political stability (pp. 126–27), he believes that the institution obviates the need for unrepublican standing armies (pp. 127–28).[48] He also believes that Southern whites need not fear that the institution will be a source of instability in times of war because, again, their slaves heretofore have shown little inclination to revolt (pp. 128–29).[49] And even if free labor may be the more profitable economic system for individual employers, Hammond is certain that slave labor is the more profitable economic system for the community as a whole because of the way that it immunizes a society against the ill effects of chronic underemployment (pp. 140–41).[50]

Hammond even argues that Southern slavery is important, if not essential, to the economic well-being of the North as well as the rest of the world. He explains that the North gains from the tariffs by which it "taxes" the South's slave-grown cotton exports (pp. 129, 155) and that those exports, in turn, fuel the world economy (p. 187). Abolish Southern slavery, and, Hammond warns, "no calamity could befall the world at all comparable to the sudden loss of two millions of bales of cotton annually. From the deserts of Africa to the Siberian wilds—from Greenland to the Chinese Wall, there is not a spot on earth but would feel the sensation" (p. 187).[51] In the Clarkson letters, Hammond presents the Southern institution of racial slavery in a very positive light indeed. On consequentialist grounds, his defense of the institution is more proslavery than it is antiabolitionist. On deontological grounds, despite his refusal to defend the institution in the abstract, he never hints that it might be an unjust institution. To the contrary, he portrays it as an institution that is perfectly defensible on the basis of biblical and, in particular, liberal principles. On contextualist grounds, he therefore does not portray the union as a house divided over liberal principles but, rather, the reverse.

Notwithstanding his vigorous attacks on the abolitionists in these letters, Hammond does not present the North as a generically different society than the South but merely suggests that the two sections of the country manage their labor relations in different ways (pp. 159, 185). In fact, the rhetorical thrust of the letters is to isolate the abolitionists as unrepresentative of the North and as "the apple of discord" in the union. Unlike in his "gag rule" speech, Hammond makes no threats of disunion, nor does he claim that the North and the South are a house dividing over the fate of slavery. Hammond remains a conditional unionist—as concerned about the fate of the union as of slavery—but now with more faith in the union.[52]

Hammond's conditional unionism emerges in several different forms in the Clarkson letters. It emerges negatively in his warning to the North that the South would rather abandon the union than slavery (p. 162), a warning that places the fate of the union directly in the hands of the North (p. 193). Hammond's conditional unionism emerges more positively in his advice to the North on how it should handle this great responsibility: it should choose union over disunion because disunion would harm the North more than it would harm the South (pp. 126, 162, 192–93). To choose union, though, would be to repudiate the abolitionists. According to Hammond, they, not the slaveholders, are the real disunionists (pp. 126, 162). The slaveholders are actually very favorably disposed toward the union, despite the heavy financial burdens it imposes on them (pp. 192–93). After all, "the South venerates the Constitution, and is prepared to stand by it forever, *such as it came from the hands of our fathers*" (p. 192); it is the abolitionists who denounce "'the shameful compromises' of our Constitution" (p. 191).[53]

Hammond's conditional unionism emerges most strongly when he criticizes Clarkson and his fellow British abolitionists for meddling in American affairs (pp. 154, 160, 190–91, 196–97). Hammond especially objects to Clarkson's opening reference to the United States in his circular as "'a nation whose character is *now so low* in the estimation of the civilized world'" (p. 190). Hammond replies that such attitudes may be prevalent among British abolitionists but he doubts that most Americans are so "destitute of patriotism or pride of country" (p. 190).

To the contrary, there is a vast body of people here beside slaveholders, who justly "deem their own land of every land the pride, Beloved by heaven o'er all the world beside" (p. 191).

Apparently, then, the presence of racial slavery on American soil does not cause most Americans to despair of their nation's special mission in history. At least in Hammond's case, this attitude depends on refuting the idea that racial slavery is an illiberal or unrepublican institution. When speaking of the possibility of disunion, he contends that "the fate of the Union then—but thank god not of Republican Government—rests mainly in the hands of the [Northern] people" (p. 193). The implication is that the fate of republican government is in good Southern hands despite, or rather because of, the continued existence of racial slavery in the South and that the fate of the union would be in good Northern hands if only the people of the North would repudiate the abolitionists. The American abolitionists mimic the British abolitionists in insisting that the presence of racial slavery on American soil undercuts the force of the nation's liberal exemplar in other countries around the world and in meddling in other people's affairs (pp. 130, 152, 154, 162).[54] Hammond thus rejects the antislavery version of the "American exemplar" argument, as he (now) rejects the antislavery version of the "house divided" argument.

Hammond also rejects the antislavery version of the "human progress" argument. First, he believes that slavery is not necessarily being swept aside by the forces of progress because "in some form or other," it is a universal institution that rests on "essential principles of human association revealed in history, both sacred and profane" (p. 176).[55] Second, he believes that the institution is a progressive institution in its own right, so much so that the Southern slaveholders "stand in the broadest light of the knowledge, civilization and improvement of the age" (p. 172). Hammond suggests that slavery has been a civilizing, even a liberalizing, force in history (p. 118). Abolishing the institution at this time would have a regressive impact on Southern civilization, not a progressive one. It would return the region to the "barbaric ignorance" of a preliberal state of nature (p. 182).

Notwithstanding his conservative, Burkean stance against the present "transcendental" (pp. 170–71) and "fanatical" (pp. 194–95) age, Hammond applauds the self-proclaimed progressive influence that he and his fellow slaveholders have had on history. The abolitionists, in contrast, conform to the present age, but they promise to have a regressive influence on history. According to Hammond, they are not part of any genuine age of improvement, for they seek to destroy, not improve, existing institutions (pp. 126, 162, 184, 194). He, therefore, presents himself and other defenders of slavery as salutary antidotes to the abolitionists: practical-minded progressive liberals who understand the need for people to limit their (natural) liberty in order to better secure their (civil) liberty.[56]

As the abolitionists increasingly invoked the "house divided," "American exemplar," and "human progress" arguments against Southern slavery, Hammond must have felt compelled to rebut their versions of those arguments and embrace a more "positive good" defense of the institution. His primary defense of the institution was no longer the argument that Northern antislavery agitation and continued union were incompatible. It was the argument that Southern slavery and continued union were *not* incompatible, not only on the consequentialist grounds that the continued existence of the institution benefited the whole nation, but also on the contextualist grounds that it was a liberal institution perfectly consistent with the nation's progressive mission in history. At the beginning of the next decade, however, Hammond found himself once again accentuating, instead of attentuating, the "house divided" argument. Indeed, during the 1850s, that argument received his (almost) undivided attention. This development further exposed the conditionality of his unionism. Ironically, it also placed him on a similar footing with the Garrison abolitionists, who earlier had shifted in a disunionist direction.

Reasserting the "House Divided" Argument

After John C. Calhoun died in March 1850, the Charleston city council chose Hammond to deliver one of its two official funeral orations.[57] In his speech, not delivered until November 21, Hammond naturally focuses on Calhoun's political career and personal character, ultimately portraying him as "a Philosophical Statesman—the only true and real Statesman" (p. 299). Hammond presents Calhoun's career and character as being intertwined with the fate of the union, thereby providing him with a rationale for offering his own assessment of the state of the union at midcentury.

By all accounts, Calhoun was the leading South Carolina statesman that Hammond always wanted to be but never could.[58] Nonetheless, Hammond's funeral oration is a thinly veiled critique of Calhoun for his "almost superstitious" attachment to the union (p. 262). This criticism does not mean that Hammond has no attachment to the union, for Hammond uses Calhoun's unionism as both an accusation against him and an excuse for his errors in political judgment (pp. 247, 262, 271, 286–87). Hammond, moreover, is not ready to recommend disunion in 1850, any more than Calhoun was. His criticism of Calhoun "merely" means that he is more of a conditional unionist than Calhoun was.[59] Now, in 1850, Hammond's emphasis is not on how divided the union really is *not* but on how divided it really *is*. In his view, the "house divided" argument seems to have more validity than it ever has had before.

Obviously, 1850 was a critical year in North-South relations. Although Calhoun died during the battle over the Compromise of 1850, Hammond does not take a position on that particular compromise in his funeral oration.[60] He does praise Calhoun's last major speech against the compromise measures (pp. 285–86) but then rebukes Calhoun for seeking a constitutional remedy to a problem that is not constitutionally remediable (p. 287).[61] Hammond urges instead a "return" to intersectional comity as the best and only solution to the problem of continuing sectional conflict in the United States (p. 288). This proposal, which, according to Hammond, is embodied in the Constitution of "our fathers," was clearly foreshadowed in his earlier works. His basic position on the union has not changed, for he always has favored preserving a "Constitutional Union, which is the only Union a patriot can desire to preserve" (p. 262). What has changed is how conditionally he states his unionism. Hammond is not sanguine about the efficacy of his own proposal for intersectional comity because, as he noted as far back as 1836, it would require the North to crush "the fell spirit of Abolitionism" (p. 288). As in 1836, he seems now to view the union as a house in the process of dividing. Yet he still has some hope for the union, and he still believes that it would be one if it were not for Northern antislavery agitation. Thus, now more than ever, the task is not so much to defend slavery as to save the union by attacking the abolitionists. In this effort, Hammond portrays himself as one with Calhoun.

Hammond's funeral oration recounts Calhoun's political career in great detail and in chronological order until it comes to his opposition to the Mexican War on the grounds that the war was likely to exacerbate sectional conflict in the United States (pp. 275–76).[62] Until then, Hammond does not even mention slavery. But after discussing Calhoun's opposition to the Mexican War, he backtracks to explicitly consider the role of slavery in American politics and offer a substantially different picture of American history than he has up to that point.[63]

This "interlude" begins with the Federal Convention of 1787. Hammond contends that the Southern states never would have entered into the union without obtaining some strong guarantees in the Constitution for their institution of racial slavery (p. 278).[64] He then considers the Missouri crisis of 1819–20, which first disturbed the constitutional consensus on slavery but which, from his perspective, also was satisfactorily settled (p. 278). He next summarizes the congressional debates over the reception of the abolitionist petitions in the mid-1830s, which, of course, was the controversy that brought Hammond himself to national attention.[65] He points out that Calhoun opposed the reception of the abolitionist petitions on the same grounds he did: as a threat to continued union (p. 280). He also points out that this controversy elicited a "positive good" defense of slavery from Calhoun that "scouted the idea of natural freedom and equality" (p. 281).[66] Here, Hammond anticipates his broader conclusion about Calhoun's career by observing that Calhoun was mistaken in believing he could "reason with enthusiastic Abolitionists, or with the masses of the non-Slaveholders, equally bigoted in their abstract notions of morality, freedom, and equality" (p. 281).[67] Hammond's ensuing analysis of Northern antislavery politics (pp. 281–83) brings the speech back to its original chronological order as he turns to examining how the Mexican War aggravated sectional conflict over the status of slavery in the territories, just as Calhoun warned it would (pp. 283–86).[68] In discussing Calhoun's opposition to the proposed compromise to that conflict, Hammond again insists that mere words—even in the form of a constitutional amendment—will not dissuade the abolitionists, nor will they repair a house divided (pp. 287–89).

At this point in the speech, Hammond suggests his own alternative policy of intersectional comity. He assumes that the union is not held together by the Constitution but "by habit; by recollections of the past, and a common reverence for the patriots and heroes of the Revolution; by the ties of political parties, of religious sects, and business intercourse" (p. 288). He also assumes that many of these cords of union already have been "snapped asunder. The religious bonds have been nearly all ruptured; party ties are going fast; those of business are seriously endangered" (p. 288). For Hammond, unlike Calhoun, who had presented a similar analysis of the current state of sectional controversy in his last major speech, the lesson is not to paper over those divisions with a constitutional amendment.[69] It is to frankly recognize that "we have at least two separate, distinct, and in some essential points, antagonistic social systems, whose differences can never be reconciled and subjected to one equal and just Government" (p. 288). Hammond believes that the only hope for continued union is to ensure that "our respective industrial enterprises are left free from every shackle, and the fell spirit of Abolitionism crushed and entirely eradicated" (p. 288). What exactly this solution entails and why exactly it is not a constitutional solution are far from clear. What is clear is that Hammond views it as the only way that the union can endure as a house divided.

Hammond does not hold out much hope for his own policy, admitting that "providential interposition" might be necessary to preserve the union (p. 288). He further tempers any expectations he might have raised when he states that "whatever may be the ultimate result," it still is "the sacred duty of the statesman . . . to propose the best remedies he can" (pp. 288–89). At least Calhoun, and now Hammond, has fulfilled that duty (p. 289).

The speech finishes with a glowing paean to Calhoun's personal character (pp. 290–300), capped by Hammond's portrait of him as a philosophical statesman, "a genuine apostle" of "free and popular Government" (pp. 299–300).[70] Hammond thus does not view Calhoun as an illiberal statesman for denying natural freedom and equality in the process of defending Southern slavery but, rather, as a liberal statesman for attempting, through his theory of the concurrent majority, to restrain sectional majorities that disagree over the fate of the institution (pp. 299–300).[71] The speech is liberal not in the way that it defends Southern slavery but in the way that it defends a particular political process. At least implicitly, Hammond argues that liberal principles reside in people's beliefs about the appropriate way of settling disputes over the fate of slavery and other social institutions, not in their beliefs about the propriety of those institutions themselves. The lesson of the speech is that free and popular government rests on the willingness of people to agree to disagree, which, if present, obviates the need for Calhoun's concurrent-majority system and, if absent, renders it ineffectual. The system, then, cannot itself solve the recurrent crises of union.

The central objective of Hammond's funeral oration for Calhoun, however, is not to defend a particular political process or Southern slavery or the union, on either deontological or consequentialist grounds. It is to test how, on contextualist grounds, Southern slavery and the union can coexist together in the face of the deep sectional differences that have emerged over the fate of the institution and that were further exposed during the most recent crisis of union. Hammond is plainly pessimistic about the long-term prospects of the union. But as he closes the speech, he reiterates his belief that statesmen do have "high and sacred duties" to propose solutions to such crises and, because of an "unshaken confidence in the Providence of God," claims not to be without hope in the efficacy of those solutions (p. 300).

By 1858, whether because of Providence or other causes, North-South relations were even more strained than they had been in 1850. Stephen A. Douglas's Kansas-Nebraska bill reopened sectional controversy over the status of slavery in the territories, and by 1858 the slavery issue, at least for Congress, had assumed the form of whether to admit Kansas into the union under the proslavery Lecompton constitution. During the debate over that question, Hammond, who only recently had been appointed to the Senate, delivered his "Mudsill" speech. Denouncing both Douglas's "popular sovereignty" and William H. Seward's "irrepressible conflict" doctrines, the speech calls for Senate approval of the Lecompton constitution (pp. 302–5). Hammond's support for that constitution, however, is fairly tepid (pp. 307–8).[72] The speech is much less a defense of any particular course of action on the slavery issue than it is a discourse on the "house divided" argument. Somewhat paradoxically, Hammond both accepts and rejects Seward's claim that the free North and the slave South are locked in an irrepressible conflict with each other.[73]

Behind the idea of an irrepressible conflict is the "house divided" argument. Seward's conclusion to that argument is that the union will become all free as the North remakes the South in its own image. Accordingly, Hammond accuses Seward of threatening to remake the South in the North's image as "a conquered province" (p. 310).[74]

Hammond answers this perceived threat to the South and its institution of racial slavery in several different, not necessarily consistent, ways in the speech.

Hammond's initial response to this threat is to declare that the South never will allow the North to remake the South in its own image. If the North is intent on doing so, Hammond suggests that it might well come to disunion and civil war, especially since the South no longer can rely on the North's good faith (pp. 310–11). He certainly offers no concrete proposal for reversing the current course of events.[75] Hammond seems to accept the "house divided" argument in this speech and to view the union as a house in the process of dividing along its sectional fault lines.

Hammond's speech, though, is also a plea to the North not to try to remake the South in its own image and thus invite disunion and civil war. The North should be satisfied with an indefinitely divided house, as the South is. Hammond insists that the North not only needs the union more than the South does but also benefits from it more (pp. 320–22). Unlike the North, the South can stand alone; any Southern commitment to the union must be highly conditional (pp. 311–18). In this speech, Hammond wavers between imagining the union as a house divided that can stand and as a house divided that cannot, and perhaps should not, stand.

Hammond's defense of Southern slavery in the speech proceeds largely on the grounds that the institution is a powerful regional asset that permits the South, unlike the North, to stand alone in the case of disunion (pp. 317–18). But he also suggests that the institution is a powerful national asset in the case of continued union (pp. 321–22). In these terms, Southern slavery does not create a house divided; only Northern misperceptions of the institution do. Most radically, Hammond denies that the union is even a house divided in this speech.

In its defense of slavery, Hammond's "Mudsill" speech harks back to his Clarkson letters. As he did in those letters, he promises to defend the institution not in the abstract but "as a *practical thing*, as a thing that *is* and *is to be*" (p. 309). Now, however, his focus has shifted even further away from defending the institution in itself to examining "its effect upon our political institutions" and ascertaining "how long those institutions will hold together with slavery *ineradicable*" (pp. 309–10). This focus initially means defending the institution as one of the South's major regional assets that would make it an empire unto itself in the case of disunion.

According to Hammond, the South's major regional assets include its geography (pp. 311–12), manpower (pp. 312–13), and economy (pp. 313–16), leading up to the claim that no country would make war on an independent South because "Cotton is King" of the international economy (pp. 316–17).[76] Yet Hammond contends that "the greatest strength of the South arises from the harmony of her political and social institutions" (p. 317).[77]

Hammond argues that this harmony provides the South with "an extent of political freedom, combined with entire security, such as no other people ever enjoyed upon the face of the earth" (pp. 317–18). He goes on to demonstrate how the institution of racial slavery produces this beneficent harmony and offers the South a comparative advantage over the North. In that demonstration, he assumes that every society is built on a "mud-sill" class that performs the menial work of that society (p. 318). The South's comparative advantage lies in the fact that it "found" members of an "inferior" race who were perfectly adapted to composing such a class and who were already slaves by "the common 'consent of mankind'" (pp. 318–19).[78] He contends that the people of the South actually have elevated Africans by making them their slaves (p. 319). As Southern "mud-sills," they are, furthermore, "happy, content, unaspiring, and utterly incapable, from intellectual weakness, ever to give us any trouble by their aspirations" (p. 320).

The North's "mud-sills" are, in contrast, not happy, content, or unaspiring but, rather, "galled by their degradation." They also are "equals in natural endowment of intellect" to their "masters," belong to the same race, and enjoy the right to vote (p. 320). Hammond warns of a working-class revolution in the North, an indication of precisely how insecure he believes Northern liberty to be when compared to Southern liberty (pp. 320–21).[79] The North has been saved from such tumults only by "transient and temporary causes" (p. 321). In particular, Hammond believes that the frontier has dissipated social tensions in the North and that its connection to the more conservative South also has enhanced its economic and political stability (p. 321).[80] Earlier in the speech, he offered the common proslavery argument that Northern free laborers are slaves in everything but name and, in practice, are worse off than Southern slaves.

> The difference between us is, that our slaves are hired for life and well compensated; there is no starvation, no begging, no want of employment among our people, and not too much employment either. Yours are hired by the day, not cared for, and scantily compensated, which may be proved in the most painful manner, at any hour in any street in any of your large towns. Why you meet more beggars in one day, on any single street of the city of New York, than you would meet in a lifetime in the whole South. (P. 319)[81]

Hammond's point, however, is not that Northern free laborers should be (re)enslaved. He does not think that "whites should be slaves either by law or necessity" (p. 319). His point, once again, is that because of its institution of racial slavery, the South compares favorably to the North in how it handles its labor relations and in the quality of life of its free (white) laborers.

Relative to his defense of slavery in the Clarkson letters, Hammond's defense of the institution in the "Mudsill" speech is more liberal. He emphasizes that the institution, deontologically, is based on the "consent of mankind" and, consequentially, maximizes the liberty and equality of Southern whites. His defense of slavery is also more "positive good." Even though he vows to defend the institution as a "practical thing," he neglects the centerpiece of such "practical" defenses of slavery: antiabolitionist arguments dwelling on the worst-case scenarios of what might occur if the institution were ever abolished. Finally, his defense of slavery is more contextualist. He concentrates less on defending the institution in itself and more on defending it in the broader context in which it exists in both the South and the nation as a whole. Hammond thus portrays the institution as a powerful regional asset in the case of disunion and as a powerful national asset in the case of continued union.

The striking ambivalence of Hammond's views toward the union in this speech reflects his conditional unionism. Still, it is somewhat surprising that he does not close the speech with a warning about disunion but instead with a tribute to the union, its special mission in history, and the leading role of "the slaveholders of the South" in transforming it into what it is today: "boundless in prosperity, incalculable in her strength, the wonder and admiration of the world" (pp. 321–22).[82] This conclusion foreshadows the dramatic "shift" in his views toward the union that he announces to his constituents a mere seven months later.

Denying the "House Divided" Argument

On October 29, 1858, before returning to the Senate, Hammond reported on the state of national affairs to his constituents in Barnwell, South Carolina. In the interim, Congress rejected the Lecompton constitution, and the compromise English bill was rejected by the people of Kansas.[83] Despite these proslavery setbacks, Hammond now appears much more optimistic about the future of the union and even claims to have shifted from disunionism to unionism. Perhaps this shift is an artifact of the different audiences of the "Mudsill" and "Barnwell" speeches.[84] The two speeches, though, actually share the same theme. In the "Barnwell" speech, Hammond is arguing the same point he has been arguing throughout the decade, that under certain conditions, the union can survive its divisions over slavery. His theme remains conditional unionism. He professes to be more optimistic about the long-term prospects of the union not because he considers it less of a house divided but because he considers the South more of a house united. What he is denying in this speech is not a disunionism he never really adopted but a "house divided" argument he never wholly accepted.

Hammond begins the speech by insisting that "our battle" is the same in 1858 as it was in 1833: to maintain "the Constitution and our rights, in the Union, if possible—out of it, if need be" (p. 323). After defending his course of action in the Senate on the Kansas question (pp. 325–33),[85] he predicts that "an overwhelming majority of the South" would prefer to remain in the union "if assured that this government was hereafter to be conducted on the true principles . . . of the Constitution" (p. 333). It is at this point in the speech that he announces his newfound unionism.

> I confess that, for many years of my life, I believed that our only safety was the dissolution of the union, and I openly avowed it. I should entertain, and without hesitation express the same sentiments now, but that the victories we have achieved and those that I think we are about to achieve, have inspired me with the hope, I may say the belief, that we can fully sustain ourselves in the union and control its action in all great affairs. (P. 334)[86]

Hammond then asks, rhetorically, how he can entertain such sentiments when both houses of Congress now have Northern majorities,

majorities that he expects only to grow larger in the future (pp. 334–39).[87]

Hammond offers the same answer to that question as he offered in the "Mudsill" speech to the question of how the South would fare as an independent nation: it need not dread either eventuality because it is an empire onto itself (p. 339). The South's powerful regional assets allow it to remain in the union or exist outside the union as it sees fit (p. 340). The rest of the "Barnwell" speech is then similar to the "Mudsill" speech in magnifying the power of those regional assets, except for its emphasis on the fact that the basis of both the South's options is its own internal unity. The two speeches also are similar in advocating continued union at the present time, although the "Barnwell" speech is much more optimistic about the long-term viability of that option.

In underscoring the need for Southern unity, Hammond claims that most of the South's wounds have been self-inflicted (p. 343). When the South has been united, it has been able to dictate terms to the North, as on the tariff, internal improvements, and the national bank (pp. 341–42).[88] Hammond observes that in the past, the South was divided over the future of its institution of racial slavery, since many of its leading citizens thought of the institution as a necessary evil (p. 344).[89] The abolitionist movement, though, has "succeeded" in uniting the South behind a "positive good" ideology (pp. 344–45). It should now also be able to dictate terms to the North on the fate of slavery because "the sense of danger and the love of cotton and tobacco would, with our northern brethren, in every crisis override their love of negroes" (p. 340).

After Hammond presents his own "positive good" defense of Southern slavery as an institution "sustained by the religion of the Bible, . . . [opposed by] neither humanity nor sound philosophy, . . . [and] a social, political, and economical benefit to the world" (p. 348),[90] he further debunks Northern antislavery sentiment. He contends that antislavery sentiment is already receding in Europe (p. 348) and will soon also begin receding in the North (p. 349; see also p. 346).[91] He also predicts that once the Kansas question is settled, the abolitionists no longer will have a concrete issue to agitate (p. 349) and that they will be reduced to an insignificant minority in the North if the Republican Party does not win one of the next two presidential elections (p. 350).[92] According to Hammond, the Republican leadership does not "care anything for African slavery" (p. 350). He accuses the party of exploiting the slavery issue solely for political gain and believes that it will stop doing so once it sees that nothing more can be gained from it (p. 350).

Hammond's belief in the waning and insincerity of antislavery sentiment bolsters his confidence that the South will be able to dictate terms to the North on the fate of slavery. Success, however, will not be measured in terms of uniting the house on the ultimate justice of the institution but in terms of maintaining the status quo of a house divided over that issue. As he had in his funeral oration for Calhoun, Hammond holds out intersectional comity as the key to the future of the union. He insists that the South retain the fate of slavery in its own hands (p. 351) and warns of disunion if Congress ever legislates on the subject, which in turn could precipitate a worldwide apocalypse (pp. 351–52).[93] Both scenarios presume a united South (p. 352).

But Hammond quickly retreats from these images of a union rent "into fragments" and a world plunged "in ruin" (p. 351) to envision a more glorious future for the South. He claims that a united South has no reason to be apprehensive about holding the fate of slavery in its own hands (p. 352). The South still effectively controls the federal government because it still has faithful allies in the North (pp. 352–53).[94] This topic leads Hammond into defending his own course of action in the Senate as a "National Democrat" who was, and is, willing to work with the "true" Democrats of the North (pp. 353–55).[95] After reasserting the need for Southern unity and again thanking the abolitionists for helping achieve it (p. 356), Hammond contrasts a Southern "union" with the national union, identifying the former, not the latter, as the exemplary liberal polity for his constituents.

> The union of these States, from the Canadas to the Rio Grande, and from shore to shore of the two great oceans of the globe, whatever splendor may encircle it, is but a policy and not a principle. It is subordinate to rights and interests. But the union of the slaveholders of the South is a principle involving all our rights and all our interests. Let that union be perfect and perpetual. It constitutes our strength, our safety and prosperity. Let us frown down every proposition that might seriously divide us, and present to our assailants from every quarter a solid and impregnable phalanx. (Pp. 356–57)

Hammond, however, leaves open, and actually encourages, the option of the South's "asserting our great power in this great confederacy" (p. 357). While he presents disunion as a more viable option for the South in the "Barnwell" speech than he has in any of his earlier works, he also presents continued union as a more viable option. Hammond remains a conditional unionist who is attracted by the "splendor" of the union and whose hopes that it can endure its divisions over the fate of slavery outweigh his fears that it will not. He tailors his "positive good" defense of Southern slavery and his strong advocacy of Southern unity in the speech less to the possibility of disunion than to the possibility of the continuing existence of the union as a house divided over the fate of the institution. He accordingly calls into question the validity of the "house divided" argument, an argument he long has asserted but, apparently, never wholeheartedly.

By November 8, 1860, two days after Lincoln's election, the house had already divided, at least as far many people in South Carolina were concerned. The state's "hot spurs" had worked diligently throughout the year to make the election of a Republican president the sine qua non of secession, and they had been very successful in their campaign.[96] Hammond, though, hung back. In a speech prepared for the eventuality of Lincoln's election but never delivered, he reiterated the "Southern unity" theme of the "Barnwell" speech.[97] Southern unity now, however, had become the precondition for disunion rather than for continued union. Southern unity had also become more problematic than it was in 1858. Hammond seems much more anxious about the viability of disunion than he was then, perhaps because it now appeared inevitable and he never really had desired it in the first place.

In this, his last major "speech," Hammond offers many pieces of advice to South Carolina, but in the end, it is unclear exactly how he is advising his state to act.[98] Even his two main pieces of advice—that Lincoln's election is not in itself sufficient grounds for secession and that South Carolina should wait for other Southern states to act before deciding whether or not to secede—are rendered ambiguous during the speech. Hammond remains a conditional unionist. The ambiguities of the speech are the ambiguities of that position.[99]

Hammond begins this speech by quoting from his "Barnwell" speech to the effect that the union is a matter of policy, not principle, for the South and that the South holds its destiny in its own hands (p.

2).[100] He still claims to subscribe to those views. The twin themes that the union is only a matter of policy for the South and that the South, if united, need not fear either disunion or continued union also become recurrent themes in this later speech (pp. 20, 22–24, 29–30, 32).

Hammond's most extensive treatment of these themes occurs while arguing, much more explicitly than he has in the past, that disunion would actually be advantageous to the South. Nearly two-thirds of the way through the speech, Hammond confronts the objection that "the union is a great blessing to the South, and that nothing but evil for her would follow its dissolution" (p. 22). He acknowledges that at its inception and for a long time afterward, the union was a great blessing to the South as well as to the North but that "ever since the South has been strong enough to stand alone, I have believed that its advantages are mainly with the North, and that well out of it and properly reorganized the South would be better off" (p. 22).[101] He goes on to paint a very bleak picture of the union from the South's perspective. He contends that "the union has for a long time been smothering the South. It kills our commerce, our manufactures, and our mechanic arts; it drains us of our money" (p. 22). With disunion, Hammond insists that the South "would at least be freed from the Anti-Slavery agitation" because, he believes, Northern politicians no longer would have any incentive to pursue it (pp. 22–23).[102]

At this point in the speech, Hammond asks, and the question is certainly pertinent, "But why should we continue to be annoyed, scandalized, and injured—denounced as feeble when we furnish three fourths of the life blood of this union, and threatened with conquest by Northern armies which we can beat on any battlefield, at odds" (p. 24).

Hammond answers that Lincoln's election is not in itself sufficient cause for disunion because it would place the South in the false position of disrupting the union on the occasion of a presidential election that took place in a perfectly constitutional manner (p. 25).[103] He claims that the South would have been justified in seceding from the union in 1828, with the passage of the "tariff of abominations," or in 1820, at the time of the Missouri controversy, or at any time since 1833, when Northern antislavery societies started to actively attack "our social system," because those events, unlike Lincoln's election, were unconstitutional aggressions against the South (p. 26). Just as the South weathered those events, Hammond believes that it can weather

Lincoln's election. He already has reassured his "audience" that Lincoln will be only a one-term president and therefore unlikely to "accomplish anything seriously detrimental to us" (p. 24).[104]

Yet Hammond undercuts these and other arguments against Southern secession in the short history of the United States he presents in the speech. The initial premise of this history is that the framers of the Constitution were almost miraculously able to reconcile two quite different social systems under one government.[105] If their successors had strictly followed the Constitution, the union would have lasted "for untold ages," and the American people would have become a liberal empire unto itself: "the freest, most prosperous and most powerful people that the world has ever known" (p. 27). The North, unfortunately, disregarded the Constitution from the first. It also abolished slavery, further differentiating the two social systems.[106] Soon after abolishing slavery, it began to make war on the institution in the South, eventually organizing its own sectional party (pp. 27–28).[107] That party, which is committed to destroying the South "by setting free our slaves, and in order to do this, to instigate . . . civil and servile war," now has seized control of the executive branch of the federal government (pp. 28–29).[108] Hammond concludes his history lesson by contending that this Republican conspiracy against the South—and not Lincoln's election per se—provides the rationale for disunion at this time (p. 29). That, however, now seems to be a distinction without a difference, especially since the conspiracy actually predates the Republican Party and presumably would have justified Southern secession at any time between 1833 and 1860.

Hammond soon returns to his conspiracy theory. He declares that since he has

> ever been indifferent to the union, if it is believed that the policy . . . of an "irrepressible conflict" between free and slave labor—which is as false as it would be barbarous and brutal—is the settled and permanent policy of this government, I would not advise the state to await an "overt act" to secede from the union. (P. 30)[109]

But now that Hammond has undermined his prior antisecessionist logic, he reverses himself and undermines this new prosecessionist logic. He contrasts the English and American revolutions with the French and Mexican revolutions as the difference between successful revolutions that were prepared judiciously over long periods of time and unsuccessful revolutions that erupted spasmodically under intense popular excitements (pp. 33–34). He then closes the speech by urging the South to heed these historical examples and to wait at least until Lincoln's inauguration before deciding whether or not to secede (p. 34).[110] Hammond also had anticipated this final cautionary tone when he prefaced his conspiracy theory by stating that "I do not regard our circumstances in the union as desperate now and I would not myself advise rash and desperate remedies" (pp. 30–31).

Indeed, the entire speech follows this point/counterpoint pattern. For every reason to secede, a corresponding reason exists not to secede: (1) the South need not await the first blow to secede (pp. 30–31); all successful revolutions require time to mature (pp. 33–34); (2) a Republican conspiracy against the South would dictate South Carolina's immediate secession from the union (p. 31); South Carolina should not secede without the cooperation of the other Southern states (pp. 11–13, 17);[111] (3) a Republican presidency endangers the South's future well-being (pp. 28–29); Lincoln's election does not, in itself, justify secession (pp. 25–26); (4) a Republican administration threatens to abolish the South's institution of racial slavery (p. 29); a worldwide reaction is taking place in favor of slavery, especially among the commercial classes of the North (pp. 3, 20);[112] (5) an independent South need only reorganize itself under the existing Constitution to stand against the world (pp. 17–18); this process of political reorganization could easily fall prey to popular excitements (pp. 18–19);[113] (6) a united South need not fear disunion (pp. 2–3); the recent presidential canvass has frayed Southern unity (pp. 4–5); and (7) the union is a matter of indifference or, worse, misfortune to the South (pp. 2, 22, 30); safely secured in a true, constitutional union, the United States would be a world power with its world-historic mission for the cause of human freedom unimpaired (p. 27).

This pattern has baffled scholars, as it undoubtedly would have baffled its intended audience.[114] It is, however, the pattern one would expect from a conditional unionist. From Hammond's perspective, the only hope for continued union rests in the North's willingness to honor the principles of intersectional comity underlying the Constitution and not to interfere with the South's institution of racial slavery. In this way, the union might again benefit the South as well as the North and continue to exist indefinitely into the future, despite its divisions over the fate of the institution. Even though Hammond, not surprisingly, considers this possibility more remote now than he ever has before, he still favors it. He holds out hope for the union because except for Northern aggressions against Southern slavery, "we almost are" what "we should have been": the freest, most prosperous, and most powerful people in the world (p. 27). Hammond thus never abandoned hope of identifying the union as the exemplary liberal polity for his constituents and the whole world beside.

Conclusion

"Except for Northern aggressions against Southern slavery we are one" might well have been the main theme of Hammond's writings and speeches from 1836 to 1860. He believed that the North and the South were equally committed to liberal principles and jointly constituted the freest people in the world, notwithstanding the continued existence of racial slavery in the South. He also believed that racial slavery could be defended on the basis of liberal principles as actually contributing to the aggregate liberty and happiness of the American people. Finally, he believed that racial slavery had created a house divided in the United States only because the liberal face of the institution had been ignored by the people of the North, a people who had little personal experience with the institution and who wrongly thought liberal principles and the nation's unique dedication to those principles required its abolition.[115] This set of beliefs explains Hammond's rhetorical emphasis on slavery and union rather than on slavery per se.

For Hammond, the key question was not how Southern slavery could survive in an increasingly hostile world but how the union could endure as a house increasingly divided over the fate of the institution. He offered various answers to that question during his political career. But those answers all revolved around the same point: the union could endure indefinitely as a house divided over slavery if Americans honored the Constitution of "our fathers," a constitution that, according to Hammond, mandated intersectional comity and, in particular, Northern noninterference with Southern slavery. Hammond's views on how divided the house really was and whether it would be able to survive its divisions over slavery also changed over time. He alternated between optimism and pessimism about the future of the union. Yet he never despaired over its future, and he never advocated disunion.

As a conditional unionist, Hammond favored continued union as long as the price was not Southern slavery. He had often defended the institution in the past as a positive good on both deontological and consequentialist grounds, but the flow of events "diverted" his attention to the contextualist conundrum of how a South increasingly determined to preserving the institution could remain in union with a North increasingly committed to abolishing it. Hammond was never completely convinced that the price of continued union was Southern slavery. As he insisted in his last major "speech," Lincoln's election should mean disunion only if Lincoln and the Republican Party were conspiring to destroy the institution. Lincoln himself professed otherwise. He disavowed any intention to interfere with the institution in those states where it already existed.[116] Hammond was probably no more convinced by Lincoln's disavowals than other Southern leaders were. Unlike Hammond, however, many Southern leaders interpreted Lincoln's election not simply as further evidence that the "house divided" argument might be prophetic but as the fruition of its prophecy. It was, after all, an argument that Hammond as well as Lincoln had asserted previously under far less trying circumstances.

Part IV

7

The "House Divided" and Civil-War Causation

In the midst of the Civil War, Abraham Lincoln suggested a theory of civil-war causation based on a fundamental antagonism between Northern and Southern definitions of liberty.

> The world has never had a good definition of the word liberty, and the American people, just now, are much in want of one. We all declare for liberty; but in using the same *word* we do not all mean the same *thing*. With some the word liberty may mean for each man to do as he pleases with himself, and the produce of his labor; while with others the same word may mean for some men to do what they please with other men, and the produce of other men's labor. Here are two, not only different, but incompatable [*sic*] things called by the same name—liberty. And it follows that each of the things is, by the respective parties, called by two different and incompatable [*sic*] names—liberty and tyranny.[1]

Lincoln believed that the Northern definition of liberty was clearly the superior one, since it was the definition of the sheep, as opposed to the definition of the wolf. The shepherd who armed himself with the first definition to drive "the wolf from the sheep's throat" seemed to have the better of the argument, although his advantage was not as great as he or the sheep might have wished. Southern proslavery figures obviously would have presented their definition of liberty in a nobler light than Lincoln did. But they would have agreed with him that they applied liberal principles to the Southern institution of racial slavery in a quite different way than he and other Northern opponents of the institution did.[2]

The question Lincoln left unanswered in this speech was why the nation could not have existed as a house divided, with each section allowing the other to pursue its own definition of liberty in its own way. He had offered an answer to that question six years earlier, before the beginning of the Civil War, when launching an unsuccessful campaign to unseat his longtime rival, Stephen A. Douglas, as senator from the state of Illinois.

> "A house divided against itself cannot stand." I believe this government cannot endure permanently half slave and half free. I do not expect the Union to be dissolved—I do not expect the house to fall—but I do expect it will cease to be divided. It will become all one thing, or all the other. Either the opponents of slavery will arrest the further spread of it, and place it where the public shall rest in the belief that it is in the course of ultimate extinction; or its advocates will push it forward, till it shall become alike lawful in all the States, old as well as new—North as well as South.[3]

The irony is that neither of these alternatives became a reality; neither, as Lincoln preferred, a house united against slavery nor, as he feared, a house united for slavery. Nor did the possibility that he intended to exclude through his "house divided" speech become a reality, that of an indefinitely divided house. It was a fourth possibility—one that he claimed not to expect in the speech and one that he certainly did not desire—that became a reality: disunion and then a long, bloody civil war.[4]

Lincoln's "house divided" speech, however, played an important role in unleashing this chain of events. His election as president of the United States in 1860 was the occasion for Southern secession because many Southern leaders interpreted his election as signaling the North's acceptance of the "house divided" argument and of Lincoln's own particular conclusion to it. They feared that his election portended the imposition of Northern liberty on Southern liberty and thus acted to conclude the argument in a way that they found more acceptable to themselves. They physically divided the house.

If this analysis is correct, it places the burden of disunion and civil war on Lincoln and, through him, the Northern majority who voted for him for president. Why did they finally accept the "house divided" argument, an argument that the abolitionists had been promulgating for more than two decades?[5] Alternatively, why could they no longer accept living in a house divided over the fate of slavery, a solution that still, as late as 1860, seemed to be preferred by a majority of Southern voters as well as the sizable Northern minority who voted for Douglas for president?[6]

The answer to those questions lies in the way that Lincoln elaborated the "house divided" argument during his earlier Senate campaign against Douglas.[7] He emphasized that the union could not survive its divisions over such a fundamental issue as the fate of slavery, as distinct from the way that it could survive its "divisions" over less fundamental issues such as the propriety of laws regulating various agricultural products. He insisted that only the former, and not the latter, created a house divided.[8] Douglas countered that the union had survived as a house divided over the fate of slavery for seventy years, ever since it was founded, and there was no reason to believe that it could not continue to do so, except for the way Lincoln and other "Black Republicans" were aggressing against the constitutional rights of the Southern states to choose their own domestic institutions for themselves.[9] Lincoln denied Douglas's premise. He contended that until recently the union had not been a house divided over the fate of slavery because most Americans, North and South, had agreed with the founders that it was an evil institution "in the course of ultimate extinction." He also contended that the union could not possibly survive the loss of this founding consensus.[10]

If most Northern voters accepted Lincoln's analysis as superior to Douglas's—and the results of the 1860 presidential election stand as evidence of that acceptance—then it precluded the possibility of an indefinitely divided house. This left them with three options: to unite the house against slavery, to unite the house for slavery, and to physically divide the house (or allow the Southern states to do so). Even though Lincoln presented in his Senate campaign the second option as a distinct possibility, he also anticipated that the election of a Republican president two years hence would be the death knell of that option.[11] He never seriously raised the possibility of disunion in his Senate campaign, apparently assuming that the North's militant nationalism precluded it. According to Lincoln's analysis, only the first option of uniting the house against slavery remained a viable one for the people of the North. For his purposes, the asymmetry of the "house divided" argument was extremely useful because it also seemed to leave the people of the South with only that same option. If the North never united with the South for slavery and if the South's own militant nationalism precluded disunion, then it, too, had to accept uniting the house against slavery. Lincoln tried to cushion that prospect by being very vague about what exactly uniting the house against slavery entailed as well as by insisting that the Republican Party did not intend to interfere with the institution in those states where it already existed.[12]

Unfortunately, Lincoln's reading of Southern intentions was only partially correct. The South chose disunion over continued union with a North determined to unite the house against slavery. But this option was not the first choice of most Southern voters.[13] Rather, their first choice was continued union with a North determined *not* to unite the house against slavery but to honor intersectional comity in a house indefinitely divided over the fate of the institution. While Lincoln's disavowals of any intention to interfere with slavery in the states where it already existed seemed to honor intersectional comity, those disavowals simply did not match his insistence on uniting the house against the institution.[14] No matter how vaguely he spoke of the actions required to "extinguish" Southern slavery and how long they might take, the fact remained that some actions against the institution had to be contemplated at some time in the future. Those actions, moreover, would violate intersectional comity, unless it was assumed that the Southern states would voluntarily undertake or welcome such actions. Most Southern leaders knew otherwise, that their states were now determined *not* to abolish racial slavery. The asymmetry of the "house divided" argument induced many of them to reject the argument at the same time as they met the North's acceptance of the argument with efforts to disrupt the union.[15] Not surprisingly, in order to advance their cause, those Southern leaders most dedicated to disunion referred repeatedly to Lincoln's "house divided" speech during the 1860 presidential campaign.[16]

The South, in effect, chose slavery over union. This choice, however, was not an easy one for most people in the South to make, and it was not a choice they wanted to have to make. They tended to be as nationalistic as were the people of the North who refused to accept their choice and went to war to "nullify" it.[17] Furthermore, they did not view it as choosing slavery over liberty but as choosing Southern liberty over Northern tyranny. The antebellum debate over the fate of slavery had pressed Southern proslavery figures into developing more positive, liberal defenses of the institution that associated Southern slavery with Southern liberty and Northern abolitionism with Northern tyranny. Most people in the North could not accept such defenses of slavery as readily as they could the more negative, racist defenses of the institution that Southern proslavery figures had previously favored.[18] It was therefore the South's move toward a more aggressive defense of racial slavery in the 1850s that first created a house divided in the United States, although more from the North's than from the South's perspective. This house divided, in turn, fortified the North's determination to unite the house against slavery as well as the South's counterdetermination not to allow that to happen.

If the key to civil-war causation was the collapse of the middle in both the North and the South by the late 1850s, then the use of the "house divided" argument by more extreme groups in each section of the country played an important role in causing the Civil War.[19] The "house divided" argument increased the pressure on the middle in both sections of the country to move away from the "necessary evil" position that defined, on deontological grounds, the Southern institution of racial slavery as an evil institution and yet claimed, on consequentialist grounds, that abolishing the institution would lead to even less desirable conditions in the future. The argument, correspondingly, increased pressure on the middle in both sections of the country to move toward either a more antislavery or a more proslavery position by portraying, on contextualist grounds, the status quo of a nation half free and half slave as an unsustainable situation. Northern moderates, of course, moved toward a more antislavery position, and Southern moderates, a more proslavery position, thereby creating a truly unsustainable situation. Lincoln did not expect or hope to strengthen the proslavery forces in the South, but he did expect and hope to strengthen the antislavery forces in the North. During his 1858 Senate campaign, he certainly had pressed Douglas's Democratic supporters and even Douglas himself to move toward the moderate antislavery position of the Republican Party by charging that their "I don't care" position on the fate of slavery was, in effect, a proslavery position.[20] In sum, Lincoln's theory of civil-war causation was basically correct, but he had helped make it so. The "house divided" argument did become a self-fulfilling prophecy.

Broadly speaking, there are two alternative views of civil-war causation: the "blundering generation" thesis and the "irrepressible conflict" thesis.[21] The proponents of the first thesis, such as revisionist historians James Randall and Avery Craven, claim that the Civil War was not inevitable but was the result of a series of miscalculations by inept political leaders on both sides that escalated a manageable conflict into a civil war.[22] These historians assume that the nation could have remained indefinitely a house divided, half free and half slave, and that

Southern slavery would eventually have died of its own accord. Accordingly, they tend to discount the differences between the antebellum North and South, especially over the fate of slavery, and to stress what the two sections of the country had in common.

The "blundering generation" thesis is persuasive in several ways. Political leaders on both sides miscalculated. Northern leaders underestimated the disposition of Southern leaders to disrupt the union, and Southern leaders underestimated the disposition of Northern leaders to preserve it. But every generation of political leaders miscalculates in some ways. Their miscalculations usually do not lead to civil war unless some substantial differences exist between them. It also is true that the two sections of the country had much in common, including strong commitments to liberal principles. Yet as Lincoln pointed out, Northern and Southern leaders had come to define those principles in very different, if not incompatible, ways. Their shared liberalism became a source of conflict rather than of compromise. Beyond any misperceptions they may have had of each other, political leaders in both sections of the country entertained real fears of each other.[23] Northern leaders feared that the institution of racial slavery had become so entrenched in the South that it was changing the whole tenor of American society in illiberal directions; Southern leaders feared that the North was determined to resolve that state of affairs in ways that threatened to destroy their own liberty. Neither side seemed to believe that Southern slavery would die of its own accord. Conflict, at some level, did seem irrepressible.

The "irrepressible conflict" thesis, however, also suffers from several weaknesses. The question of timing is a troublesome one for its proponents. As Douglas and other moderate Democrats at the time might have asked, when did an "irrepressible" conflict in a nation that had long been half free and half slave become no longer repressible? The thesis also has an unpersuasive aura of historical inevitability to it. Are any conflicts truly irrepressible?

The proponents of this thesis, such as neo-Progressive historians Arthur Cole and Allan Nevins, assume that the conflict was irrepressible only because it was defined and accepted as such by a sufficient number of people in both the North and the South.[24] They also assume that it took time for that definition and acceptance to emerge, even if they were encoded into the "original" sectional differences and the divergent paths of political development that the two sections of the country subsequently followed. Within that "iron cage," human agents nevertheless made choices, choices that, while bounded and explicable in relation to each other, were historically contingent. It was not inevitable that the Northern states would abolish racial slavery in the post-Revolutionary period and that the Southern states would not do so, although those choices are often portrayed in that light.[25] It also was not inevitable that during the antebellum period, the opponents of racial slavery would oppose the institution in the manner that they did or that the defenders of the institution would defend it in the manner that they did. The irrepressibility and timing of the conflict depended crucially on such historically contingent choices.

More recently, scholars have tried to synthesize the "blundering generation" and "irrepressible conflict" theses by looking at the institutional boundaries within which individual political choices were made. Proponents of this "institutional failure" thesis claim that the roots of the Civil War lay in the failure of national political institutions to respond adequately to continuing sectional conflict over the fate of slavery, thereby transforming a repressible conflict into an irrepressible one in a way that transcended the miscalculations of individual political leaders. Michael Holt's version of this thesis is the most persuasive one. He argues that the key factor in the mutual escalation of sectional conflict over the fate of slavery beyond repressible dimensions was the breakdown of the second-party system during the early 1850s. Before that time, the second-party system had successfully repressed sectional conflict through competing intersectional party coalitions, but by the early 1850s, the system had lost its momentum through the settlement of the "old" party issues of banks, internal improvements, and tariffs.[26] Yet as Kenneth Greenberg argues in his review of Holt's book, it seems more likely that the mutual escalation of sectional conflict over the fate of slavery beyond repressible dimensions caused the breakdown of the second-party system than the reverse.[27]

This critique points to the need to look also at the cultural boundaries on individual political choices.[28] Louis Hartz's work becomes invaluable here, though, on the question of civil-war causation, in ways that depart from his own analysis. According to Hartz's "liberal consensus" thesis, a widely shared set of liberal principles established the boundaries within which individual political choices were made in the antebellum United States, including, I would add, the choices that led to disunion and civil war. A national liberal consensus shaped how the opponents of racial slavery opposed the institution and how the defenders of the institution defended it. It also shaped how the antislavery and proslavery arguments reacted to each other to spread the closely related ideas of a house divided and an irrepressible conflict from the sectional extremes to the middle. Finally, it shaped how Lincoln's election on a platform of uniting the house against slavery would be interpreted in the South and thus how his election could precipitate disunion and civil war. While the thesis does not explain precisely how and why those events occurred, it does offer an interpretation of them that, I think, best synthesizes the "bumbling generation" and "irrepressible conflict" theses.

This extension of Hartz, however, hinges on understanding liberalism as a historically contingent phenomenon, as a loose set of arguments that can be used to defend a diverse set of social practices. Even though a liberal consensus does not determine what arguments will be used to defend what practices, it does establish historically significant boundaries on what arguments can be used and what practices can be defended. And even though a liberal consensus does not determine when and if liberals will come to blows, it does indicate how they might do so and how they might do so when people of other persuasions might not. The Civil War was a testament to consensus, not a denial of it.[29]

Lincoln's theory of civil-war causation was, in essence, a "liberal consensus" view. At the core of the conflict, he saw two contested forms of liberalism: a proslavery and an antislavery liberalism. But Lincoln was not a historian who was primarily interested in the accuracy of particular theories of historical causation. He was a political actor who was primarily interested in the justice and expediency of particular political principles and practices.[30] The mainspring of his political action was exposing proslavery liberalism as the proverbial wolf in sheep's clothing. He concluded that this course of action was a necessary first step to "extinguishing" the patently unjust and inexpedient Southern institution of racial slavery. In all these ways, Lincoln seems to have seen and acted correctly, even if somewhat hesitantly and belatedly when compared with the abolitionists.

If liberalism is itself a historically contingent phenomenon, then at any point in time, people who believe in liberal principles will be engaged in disputes over the nature of those principles and how best to apply them to their own concrete social settings. As social scientists, we should not be surprised by such disputes, and we need not look to "multiple traditions" to try to explain them. As political actors, we should not skirt such disputes but face them boldly to help ensure that our side—the most just side, we presume—triumphs. Lincoln and, even more, the abolitionists achieved such a triumph, although it was admittedly not quite the triumph they hoped to achieve.

Notes

NOTES TO CHAPTER 1

1. This period was defined by, on the one hand, the rise of Garrison abolitionism in the North and, on the other, the outbreak of the Civil War.

2. See Louis Hartz, *The Liberal Tradition in America: An Interpretation of American Political Thought since the Revolution* (New York: Harcourt Brace Jovanovich, 1955). Hartz, of course, did not establish this new paradigm alone, but he now appears preeminent. See J. David Greenstone, *The Lincoln Persuasion: Remaking American Liberalism* (Princeton, N.J.: Princeton University Press, 1993), p. 38; Daniel T. Rodgers, "Republicanism: The Career of a Concept," *Journal of American History* 79, no. 1 (1992): 13–14; Rogers M. Smith, *Civic Ideals: Conflicting Visions of Citizenship in U.S. History* (New Haven, Conn.: Yale University Press, 1997), p. 26; James P. Young, *Reconsidering American Liberalism: The Troubled Odyssey of the Liberal Idea* (Boulder, Colo.: Westview Press, 1996), pp. 2–3.

3. See especially Charles A. Beard, *The Rise of American Civilization* (New York: Macmillan, 1927).

4. See Bernard Bailyn, *The Ideological Origins of the American Revolution* (Cambridge, Mass.: Belknap Press, 1967); Gordon S. Wood, *The Creation of the American Republic, 1776–1787* (Chapel Hill: University of North Carolina Press, 1969); J. G. A. Pocock, *The Machiavellian Moment: Florentine Political Thought and the Atlantic Republican Tradition* (Princeton, N.J.: Princeton University Press, 1975). For republican revisionism as a paradigm shift, see Peter S. Onuf, "Reflections on the Founding: Constitutional Historiography in Bicentennial Perspective," *William and Mary Quarterly*, 3d series, 46, no. 2 (1989): 346–47; Rodgers, "Republicanism," pp. 11–12; Robert E. Shalhope, "Toward a Republican Synthesis: The Emergence of an Understanding of Republicanism in American Historiography," *William and Mary Quarterly*, 3d series, 29, no. 1 (1972): 49–80; Robert E. Shalhope, "Republicanism and Early American Historiography," *William and Mary Quarterly*, 3d series, 39, no. 2 (1982): 3–26. Except for Pocock, the republican revisionists generally acknowledge the emergence of a liberal consensus at some later point in American history, certainly by the end of the Civil War.

5. See James T. Kloppenberg, "The Virtues of Liberalism: Christianity, Republicanism, and Ethics in Early American Political Discourse," *Journal of American History* 74, no. 1 (1987): 9–33. See also Isaac Kramnick, "The 'Great National Discussion': The Discourse of Politics in 1787," *William and Mary Quarterly*, 3d series, 45, no. 1 (1989): 3–32; Onuf, "Reflections on the Founding," pp. 350–51, 353–54; Young, *Reconsidering Liberalism*, p. 91.

6. Besides his book *Civic Ideals*, see Rogers M. Smith, "Beyond Tocqueville, Myrdal, and Hartz: The Multiple Traditions in America," *American Political Science Review* 87, no. 3 (1993): 549–66; "Response to Karen Orren," *Journal of Policy History* 8, no. 4 (1996): 479–90; "Beyond Morone, McWilliams, and Eisenach?: The Multiple Responses to *Civic Ideals*," *Studies in American Political Development* 13, no. 1 (1999): 230–44; "Liberalism and Racism: The Problem of Analyzing Traditions," in *The Liberal Tradition in American Politics: Reassessing the Legacy of American Liberalism*, ed. David F. Ericson and Louisa Bertch Green (New York: Routledge, 1999), pp. 9–27. By ascriptive ideas, Smith means those that either assert or imply the legitimacy of social inequalities based on race, gender, religion, ethnicity, or birthright. For another multiple-traditions approach, see Richard J. Ellis, *American Political Cultures* (New York: Oxford University Press, 1993).

7. In this section, I use the "multiple traditions" label to refer to Hartz's critics, but I include scholars who subscribe to "discursive pluralism." I also assume that, to use Rodgers's figure of speech, republican revisionism has come to the end of its career as a competing metanarrative of American history. See Rodgers, "Republicanism," pp. 37–38.

8. A point of clarification here: these traditions are constructs. Neither side of this historiographical debate contends that the issue is whether there was one or more than one tradition of political ideas within which historical actors consciously placed themselves. The issue, rather, is whether we can better understand American history by constructing one or more than one tradition of political ideas within which we can place historical actors. See Hartz, *Liberal Tradition*, pp. 21, 63; Rodgers, "Republicanism," pp. 35–37; Smith, "Liberalism and Racism," pp. 11–14; Young, *Reconsidering Liberalism*, pp. 52–54, 67–68, 327–28. Hence, what we call the tradition(s) and whether the actors themselves used different labels for their own traditions and ideas or no labels at all are immaterial as long as we, and they, are referring to the same general set of ideas. By convention, we now use the term *liberal* to refer to the general set of ideas that asserts the "virtues" of personal freedom.

9. Recall that Hartz's argument is a comparative one.

10. An incomplete list of the (clearly overlapping) intellectual traditions that scholars have used to analyze American history would include liberalism, republicanism, Protestantism, such ascriptive ideologies as racism and sexism, dialectics between democratic and aristocratic ideals as well as between com-

mercial and agrarian ones, the Scottish Enlightenment, nationalism, federalism, capitalism, and the frontier myth.

11. See Smith, "Beyond Tocqueville," p. 550; Hartz, *Liberal Tradition*, p. 63.

12. In his influential essay "The State of the Art," Pocock epitomizes as he tries to justify this tendency. See J. G. A. Pocock, "The State of the Art," in his *Virtue, Commerce, and History* (Cambridge: Cambridge University Press, 1985), pp. 1–34. Both Eldon Eisenach and Karen Orren criticize Smith for the same tendency, though they pursue their critiques in very different directions than I would. See Eldon Eisenach, "Liberal Citizenship and American National Identity," *Studies in American Political Development* 13, no. 1 (1999): 208; Karen Orren, "Structure, Sequence, and Subordination in American Political Culture: What's Traditions Got to Do with It?" *Journal of Policy History* 8, no. 4 (1996): 470.

13. However, as we will see, this image is not quite the one that Hartz himself presents.

14. At this point, I might add that these different sets of ideas never have seemed that distinct to me, especially liberal and republican ideas, as I argued in my first book, *The Shaping of American Liberalism: The Debates over Ratification, Nullification, and Slavery* (Chicago: University of Chicago Press, 1993), chaps. 1–2. What Smith identifies as liberal and as ascriptive ideas do seem distinct to me, but my argument on this point is that for *most* political actors throughout American history, liberal ideas were primary and ascriptive ideas were secondary (or less); they usually tried to justify ascriptive ideas by means of liberal ones rather than to use the two sets of ideas coequally. Finally, the relationship between Protestant and liberal ideas is more complex, but several important works have argued, in a variation on Max Weber's "spirit of capitalism" thesis, that Protestant ideas—while not themselves liberal—created a favorable milieu for the acceptance of liberal (and republican) ideas. See Greenstone, *Lincoln Persuasion*, pp. 55–58, 61–62; Edmund S. Morgan, "The Puritan Ethic and the American Revolution," *William and Mary Quarterly*, 3d series, 24, no. 1 (1967): 3–43; Young, *Reconsidering Liberalism*, pp. 3–4, 13, 48–50, 327. Hartz and Smith do not necessarily share this view. See Hartz, *Liberal Tradition*, pp. 4, 23; Smith, "Liberalism and Racism," pp. 23–24. See also John P. Diggins, *The Lost Soul of American Politics: Virtue, Self-Interest, and the Foundations of Liberalism* (Chicago: University of Chicago Press, 1984); Barry Alan Shain, *The Myth of American Individualism* (Princeton, N.J.: Princeton University Press, 1994).

15. Another point of clarification: the consensus view is that most, not *all*, political actors throughout American history shared the same general set of ideas, although how many is most for purposes of defining a consensus is an open question. Hartz's claims here are somewhat more modest than his critics

interpret them as being. Hartz does not (nor do I) contend that everything American is liberal. Compare Hartz, *Liberal Tradition*, pp. 4, 21–23; Smith, "Liberalism and Racism," pp. 18–20.

16. The abolitionists did not favor a military option for abolishing racial slavery—until events forced it on them—in part because they thought it would circumvent this decision process and decrease the chances that a postemancipation society would be racially egalitarian. See Lawrence J. Friedman, *Gregarious Saints: Self and Community in American Abolitionism* (Cambridge: Cambridge University Press, 1982), chap. 7; Aileen S. Kraditor, *Means and Ends in American Abolitionism: Garrison and His Critics on Strategy and Tactics* (Chicago: Elephant, 1989 [1969]), pp. 255–60; Lewis Perry, *Radical Abolitionism: Anarchy and the Government of God in Antislavery Thought* (Ithaca, N.Y.: Cornell University Press, 1973), chap. 8; Ronald G. Walters, *The Antislavery Appeal: American Abolitionism after 1830* (New York: Norton, 1978), pp. 25–33.

17. See especially Eric Foner, *Reconstruction: America's Unfinished Revolution, 1863–1877* (New York: Harper & Row, 1988).

18. Scholars, however, also have observed illiberal tendencies on the antislavery side. In fact, both the proslavery and antislavery movements have received at least one major interpretation from each of the four perspectives at issue. See James Oakes, *Slavery and Freedom: An Interpretation of the Old South* (New York: Knopf, 1990) (proslavery liberalism); David Brion Davis, "The Emergence of Immediatism in British and American Antislavery Thought," *Mississippi Valley Historical Review* 49, no. 2 (1962): 209–30 (antislavery liberalism); Kenneth S. Greenberg, *Masters and Statesmen: The Political Culture of American Slavery* (Baltimore: Johns Hopkins University Press, 1985) (proslavery republicanism); Eric Foner, *Free Soil, Free Labor, Free Men: The Ideology of the Republican Party before the Civil War* (New York: Oxford University Press, 1970) (antislavery republicanism); Eugene D. Genovese, *A Consuming Fire: The Fall of the Confederacy in the Mind of the White Christian South* (Athens: University of Georgia Press, 1998) (proslavery Protestantism); Gilbert Hobbs Barnes, *The Antislavery Impulse, 1830–1844* (Gloucester, Mass.: Peter Smith, 1957 [1933]) (antislavery Protestantism); John Ashworth, *Slavery, Capitalism, and Politics in the Antebellum Republic: Volume 1: Commerce and Compromise, 1820–1850* (Cambridge: Cambridge University Press, 1995) (proslavery illiberalism); Richard J. Ellis, *The Dark Side of the Left: Illiberal Egalitarianism in America* (Lawrence: University Press of Kansas, 1998), chap. 1 (antislavery illiberalism). Smith detects ascriptive elements on both sides, although much more on the proslavery than on the antislavery side. See Smith, *Civic Ideals*, pp. 204–5, 249. But he does not dwell on this particular case, since he wants to stress that the impact of ascriptive ideas on American history extended far beyond the slavery issue.

19. See Hartz, *Liberal Tradition*, chap. 6.

20. Hartz saw the proslavery movement as somewhat less firmly in the illiberal camp because he saw it as somewhat ambivalent about abandoning liberal ideas in order to defend an institution that, to him, could not possibly be defended on liberal grounds. See Hartz, *Liberal Tradition*, pp. 153–54, 166–67, 180, 189–90.

21. See Hartz, *Liberal Tradition*, pp. 148, 172–73, 176–77, 182–83.

22. This topic is beyond the scope of this study, yet it is clear that many of the arguments used to defend racial slavery before the Civil War were used after the war to defend continuing forms of racial oppression. See George M. Fredrickson, *The Black Image in the White Mind: The Debate on Afro-American Character and Destiny, 1817–1914* (Middletown, Conn.: Wesleyan University Press, 1987 [1971]), pp. 187–89; Eugene D. Genovese, *The Southern Tradition: The Achievement and Limitations of an American Conservatism* (Cambridge, Mass.: Harvard University Press, 1994), pp. 7–8, 23; William B. Hesseltine, "Some New Aspects of the Proslavery Argument," in *Sections and Politics: Selected Essays by William B. Hesseltine*, ed. Richard N. Current (Madison: State Historical Society of Wisconsin, 1968), pp. 83–84; George B. Tindall, "The Central Theme Revisited," in *The Southerner as American*, ed. Charles Grier Sellers Jr. (New York: Dutton, 1966), pp. 109–12. It also is clear that many of these arguments were, as Smith shows, ascriptive. See Smith, *Civic Ideals*, chaps. 10–11. But I again would note that the "liberal consensus" view does not commit one to the claim that everything American is liberal. I also would place greater emphasis than Smith does on the degree to which these inegalitarian movements did offer liberal arguments. Compare Carol Horton, "Liberal Equality and the Civic Subject: Identity and Citizenship in Reconstruction America," in Ericson and Green, eds., *Liberal Tradition in American Politics*, pp. 115–36.

23. It is especially surprising Hartz did not take the "liberal" route in interpreting the proslavery movement because he did not seize the one advantage that the "illiberal" route he did take offered him: the ability to account for the Civil War. Instead, he admitted that one of the things his thesis could not account for was the Civil War. See Hartz, *Liberal Tradition*, pp. 18–19. It also is surprising that this whole historiographical debate has largely bypassed the question of civil-war causation. Even though this is one area in which the multiple-traditions approach appears to enjoy a clear advantage, its proponents have not criticized Hartz very vigorously for his "failure" to account for the Civil War, which is not to say that he has received no criticism on this score. See Richard J. Ellis and Aaron Wildavsky, "A Cultural Analysis of the Civil War," *Comparative Studies in Society and History* 32, no. 1 (1990): 91; Greenstone, *Lincoln Persuasion*, p. 55; Major L. Wilson, *Space, Time, and Freedom: The Quest for Nationality and the Irrepressible Conflict* (Westport, Conn.:

Greenwood Press, 1974), p. 239 (n. 2); Young, *Reconsidering Liberalism*, pp. 4, 328.

24. See Hartz, *Liberal Tradition*, pp. 147–48, 169–70. In the sequel, Hartz ventured that the defenders of slavery could place the institution on liberal grounds by denying the humanity of the slaves. See Louis Hartz, *The Founding of New Societies: Studies in the History of the United States, Latin America, South Africa, Canada, and Australia* (New York: Harcourt, Brace, 1964), pp. 50, 61. But as Smith rightly points out (*Civic Ideals*, pp. 24–26), this strategy does not seem very liberal, and as I insist, it was not the dominant proslavery strategy for that very reason.

25. See Hartz, *Liberal Tradition*, pp. 166–67, 172–73. As propounded by others, this view has been labeled the "guilty conscience" thesis. See Ashworth, *Slavery and Capitalism*, pp. 194–95, 215, 281; Gaines M. Foster, "Guilt over Slavery: A Historiographical Analysis," *Journal of Southern History* 56, no. 4 (1990): 665–94; Charles Grier Sellers Jr., "The Travail of Slavery," in Sellers, ed., *Southerner as American*, pp. 40–71; Tindall, "Central Theme Revisited," pp. 116–19.

26. For these reasons, Greenstone and Young proposed, as I did in my first book, that we understand liberalism in nonessentialist terms as a historical phenomenon that has assumed multiple forms in American history. See Ericson, *Shaping of Liberalism*, chap. 2; Greenstone, *Lincoln Persuasion*, pp. 50–63; Young, *Reconsidering Liberalism*, pp. 6–9, 91, 345 (n. 30). (However, none of these works proposed, as I am now doing, proslavery liberalism as one of those forms.) Smith is on solid methodological grounds in insisting that we use Hartz's definition of liberalism to test the validity of Hartz's thesis ("Beyond Morone," p. 231; "Liberalism and Racism," p. 20), except that in doing so, he actually accentuates Hartz's ahistoricism. The irony here is that Hartz—as Smith and nearly everyone else who has read *The Liberal Tradition in America* have noted—did not define liberalism in the book, nor did he rigidly apply a definition of liberalism to his historical cases, as Smith does in *Civic Ideals*. In practice, Smith is much more ahistorical than Hartz was. See James A. Morone, "The Other's America: Notes on Rogers Smith's *Civic Ideals*," *Studies in American Political Development* 13, no. 1 (1999): 190; Karen Orren, "Reply to Rogers Smith," *Journal of Policy History* 8, no. 4 (1996): 492–93. In making this criticism of Smith, I am not claiming that scholars in this area of research do not, or should not, use working definitions of liberalism. Hartz did seem to use such a definition in *The Liberal Tradition in America*, and Smith rightly tries to tease it out of the book. Rather, I am claiming that it is ahistorical to rigidly apply such a definition without taking into account how specific arguments made by specific actors in specific writings and speeches function in specific contexts.

27. As we shall see, antislavery and proslavery figures did read and respond

to one another's arguments even if, as seems likely, they were not attempting to convert one another but, rather, more moderate publics in their respective sections of the country. See Hesseltine, "Some New Aspects," pp. 79–83; Ralph E. Morrow, "The Proslavery Argument Revisited," *Mississippi Valley Historical Review* 48, no. 1 (1961): 81–83; Ronald G. Walters, "The Boundaries of Abolitionism," in *Antislavery Reconsidered: New Perspectives on the Abolitionists*, ed. Lewis Perry and Michael Fellman (Baton Rouge: Louisiana State University Press, 1979), pp. 21–22; Bertram Wyatt-Brown, "William Lloyd Garrison and Antislavery Unity: A Reappraisal," *Civil War History* 13, no. 1 (1967): 22–23.

28. Friedman divides the abolitionists into three "circles": (1) a more perfectionist New England circle led by William Lloyd Garrison, (2) a more political upstate New York circle led by Gerrit Smith, and (3) a more evangelical New York City and Ohio circle led by the Tappan brothers and Theodore Weld. See Friedman, *Gregarious Saints*, chaps. 2–4. Child, who was a popular novelist at the time she wrote the *Appeal*, was inspired to write it by her initial contacts with Garrison. Her husband, David Lee, was one of the twelve founding members of the New England Anti-Slavery Society, Garrison's first antislavery organization. Child never formally joined that organization or any other antislavery organization, and both she and her husband found themselves the targets of Garrisonian orthodoxy during the 1840s for their more favorable views toward the union and political party organization. See Carolyn L. Karcher, *The First Woman in the Republic: A Cultural Biography of Lydia Maria Child* (Durham, N.C.: Duke University Press, 1994), chaps. 8, 12.

29. In the early 1840s, soon after escaping from slavery and settling in New Bedford, Massachusetts, Douglass became associated with the Garrison circle. By the early 1850s, however, he had broken with Garrison, moved to Rochester, New York, to start his own antislavery paper, and become associated with the Smith circle. Two major points of dispute had arisen between Douglass and Garrison: (1) Douglass's decision to start his own antislavery paper and (2) Douglass's increasingly favorable views toward the Constitution and union, the use of violent means to end slavery, and political party organization, views more congruent with the Smith circle than the Garrison circle. The Douglass-Garrison "break" has received an extensive airing in the large secondary literature on Douglass. Perhaps the best treatment is John R. McKivigan's essay, "The Frederick Douglass-Gerrit Smith Friendship and Political Abolitionism in the 1850s," in *Frederick Douglass: New Literary and Historical Essays*, ed. Eric J. Sundquist (Cambridge: Cambridge University Press, 1990), pp. 205–32.

30. Unlike Child and Douglass, Phillips remained an orthodox Garrisonian almost to the very end of the abolitionist movement. Phillips and Garrison finally did "split" in 1865 over the decision not to disband the American Anti-Slavery Society after ratification of the Thirteenth Amendment. The majority

sided with Phillips, against Garrison, in voting not to disband the society at that time. Garrison then resigned as president of the society, and Phillips was elected the new president. The society voted to disband in 1869, after Congress passed the Fifteenth Amendment. See Irving G. Bartlett, *Wendell Phillips: Brahmin Radical* (Westport, Conn.: Greenwood Press, 1961), pp. 287–90, 314–15; James Brewer Stewart, *Wendell Phillips: Liberty's Hero* (Baton Rouge: Louisiana State University Press, 1986), pp. 264–66, 293–95.

31. Dew was a professor of political economy and law at the College of William and Mary. He wrote a critical review of the 1831–32 debate in the Virginia legislature over the fate of racial slavery in the state, at the suggestion of Governor John Floyd, who apparently was concerned about the divisive nature of the debate. Dew subsequently became president of William and Mary and died prematurely in 1846 from a fall while vacationing in England. See Drew Gilpin Faust, ed., *The Ideology of Slavery: Proslavery Thought in the Antebellum South, 1830–1860* (Baton Rouge: Louisiana State University Press, 1981), pp. 21–22.

32. Fitzhugh became a small slaveholder through marriage and assumed the role of proslavery polemicist rather late in life. He was an avid reader of abolitionist tracts and British "social criticism" and liberally quoted from them in his own writings. Beginning in the late 1840s, he published a steady stream of proslavery essays in several major Virginia newspapers and Southern literary journals as well as two books: *Cannibals All!* and *Sociology for the South, or the Failure of Free Society* (1854). Harvey Wish's biography of Fitzhugh remains the definitive one. See Harvey Wish, *George Fitzhugh: Propagandist of the Old South* (Gloucester, Mass.: Peter Smith, 1962 [1943]).

33. Hammond served in both chambers of Congress and as governor of South Carolina. Faust's biography of Hammond remains the definitive one. See Drew Gilpin Faust, *James Henry Hammond and the Old South: A Design for Mastery* (Baton Rouge: Louisiana State University Press, 1982).

34. Political and intellectual elites are clearly the objects of this particular historiographical debate. See Pocock, "State of the Art," p. 18; Smith, *Civic Ideals*, pp. 7–8.

35. The possible exceptions, such as Ashworth's *Slavery and Capitalism* and Duncan Rice's *The Rise and Fall of Black Slavery* (New York: Harper & Row, 1975), still offer fairly synoptic treatments of the two sides.

36. Ashworth's *Slavery and Capitalism* is highly suggestive of this point, as is Edmund S. Morgan's classic study, *American Slavery, American Freedom: The Ordeal of Colonial Virginia* (New York: Norton, 1975).

NOTES TO CHAPTER 2

1. Given that I view liberal ideas and arguments as not being clearly distinct

from Protestant and republican ones, I follow Rogers Smith in defining nonliberal ideas and arguments as largely ascriptive ones.

2. Historically, these claims have been directed most often by men against women. But since the slavery issue was generally debated in the antebellum United States in terms of the (in)equality among men, I use masculine nouns and pronouns in the following discussion.

3. See J. David Greenstone, *The Lincoln Persuasion: Remaking American Liberalism* (Princeton, N.J.: Princeton University Press, 1993), pp. 46–50; James P. Young, *Reconsidering American Liberalism: The Troubled Odyssey of the Liberal Idea* (Boulder, Colo.: Westview Press, 1996), pp. 6, 46, 226.

4. After all, as David Brion Davis showed, until the Enlightenment, the *prima facie* case was *for* slavery. Davis also showed how while shifting the impetus to the antislavery side, Enlightenment principles still were open to defenses of slavery and were so used by specific Enlightenment philosophers, including John Locke, who has traditionally been considered the founder of modern liberalism. Davis's historical research should have foreclosed any notion that liberalism is inherently antislavery in nature. See David Brion Davis, *The Problem of Slavery in Western Culture* (Ithaca, N.Y.: Cornell University Press, 1966). Conveniently, Davis summarizes the argument of this lengthy and somewhat unwieldy book in his sequel: *The Problem of Slavery in the Age of Revolution* (Ithaca, N.Y.: Cornell University Press, 1975), pp. 39–49.

5. According to Ashworth, Southern proslavery figures invariably admitted that slavery was an evil institution in some sense, but that admission did not prevent them from defending it in a very positive manner, and increasingly so over time. See John Ashworth, *Slavery, Capitalism, and Politics in the Antebellum Republic: Volume 1: Commerce and Compromise, 1820–1850* (Cambridge: Cambridge University Press, 1995), pp. 194–97.

6. These categories, like liberalism and its "competitors," are analytic. Historical arguments do not always fit neatly into a particular category.

7. Still, no sharp distinction existed between the "necessary evil" and "positive good" positions (on the proslavery side) or the "necessary evil" and abolitionist positions (on the antislavery side). The effect of the contextualist arguments was precisely to break down those distinctions. Sectional slants also existed on the "necessary evil" position: in the North, it was more a case of antiabolitionist consequentialism, and in the South, it was more a case of proslavery consequentialism. This explanation again assumes that Northern antislavery and Southern proslavery figures increasingly targeted moderate public opinion within their respective sections of the country.

8. This explanation assumes that few Americans really wanted disunion, even among those who said otherwise. On both sides, much of the disunionist rhetoric was tactical, part of a politics of brinkmanship or a matter of stating a fundamental moral or sectional commitment instead of advocating a specific course of

action. See Aileen S. Kraditor, *Means and Ends in American Abolitionism: Garrison and His Critics on Strategy and Tactics* (Chicago: Elephant, 1989 [1969]), pp. 206–7; Charles Grier Sellers Jr., "The Travail of Slavery," in *The Southerner as American*, ed. Charles Grier Sellers Jr. (New York: Dutton, 1966), pp. 43, 70; Gerald Sorin, *Abolitionism: A New Perspective* (New York: Praeger, 1972), pp. 73–74; James B. Stewart, "The Aims and Impact of Garrisonian Abolitionism, 1840–1860," *Civil War History* 15, no. 3 (1969): 203–9; Larry E. Tise, *Proslavery: A History of the Defense of Slavery in America, 1701–1840* (Athens: University of Georgia Press, 1987), pp. 361–62; Ronald G. Walters, *The Antislavery Appeal: American Abolitionism after 1830* (New York: Norton, 1978), pp. 137–38. In any case, even if some antislavery and proslavery figures were really disunionists, most Americans clearly were not. See Hans Kohn, *American Nationalism: An Interpretative Essay* (New York: Macmillan, 1957), chap. 3; Paul C. Nagel, *This Sacred Trust: American Nationality, 1798–1898* (New York: Oxford University Press, 1971), chaps. 2–3; David M. Potter, "The Historian's Use of Nationalism and Vice Versa," *American Historical Review* 67, no. 4 (1962): 938–50; Rush Welter, *The Mind of America, 1820–1860* (New York: Columbia University Press, 1975), chap. 3.

9. One indication of this development would be the rise of less radical antislavery and proslavery groups in between the middle and the extremes in each section of the country: Free-Soil Democrats, "Conscience" Whigs, and Republicans in the North; States-Rights Democrats, "Cotton" Whigs, and Constitutional Unionists in the South (although the latter two groups did enjoy some support in the North).

10. See *Selections from the Writings and Speeches of William Lloyd Garrison* (Boston: B. F. Wallcut, 1852), pp. 62–63 (*The Liberator*, January 1, 1833).

11. Cited in Louis Ruchames, ed., *The Abolitionists: A Collection of Their Writings* (New York: Capricorn, 1964), pp. 82, 80 ("Declaration of Sentiments of the American Anti-Slavery Society," December 1833). On the combination of languages in antislavery rhetoric, see David Brion Davis, "The Emergence of Immediatism in British and American Antislavery Thought," *Mississippi Valley Historical Review* 49, no. 2 (1962): 210–14; Peter Kolchin, *American Slavery, 1619–1877* (New York: Hill & Wang, 1993), pp. 65–70; Duncan J. Macleod, *Slavery, Race and the American Revolution* (Cambridge: Cambridge University Press, 1974), pp. 17–31; Duncan Rice, *The Rise and Fall of Black Slavery* (New York: Harper & Row, 1975), pp. 159–85.

12. See Lawrence J. Friedman, *Gregarious Saints: Self and Community in American Abolitionism* (Cambridge: Cambridge University Press, 1982), pp. 197–98; Kraditor, *Means and Ends*, pp. 119–20; James B. Stewart, "Peaceful Hopes and Violent Experiences: The Evolution of Reforming and Radical Abolitionism, 1831–1837," *Civil War History* 17, no. 1 (1971): 298–99; Walters, *Antislavery Appeal*, p. 25.

13. See Eugene D. Genovese, *A Consuming Fire: The Fall of the Confederacy in the Mind of the White Christian South* (Athens: University of Georgia Press, 1998), pp. 4, 10. This study marks not only a long odyssey in Genovese's own understanding of the antebellum South but also a veritable explosion in studies of proslavery and, to a lesser extent, antislavery religion. For an overview, see John R. McKivigan and Mitchell Snay, eds., *Religion and the Antebellum Debate over Slavery* (Athens: University of Georgia Press, 1998).

14. See *Selections from the Letters and Speeches of the Hon. James H. Hammond of South Carolina* (New York: John F. Trow, 1866), p. 124 ("Two Letters on the Subject of Slavery in the United States, Addressed to Thomas Clarkson, Esq.," 1845).

15. On the combination of languages in proslavery rhetoric, see William Sumner Jenkins, *Pro-Slavery Thought in the Old South* (Gloucester, Mass.: Peter Smith, 1960 [1935]), pp. 200–7; Kolchin, *American Slavery*, pp. 190–97. I, of course, would not deny the overtly religious language of works devoted to denominational disputes over the biblical status of slavery and other, related issues. For example, see George D. Armstrong, *The Christian Doctrine of Slavery* (New York: Negro Universities Press, 1969 [1857]); Albert Barnes, *The Church and Slavery* (Detroit: Negro History Press, 1969 [1857]).

16. See Albert Bushnell Hart and Edward Channing, eds., *American History Leaflets: Colonial and Constitutional* (New York: A. Lovell, 1893), no. 10 ("Governor McDuffie's Message on the Slavery Question," 1835), pp. 4–5. Hereafter cited as McDuffie, with page numbers from this source.

17. For the Declaration's emerging consensual status, see Philip F. Detweiler, "The Changing Reputation of the Declaration of Independence: The First Fifty Years," *William and Mary Quarterly*, 3d series, 19, no. 4 (1962): 557–74.

18. See E. N. Elliott, ed., *Cotton Is King, and Pro-Slavery Arguments: comprising the writings of Hammond, Harper, Christy, Stringfellow, Hodge, Bledsoe, and Cartwright, on this important subject* (New York: Johnson, 1968 [1860]), p. 44. Hereafter cited by author of essay and page number. Ironically, proslavery figures argued that no one thought African Americans were included in the Declaration of Independence any more than they thought women were. See Chancellor Harper, *Cotton Is King*, p. 556.

19. See also Christy, *Cotton Is King*, pp. 168, 198, 226.

20. However, as we shall see, proslavery figures did contend that blacks were benefiting morally and intellectually from their enslavement to Southern whites. They also were quick to point out that it was not an "either/or" choice between enslaving and educating blacks, although they claimed that the abolitionists were forcing slaveholders into that position by "agitating" their slaves. See Hammond, *Selections*, pp. 142–43 ("Letters to Clarkson").

21. See especially George M. Fredrickson, *The Black Image in the White*

Mind: The Debate on Afro-American Character and Destiny, 1817–1914 (Middletown, Conn.: Wesleyan University Press, 1987 [1971]), pp. 58–70.

22. See John C. Calhoun, *Works* (New York: D. Appleton, 1851–56), IV:508, 511 ("On the Oregon Bill," June 27, 1848).

23. See Calhoun, *Works*, IV:511–12 ("On the Oregon Bill").

24. See William W. Freehling, "Beyond Racial Limits: Paternalism over Whites in the Thought of Calhoun and Fitzhugh," in *The Reintegration of American History: Slavery and the Civil War* (New York: Oxford University Press, 1994), pp. 82–104. Here, I am not claiming that racism did not play well in the antebellum United States but, rather, that it played better when given a liberal veneer. I therefore believe that it is a mistake to focus on the scientific racism of the Southern ethnologists, as Smith does in his gloss on the proslavery movement. See Rogers M. Smith, *Civic Ideals: Conflicting Visions of Citizenship in U.S. History* (New Haven, Conn.: Yale University Press, 1997), pp. 24–25, 203–5. In his definitive study of scientific racism, William Stanton argues that the Southern ethnologists were marginalized in the antebellum South because of clerical resistance to their "findings." Perhaps more significantly, Stanton observes that they themselves did not use their findings to defend racial slavery, since they considered themselves "objective" scientists. See William Stanton, *The Leopard's Spots: Scientific Attitudes toward Race in America, 1815–1859* (Chicago: University of Chicago Press, 1960), pp. 149, 160, 192–94. Both Fredrickson and Greenberg, moreover, argue that scientific racism was at least strongly contested by more liberal racial views in the antebellum South. See Kenneth S. Greenberg, *Masters and Statesmen: The Political Culture of American Slavery* (Baltimore: Johns Hopkins University Press, 1985), pp. 89–90; Fredrickson, *Black Image*, pp. 76–90. Finally, Genovese and Kolchin concluded that racial defenses of Southern slavery were not primary and actually receded during the antebellum period. See Genovese, *Consuming Fire*, pp. 4–5, 81–83, 91–92; Kolchin, *American Slavery*, pp. 192–93, 196–97, 234–35. Again, I would not deny Smith's "ascriptive" defenses of the institution, but I would reject the centrality he accords those defenses to the proslavery movement.

25. The defenders of Southern slavery commonly claimed that the British government was responsible for entailing the institution on its American colonies. Similarly, they charged the British government with blocking colonial efforts to end the slave trade. See Albert Bledsoe, *Cotton Is King*, p. 381; Christy, *Cotton Is King*, p. 41.

26. See Hammond, *Selections*, p. 119 ("Letters to Clarkson"). All emphases in this and subsequent quotations are in the original. In using this strategy, Hammond and other proslavery figures tended toward legal positivism, thereby denying the claims of natural law in the face of statutory law. For a discussion of this "dilemma" from the antislavery side, see Robert M. Cover, *Jus-*

tice Accused: Antislavery and the Judicial Process (New Haven, Conn.: Yale University Press, 1975). Oakes stresses that defenses of Southern slavery based on the legally sanctioned property rights of the slaveholders fit within a liberal paradigm. See James Oakes, *Slavery and Freedom: An Interpretation of the Old South* (New York: Knopf, 1990), pp. 71–72.

27. See Bledsoe, *Cotton Is King*, pp. 316, 314–15.

28. See Ashworth, *Slavery and Capitalism*, pp. 246–58; Wilfred Carsel, "The Slaveholders' Indictment of Northern Wage Slavery," *Journal of Southern History* 6, no. 4 (1940): 504–20. As we will see, some proslavery figures offered the further, identifiably liberal argument that in exchanging liberty for subsistence, the slaves did not surrender all their (natural) liberty and actually gained a greater amount of (civil) liberty in the exchange.

29. See Bledsoe, *Cotton Is King*, p. 313.

30. For a discussion of this proslavery strategy, see Greenberg, *Masters and Statesmen*, pp. 98–99.

31. See Hammond, *Selections*, pp. 318–19 ("Speech on the Admission of Kansas, under the Lecompton Constitution, delivered in the Senate of the United States," March 4, 1858); McDuffie, pp. 10–11.

32. See Merrill D. Peterson, ed., *The Portable Jefferson* (New York: Viking, 1975), p. 568 ("Letter to John Holmes," April 22, 1820).

33. See especially Tise, *Proslavery*, chap. 5.

34. See *Portable Jefferson*, p. 568 ("Letter to Holmes"). The literature on Jefferson's views on race and slavery is profuse. Especially valuable is William Cohen, "Thomas Jefferson and the Problem of Slavery," *Journal of American History* 56, no. 3 (1969): 503–26; Davis, *Problem of Slavery in the Age of Revolution*, pp. 169–83; Paul Finkelman, *Slavery and the Founders: Race and Liberty in the Age of Jefferson* (Armonk, N.Y.: Sharpe, 1996), chaps. 5–6; Winthrop D. Jordan, *White over Black: American Attitudes toward the Negro, 1550–1812* (Chapel Hill: University of North Carolina Press, 1968), chap. 12; John C. Miller, *The Wolf by the Ears: Thomas Jefferson and Slavery* (New York: Free Press, 1977); Robert E. Shalhope, "Thomas Jefferson's Republicanism and Antebellum Southern Thought," *Journal of Southern History* 42, no. 4 (1976): 3–26.

35. The African colonization movement was in full retreat by the mid-1830s because of its meager results and also because of the vigorous attacks it had sustained from both proslavery and antislavery figures. The movement then enjoyed a mini-resurgence in the 1850s, since it did seem like such a politically convenient (even if highly impractical) response to the widely accepted dilemma of how to end racial slavery without being compelled to create a racially egalitarian society. See Fredrickson, *Black Image*, pp. 25–28, 43–46, 115–17, 147–49; P. J. Staudenraus, *The African Colonization Movement, 1816–1865* (New York: Octagon, 1980), chaps. 14–18. But compare Douglas

R. Egerton, "Averting a Crisis: The Proslavery Critique of the American Colonization Society," *Civil War History* 43, no. 2 (1997): 142–56; William W. Freehling, "'Absurd' Issues and the Causes of the Civil War: Colonization as a Test Case," in *The Reintegration of American History: Slavery and the Civil War* (New York: Oxford University Press, 1994), pp. 138–57.

36. See Harper, *Cotton Is King*, pp. 616–20; McDuffie, pp. 7–10.

37. Even if emancipation went relatively smoothly, proslavery figures were certain that the freed slaves still would suffer intense racial discrimination, as they had in the North. See Hammond, *Selections*, p. 40 ("On the Justice of Receiving Petitions for the Abolition of Slavery in the District of Columbia," February 1, 1836).

38. See Daniel Mallory, ed., *The Life and Speeches of the Hon. Henry Clay* (New York: Van Ambringe and Bixby, 1844), II:375 ("Petition for the Abolition of Slavery," February 7, 1839).

39. See Christy, *Cotton Is King*, pp. 216–21.

40. See McDuffie, pp. 9–10. This version of the argument has been labeled the "Herrenvolk democracy" argument: "inferior race" slavery facilitates "superior race" democracy. See Ashworth, *Slavery and Capitalism*, pp. 216–28; Richard J. Ellis, "Legitimating Slavery in the Old South: The Effect of Political Institutions on Ideology," *Studies in American Political Development* 5, no. 2 (1991): 342–45; Drew Gilpin Faust, *A Sacred Circle: The Dilemma of the Intellectual in the Old South* (Baltimore: Johns Hopkins University Press, 1977), pp. 125–26; Fredrickson, *Black Image*, pp. 61–64.

41. See McDuffie, p. 10.

42. See Harper, *Cotton Is King*, p. 625.

43. Antislavery moderates were "necessary evil," but with a different slant than proslavery moderates. They called for the gradual abolition of Southern slavery rather than its indefinite existence. The abolitionists contended that those two positions collapsed into each other, since gradual abolition, in practice, became indefinite existence. The abolitionists, instead, called for immediate abolition. However, their position also could collapse into the gradualism of the antislavery moderates, as in the original slogan of the American Anti-Slavery Society: "immediate emancipation, gradually achieved." See John Greenleaf Whittier, *The Prose Works* (Boston: Houghton, Mifflin, 1892), III:25–26 ("Justice and Expediency: or, slavery considered with a view to its rightful and effectual remedy, abolition," 1833). Compare Davis, "Emergence of Immediatism," pp. 209–10; Kraditor, *Means and Ends*, pp. 26–29; Anne C. Loveland, "Evangelicalism and 'Immediate Emancipation' in American Antislavery Thought," *Journal of Southern History* 32, no. 2 (1966): 172–88; William Pease and Jane H. Pease, "Antislavery Ambivalence: Immediatism, Expediency, Race," *American Quarterly* 17, no. 4 (1965): 682. The challenge for the antislavery moderates was to provide some credence to their gradualism,

and they finally latched onto the "free soil" position to do so. The challenge for the abolitionists was to temper their immediatism, as they did in not offering any blueprint for "immediate" abolition. See Gilbert H. Barnes and Dwight L. Dumond, eds., *Letters of Theodore Dwight Weld, Angelina Grimke Weld and Sarah Grimke* (New York: Appleton, 1934), I:126 ("Instructions to Weld," February 24, 1834). Stanley Elkins has heavily criticized this "failure" of the abolitionists as part of a more general anti-institutionalism. See Stanley M. Elkins, *Slavery: A Problem in American Institutional & Intellectual Life* (New York: Grosset & Dunlap, 1963 [1959]), pp. 140–93. Compare Kraditor, *Means and Ends*, pp. 12–22. Ann J. Lane, ed., *The Debate over Slavery: Elkins and His Critics* (Champaign-Urbana: University of Illinois Press, 1971) contains further critiques of Elkins's anti-institutionalism thesis from Kraditor and others as well as a response from Elkins. See also Ashworth, *Slavery and Capitalism*, pp. 168–81; Merton L. Dillon, *The Abolitionists: The Growth of a Dissenting Minority* (Dekalb: Northern Illinois University Press, 1974), p. 26; Fredrickson, *Black Image*, pp. 24–25, 31 (nn. 59, 61); Walters, *Antislavery Appeal*, pp. 8–9.

44. See Whittier, "Justice and Expediency," pp. 32–33, 41–46, 52–55. The abolitionists argued that slavery even adversely affected the interests of the slaveholders. See Weld, *Letters*, I:125 ("Instructions to Weld").

45. Indeed, the abolitionists accused the defenders of slavery of not even taking the slaves' interests into account in their proslavery calculuses. See Lydia Maria Child, *An Appeal in Favor of Africans* (New York: Arno, 1968 [1833]), p. 143; Wendell Phillips, *Speeches, Lectures, and Letters* (Boston: Lee and Shepard, 1891 [1863]), I:85–86 ("Simms Anniversary," April 12, 1852).

46. See Whittier, "Justice and Expediency," p. 32.

47. See William Jay, *Inquiry into the Character and Tendency of the American Colonization and American Anti-Slavery Societies* (New York: R. G. Williams, 1838), pp. 168, 170.

48. See Whittier, "Justice and Expediency," pp. 34–41. Although the (white) abolitionists may well have been racially prejudiced, they did support the goal of racial equality. The two issues often are conflated in the secondary literature. Compare Friedman, *Gregarious Saints*, chap. 6; James M. McPherson, "A Brief for Equality: The Abolitionist Reply to the Racist Myth, 1860–1865," in *The Antislavery Vanguard: New Essays on the Abolitionists*, ed. Martin Duberman (Princeton, N.J.: Princeton University Press, 1965), pp. 156–77; Pease and Pease, "Antislavery Ambivalence," pp. 682–95; Walters, *Antislavery Appeal*, pp. 56–60. For the abolitionists' own commitment to racial equality, see Ruchames, *The Abolitionists*, p. 81 ("Declaration of Sentiments").

49. See Whittier, "Justice and Expediency," p. 57.

50. See John W. Blassingame, ed., *The Frederick Douglass Papers; Series One: Speeches, Debates, and Interviews* (New Haven, Conn.: Yale University

Press, 1979–82), IV:48 ("A Friendly Word to Maryland," November 17, 1864).

51. See William L. Barney, *The Road to Secession: A New Perspective on the Old South* (New York: Praeger, 1972), chap. 2; Eugene H. Berwanger, *The Frontier against Slavery: Western Anti-Negro Prejudice and the Slavery Extension Controversy* (Champaign-Urbana: University of Illinois Press, 1967), chap. 6; Fredrickson, *Black Image*, chaps. 2–5; Leon F. Litwack, *North of Slavery: The Negro in the Free States, 1790–1860* (Chicago: University of Chicago Press, 1961), chaps. 3–6.

52. See Ruchames, *The Abolitionists*, p. 83 ("Declaration of Sentiments"); Whittier, "Justice and Expediency," pp. 57, 29. The literature on the American mission is profuse. See especially Frederick Merk, *Manifest Destiny and Mission in American History: A Reinterpretation* (New York: Random House, 1963).

53. On the original Puritan sense of mission and its evolution over time, see Ernest Lee Tuveson, *Redeemer Nation: The Idea of America's Millennial Role* (Chicago: University of Chicago Press, 1968).

54. See Rush Welter, "The Idea of Progress in America: An Essay in Ideas and Methods," *Journal of the History of Ideas* 16, no. 3 (1955): 401–15.

55. See Elizur Wright Jr., *The Sin of Slavery and Its Remedy; containing some reflections on the moral influence of African Colonization* (New York: Wright, 1833), p. 48. Parliament's decision to abolish slavery in the British West Indies helped inspire the confidence of the American abolitionists in the ultimate victory of their cause. See Davis, "Emergence of Immediatism," pp. 226–27; Dillon, *The Abolitionists*, p. 54; Rice, *Rise and Fall*, pp. 321–22; Sorin, *Abolitionism*, pp. 53–54. For the abolitionists' own reaction to British colonial abolition, see Garrison, *Selections*, pp. 166–67 ("Words of Encouragement to the Oppressed," April 1833). A general belief in the inevitability of abolition also could hurt the antislavery cause by fostering attitudes of social quiescence. See Davis, "Emergence of Immediatism," p. 214; Martin Duberman, "The Northern Response to Slavery," in Duberman, ed., *Antislavery Vanguard*, p. 396.

56. Cited in Ruchames, *The Abolitionists*, p. 83. Gilbert Barnes's *Antislavery Impulse* remains the seminal work on the roots of the antislavery movement in the Second Great Awakening. See also Dwight L. Dumond, *Antislavery Origins of the Civil War in the United States* (Ann Arbor: University of Michigan Press, 1939), chaps. 2–3; Loveland, "Evangelicalism and Immediate Emancipation," pp. 176–79; John R. McKivigan, "'Vote as You Pray and Pray as You Vote': Church-Oriented Abolitionism and Antislavery Politics," in *Crusaders and Compromisers: Essays on the Relationship of the Antislavery Struggle to the Antebellum Party System*, ed. Alan M. Kraut (Westport, Conn.: Greenwood Press, 1983), pp. 179–80; John L. Thomas, "Antislavery and

Utopia," in Duberman, ed., *Antislavery Vanguard*, pp. 246–49. On the abolitionists' millennialism, see Lewis Perry, *Radical Abolitionism: Anarchy and the Government of God in Antislavery Thought* (Ithaca, N.Y.: Cornell University Press, 1973), pp. 37–43.

57. See Whittier, "Justice and Expediency," p. 33.

58. See Amos A. Phelps, *Lectures on Slavery and Its Remedies* (Boston: New England Anti-Slavery Society, 1834), p. 23.

59. See Walters, *Antislavery Appeal*, pp. 129–33. This division in the abolitionist ranks set up interesting linkages with antislavery moderates in the Republican Party. The Republicans agreed with the first group of non-Garrison abolitionists on the need to unite the house against slavery yet disagreed with them on whether "free soil" was sufficient to accomplish this unity without taking the "drastic" step of immediate abolition. Conversely, the Republicans agreed with the second group of Garrison abolitionists on the need to contain slavery in the South but disagreed with them on whether "free soil" was sufficient to abolish the institution without taking the "drastic" step of disunion.

60. As already noted and as discussed further in chapter 4, I also presume that even the abolitionists who supported disunion as a practical policy did so because they saw it as only a temporary measure until it "forced" the South to abandon its institution of racial slavery. It then is not surprising that if they had not done so already, most of these abolitionists distanced themselves from disunionism in the face of the real event. See Walters, *Antislavery Appeal*, pp. 139–40.

61. See Phelps, "Lectures on Slavery," p. 23.

62. One indication of this agreement was the way that antislavery moderates, such as Lincoln and William Seward, appropriated the "house divided" argument from the abolitionists.

63. See McDuffie, p. 8. Probably more apt is the quotation from Samuel Johnson: "How is it that we hear the loudest *yelps* for liberty among the drivers of negroes?"

64. See McDuffie, p. 10.

65. On proslavery views toward progress, see Eugene D. Genovese, *The Slaveholders' Dilemma: Freedom and Progress in Southern Conservative Thought, 1820–1860* (Columbia: University of South Carolina Press, 1992), pp. 10–13; Bertram Wyatt-Brown, "From Piety to Fantasy: Proslavery's Troubled Evolution," in *Yankee Saints and Sinners* (Baton Rouge: Louisiana State University Press, 1985), pp. 156, 167.

66. See Harper, *Cotton Is King*, p. 618; Hammond, p. 172 ("Letters to Clarkson").

67. See Calhoun, *Works*, III:179 ("Remarks Made during the Debate on his Resolutions, in respect to the Rights of the States and the Abolition of Slavery," January 10, 1838).

68. See Calhoun, *Works*, II:629 ("On the Reception of Abolition Petitions," February 6, 1837).

69. See Tise, *Proslavery*, pp. 361–62. Proslavery figures especially could present themselves as the true defenders of the union because, as already noted, some of the abolitionists presented themselves as disunionists.

70. See George Fitzhugh, *Cannibals All! or, Slaves Without Masters* (Cambridge, Mass.: Belknap Press, 1960 [1857]), p. 236.

71. See Christy, *Cotton Is King*, pp. 129–30.

72. But again, a house united against slavery meant different things to abolitionists and antislavery moderates. It came to mean the same thing to them only during the Civil War.

73. See Steven A. Channing, *Crisis of Fear: Secession in South Carolina* (New York: Norton, 1974), chap. 7.

74. See Potter, "Use of Nationalism," pp. 943–48. A number of scholars have argued that Southern secession did not enjoy majority support, or perhaps did only in the lower South. See Barney, *Road to Secession*, pp. 194–95; William J. Cooper Jr., *Liberty and Slavery: Southern Politics to 1860* (New York: Knopf, 1983), pp. 275–80; William W. Freehling, "The Divided South, Democracy's Limitations, and the Causes of the Peculiarly North American Civil War," in *Reintegration of American History*, pp. 212–16; William E. Gienapp, "The Crisis of American Democracy: The Political System and the Coming of the Civil War," in *Why the Civil War Came*, ed. Gabor S. Boritt (New York: Oxford University Press, 1996), pp. 121–22; Michael F. Holt, *The Political Crisis of the 1850s* (New York: Norton, 1978), pp. 219–20, 226–27; Kenneth M. Stampp, "The Irrepressible Conflict," in *The Imperiled Union: Essays on the Background of the Civil War* (New York: Oxford University Press, 1980), p. 238.

NOTES TO CHAPTER 3

1. The abolitionists recognized that the institutions of the North only imperfectly fit their (liberal) ideal, especially for free blacks. They also sought institutional change in the North, although as a subsidiary goal to ending racial slavery in the South. See especially Carleton Mabee, *Black Freedom: The Nonviolent Abolitionists from 1830 through the Civil War* (Toronto: Macmillan, 1970), chaps. 7–11.

2. See Stanley M. Elkins, *Slavery: A Problem in American Institutional & Intellectual Life* (New York: Grosset & Dunlap, 1963 [1959]), pp. 140–93.

3. See Aileen S. Kraditor, *Means and Ends in American Abolitionism: Garrison and His Critics on Strategy and Tactics* (Chicago: Elephant, 1989 [1969]), pp. 12–22.

4. See especially Jennifer L. Hochschild, *Facing up to the American Dream:*

Race, Class, and the Soul of the Nation (Princeton, N.J.: Princeton University Press, 1995).

5. Kraditor is certainly right that most of the abolitionists were not anti-institutionalists in the sense that they rejected the efficacy of political institutions and had no clear idea of the institutions they wanted to put in place of racial slavery in the South. Yet Elkins's broader point about the abolitionists neglecting the processes of institutional change stands, but because they were progressive liberals, not because they were anti-institutionalists.

6. Even Friedman, despite his analysis of the different abolitionist circles, acknowledges their fundamental unity. See Lawrence J. Friedman, "'Pious Fellowship' and Modernity: A Psychosocial Interpretation," in *Crusaders and Compromisers: Essays on the Relationship of the Antislavery Struggle to the Antebellum Party System*, ed. Alan M. Kraut (Westport, Conn.: Greenwood Press, 1983), p. 237. Walters emphasizes this unity as well as the fact that the abolitionists should be interpreted as part of the broader (liberal) culture. See Ronald G. Walters, "Boundaries of Abolitionism," in *Antislavery Reconsidered: New Perspectives on the Abolitionists*, ed. Lewis Perry and Michael Fellman (Baton Rouge: Louisiana University Press, 1979), pp. 19–22. In his larger study of the abolitionists, Walters argues that even the great schism of 1840, ostensibly over the role of women in the American Anti-Slavery Society, was more a matter of differences over tactics than over underlying philosophy. See Ronald G. Walters, *The Antislavery Appeal: American Abolitionism after 1830* (New York: Norton, 1978), pp. 9–18. See also Lewis Perry, *Radical Abolitionism: Anarchy and the Government of God in Antislavery Thought* (Ithaca, N.Y.: Cornell University Press, 1973), pp. 167–70; Bertram Wyatt-Brown, "William Lloyd Garrison and Antislavery Unity: A Reappraisal," *Civil War History* 13, no. 1 (1967): 5–24. But compare Kraditor, *Means and Ends*, pp. 9–10, 30–31; James B. Stewart, "Peaceful Hopes and Violent Experiences: The Evolution of Reforming and Radical Abolitionism, 1831–1837," *Civil War History* 17, no. 1 (1971): 293–309.

7. Of course, if the end of slavery was inevitable, then there would have been no raison d'être for an abolitionist movement. The abolitionists could always respond by claiming that they were "merely" trying to quicken the process, but as noted in the previous chapter, a general belief in the inevitability of emancipation still could have hurt their cause by fostering attitudes of social quiescence.

8. This time period stretches from the formation of a national abolitionist organization—the American Anti-Slavery Society—to the outbreak of the Civil War, which confronted the abolitionist movement with quite different challenges. What holds this period together and distinguishes it from earlier periods of antislavery reform in the United States, is Garrison's immediatism as well as the preeminent role he assumed within the movement.

9. See David Brion Davis, "The Emergence of Immediatism in British and American Antislavery Thought," *Mississippi Valley Historical Review* 49, no. 2 (1962): 210–12; Betty Fladeland, "Who Were the Abolitionists," *Journal of Negro History* 49, no. 2 (1964): 114–15; Gerald Sorin, *Abolitionism: A New Perspective* (New York: Praeger, 1972), p. 24; James B. Stewart, *Holy Warriors: The Abolitionists and American Slavery* (New York: Hill & Wang, 1976), pp. 12–13; Walters, *Antislavery Appeal*, pp. 53–54; Wyatt-Brown, "Garrison and Antislavery Unity," p. 22.

10. See Rogers M. Smith, "Liberalism and Racism: The Problem of Analyzing Traditions," in *The Liberal Tradition in American Politics: Reassessing the Legacy of American Liberalism*, ed. David F. Ericson and Louisa Bertch Green (New York: Routledge, 1999), pp. 11–14; James P. Young, *Reconsidering American Liberalism: The Troubled Odyssey of the Liberal Idea* (Boulder, Colo.: Westview Press, 1996), pp. 52–54, 67–68, 327–28.

11. Carolyn L. Karcher, *The First Woman in the Republic: A Cultural Biography of Lydia Maria Child* (Durham, N.C.: Duke University Press, 1994), pp. 183, 186–87. As represented by Karcher's biography, the growing body of secondary literature on Child focuses on her personal history and literary writings more than on her antislavery works. Although Karcher does include an analysis of Child's *Appeal* in her biography (pp. 183–91), it is fairly synoptic.

12. On Douglass's audience, see David B. Chesebrough, *Frederick Douglass: Oratory from Slavery* (Westport, Conn.: Greenwood Press, 1998), p. 106. As we shall see, there is a growing body of secondary literature on Douglass's Fourth of July oration, but my analysis departs substantially from earlier ones.

13. See Richard Hofstadter, *The American Political Tradition and the Men Who Made It* (New York: Knopf, 1948), p. 179; Robert D. Marcus, "Wendell Phillips and American Institutions," *Journal of American History* 56, no. 1 (1969): 42. Also in contrast to Child and Douglass, Phillips has not been the object of a growing body of secondary literature.

14. Phillips came from a socially prominent family—his father was the first mayor of Boston—whereas Douglass was, of course, an escaped slave, and Child's background was decidedly middle class. Her father was a baker in Medford, Massachusetts, and she and her husband—she more than her husband—constantly struggled to make ends meet. We might find more diversity if we looked at the abolitionists who were less directly influenced by Garrison, such as those belonging to Friedman's third circle of evangelical abolitionists. Barnes studied this circle as a way of asserting the Protestant roots of the abolitionist movement and denying Garrison's preeminence within it. Barnes, though, underestimates Garrison's influence on this circle as well as the degree of overall abolitionist unity. Compare Gilbert Hobbs Barnes, *The Antislavery Impulse, 1830–1844* (Gloucester, Mass.: Peter Smith, 1957 [1933]), pp. 57–58,

88–89, 174–75, 239–40 (n. 1); Wyatt-Brown, "Garrison and Antislavery Unity," pp. 7, 11, 16, 20.

15. Page references are to the 1968 reissue of Child's book published under the title of *An Appeal in Favor of Africans* (New York: Arno, 1968).

16. Here Child shows her concern for racial discrimination in the North, but she nonetheless takes the requisite position that however unfavorable conditions are for free blacks in the North, they still are better off than the Southern slaves (p. 141).

17. Karcher points out that Child hurt her literary career by publishing the book. See Karcher, *First Woman*, pp. 183, 191–92.

18. In the last chapter of her book, Child suggests several actions her readers can take to help abolish racial slavery in the United States, including ridding themselves of their own racial prejudices (pp. 195–96, 207–8), divesting themselves of any financial connections to slavery and the slave trade (p. 195), petitioning Congress to abolish slavery in the District of Columbia (p. 216), and supporting a constitutional amendment to abolish the institution throughout the rest of the country (p. 212).

19. At first, Child suggests that most Southern whites believe that slavery is a necessary evil, not a positive good (pp. 77, 92–93), but she later indicates just the opposite (pp. 100–3, 211–12).

20. In this discussion, Child confusingly lumps together nations that have undergone gradual emancipations (Colombia) with nations that have experienced immediate emancipations (Guadeloupe); nations that have abolished slavery through a legal process (Mexico) with nations that have required violent revolutions to end slavery (Haiti); and nations that have witnessed general emancipations (all the above) with nations that merely have encouraged private manumissions (South Africa). The process of abolishing slavery in the American North was, of course, very gradual and had not yet been completed by 1833. See Joanne Pope Melish, *Disowning Slavery: Gradual Emancipation and "Race" in New England, 1760–1860* (Ithaca, N.Y.: Cornell University Press, 1998), chaps. 2–3; Arthur Zilversmit, *The First Emancipation: The Abolition of Slavery in the North* (Chicago: University of Chicago Press, 1967), chaps. 5–8.

21. Child assumes that whites will never accept living in the same society as a minority to blacks. With the continuing growth of their slave population, Southern whites therefore face the alternative of a general emancipation of their slaves in the near future or a violent, geographic separation of the two races in the not-too-distant future (pp. 24, 131). Somewhat inconsistently, Child also suggests that the continuing growth of the Southern slave population might act as an incentive to emancipation by depressing the price of slaves, thus destroying their resale value, which, she believes, is the one remaining source of profit for many slaveholders (pp. 131–32).

22. Child later argues that if slaves are prone to violence, it is only because of their brutalizing experiences under slavery (pp. 191–92). She also wonders how American society can assimilate tens of thousands of European immigrants and yet so many Americans believe that it will be unable to assimilate the freed slaves, when the immigrants are less fit for citizenship than the slaves are (p. 96).

23. Here Child merely may be reflecting the ambiguity of the immediatist philosophy. As noted in chapter 2, this ambiguity was captured in the original American Anti-Slavery Society slogan of "immediate abolition, gradually achieved." Child's statements also are consistent with the original American Anti-Slavery Society interpretation of the Constitution, according to which only the Southern states, and not the federal government, can abolish slavery. (Although as Child suggests, the Constitution could have been amended to allow for the latter possibility, such an amendment would have required the support of at least some of the Southern states.) Finally, Child's statements can stand as a response to Elkins's anti-institutionalism thesis. The abolitionists saw themselves as social reformers and accorded others the task of overseeing the necessary institutional changes. See Walters, *Antislavery Appeal*, pp. 22–23.

24. Child, however, does believe that whites will never accept being a minority to blacks, which adds a certain urgency to abolition. Her attack on the American Colonization Society is another indication of the early timing of the *Appeal*.

25. Child adds that if slave insurrections do occur in the South, they will be legitimated by the injustices of slavery (pp. 143–44, 193–94). She also asserts that the members of the New England Anti-Slavery Society nevertheless do not advocate the use of violent means to end slavery, since they are firmly committed to "peace principles." She admits to initially resisting the appeal of Garrison abolitionism because she mistakenly believed that it contemplated the use of violent means to end slavery (p. 142). The abolitionists' views toward violence have been thoroughly canvassed in the secondary literature. See John Demos, "The Antislavery Movement and the Problem of Violent Means," *New England Quarterly* 37, no. 4 (1954): 501–26; Lawrence J. Friedman, *Gregarious Saints: Self and Community in American Abolitionism* (Cambridge: Cambridge University Press, 1982), chap. 7; Mabee, *Black Freedom*, chap. 5; Perry, *Radical Abolitionism*, chap. 8; Walters, *Antislavery Appeal*, pp. 26–32; Wyatt-Brown, "Garrison and Antislavery Unity," pp. 11–21.

26. See Louis S. Gerteis, *Morality & Utility in American Antislavery Reform* (Chapel Hill: University of North Carolina Press, 1987), pp. 171–73.

27. As a result, Child skips the effects of slavery on the slaves in her discussion of "the effects of slavery on all concerned" in chapter 1, although she does address the effects of the slave trade on the slaves (pp. 12–15, 32–37).

28. As Child points out, some of these evils affect a much broader population than slaveholders. She cites the passage from Jefferson's *Notes on the State of Virginia* on the corrupting effects of slavery on slaveholders' children (p. 22). She later cites the same text on Jefferson's fears of divine retribution for the continued existence of the institution (p. 71). See Merrill D. Peterson, ed., *The Portable Jefferson* (New York: Viking, 1975), pp. 214–15. As we will see, these passages were cited frequently by both antislavery (positively) and proslavery (negatively) figures.

29. See John Ashworth, *Slavery, Capitalism, and Politics in the Antebellum Republic: Volume 1: Commerce and Compromise, 1820–1850* (Cambridge: Cambridge University Press, 1995), pp. 165–66.

30. This argument is double-edged: If free labor is cheaper, then are not slaves better off (less exploited) than free laborers? As we will see in chapter 5, Fitzhugh, in particular, asserts that they are. In any case, Child believes that the relative advantages of free labor to employers has been proved by postemancipation experiences in other countries where, she claims, the freed men work harder and earn more money for their former masters than they had as slaves (pp. 84–87, 94, 97–98). She even calculates that slave labor is only two-thirds as efficient as free labor (p. 77).

31. Child also trots out the "banks of the Ohio" comparison later made famous by Tocqueville (pp. 80–81). See Alexis de Tocqueville, *Democracy in America*, ed. J. P. Mayer (New York: Anchor Books, 1969 [1835]), pp. 345–48. She does quote other European travelers on the North-South comparison (pp. 81–83).

32. Brazil was the exception to South American emancipation, but Child contends (wrongly, in retrospect) that even Brazil is closer to abolishing slavery than the United States is (p. 94). She wrote her book on the eve of the abolition of slavery in the British colonies, which becomes another source of invidious comparison for the United States (pp. 144, 208). She also claims that both the British and the Brazilians are less racially prejudiced than Americans are (p. 135).

33. Child does not seem to consider disunion an option in the "house divided" argument; see pp. 119, 212, 216. As we will see in chapter 4, this option soon proved very attractive to the Garrison abolitionists as a way of preserving Northern liberty and/or abolishing Southern slavery. But Child balked at this shift to disunionism, further loosening her ties to the Garrisonians. See Karcher, *First Woman*, pp. 283–86.

34. Note that Child does not attribute this low ranking to the racial character of modern/Southern slavery.

35. Karcher concludes her biography by stressing Child's faith in (liberal) progress. See Karcher, *First Woman*, p. 616.

36. The speech actually was delivered on July 5 because July 4 came on a

Sunday in 1852. Douglass had worked on the speech for several weeks. See John W. Blassingame, ed., *The Frederick Douglass Papers; Series One: Speeches, Debates, and Interviews* (New Haven, Conn.: Yale University Press, 1979–82), II:359.

37. Obviously, this difference can also be attributed to the difference in format between a book and a speech, but that difference does not tell us *which* antislavery arguments Douglass would emphasize in his speech.

38. This difference, however, should not be exaggerated. It seems safe to assume that Douglass knew that (1) his immediate audience would not be uniformly antislavery in sentiment (despite the group that had invited him to speak) and (2) his speech would be reported to a broader public (because of his prominence). His speech later circulated in pamphlet form. See Blassingame, *Douglass Papers*, II:359.

39. Compare Gayle McKeen, "A 'Guiding Principle' of Liberalism in the Thought of Frederick Douglass and W. E. B. Du Bois," in *The Liberal Tradition in American Politics: Reassessing the Legacy of American Liberalism*, ed. David F. Ericson and Louisa Bertch Green (New York: Routledge, 1999), pp. 99–114.

40. In the second volume of his seminal study of New England Protestantism, Perry Miller analyzes the jeremiad, an analysis that Sacvan Bercovitch extends in his provocative study of the genre. See Perry Miller, *The New England Mind: From Colony to Province* (Cambridge, Mass.: Belknap Press, 1953), chap. 2; Sacvan Bercovitch, *The American Jeremiad* (Madison: University of Wisconsin Press, 1978), especially chap. 1. Five studies of Douglass's Fourth of July oration have appeared recently: Bernard W. Bell, "The African-American Jeremiad and Frederick Douglass's Fourth of July 1852 Speech," in *The Fourth of July: Political Oratory and Literary Reactions, 1776–1876*, ed. Paul Goetsch and Gerd Hürm (Tübingen, Germany: Narr, 1992), pp. 139–53; James Jasinski, "Rearticulating History in Epideictic Discourse: Frederick Douglass's 'The Meaning of the Fourth of July to the Negro,'" in *Rhetoric and Political Culture in Nineteenth-Century America,* ed. Thomas W. Benson (East Lansing: Michigan State University Press, 1997), pp. 71–89; Neil Leroux, "Frederick Douglass and the Attention Shift," *Rhetoric Society Quarterly* 21, no. 2 (1991): 36–46; John Louis Lucaites, "The Irony of 'Equality' in Black Abolitionist Discourse: The Case of Frederick Douglass's 'What to the Slave Is the Fourth of July,'" in Benson, ed., *Rhetoric and Political Culture*, pp. 47–69; Charles W. Mills, "Whose Fourth of July? Frederick Douglass and 'Original Intent'," in *Frederick Douglass: A Critical Reader*, ed. Bill E. Lawson and Frank M. Kirkland (Oxford: Blackwell, 1999), pp. 100–42. Bell relies on Wilson Jeremiah Moses's work on the African American jeremiad as a subgenre. See Wilson Jeremiah Moses, *Black Messiahs and Uncle Toms: Social and Literary Manipulations of a Religious Myth* (University Park: Pennsylvania State University

Press, 1982). David Blight and David Howard-Pitney also explore Douglass's uses of that subgenre. See David W. Blight, "Frederick Douglass and the American Apocalypse," *Civil War History* 31, no. 4 (1985): 309–28; David W. Blight, *Frederick Douglass' Civil War: Keeping Faith in Jubilee* (Baton Rouge: Louisiana State University Press, 1989), chap. 5; David Howard-Pitney, "The Enduring Black Jeremiad: The American Jeremiad and Black Protest Rhetoric, from Frederick Douglass to W. E. B. Du Bois, 1841–1919," *American Quarterly* 38, no. 3 (1986): 481–92; David Howard-Pitney, "Wars, White America, and the Afro-American Jeremiad: Frederick Douglass and Martin Luther King Jr.," *Journal of Negro History* 71, nos. 1–4 (1986): 23–37; David Howard-Pitney, *The Afro-American Jeremiad: Appeals to Justice in America* (Philadelphia: Temple University Press, 1990), chaps. 1–2. None of these studies interprets Douglass's 1852 Fourth of July oration as a rhetorical hybrid of a jeremiad and a Fourth of July oration

41. See Bercovitch, *American Jeremiad*, pp. 141–52.

42. See Bercovitch, *American Jeremiad*, pp. 133–34.

43. For purposes of comparison, Edward Everett's 1855 Fourth of July oration at Dorchester, Massachusetts, may serve as a typical antebellum Fourth of July oration. Everett, a popular orator, former president of Harvard University, longtime Whig politician, and future vice-presidential candidate, alludes to the slavery issue by mentioning the constitutional status of slavery in the territories as one question left to the current generation to resolve. He then gently criticizes recent proslavery actions in "bleeding Kansas," but mostly he appeals for sectional harmony. By no means does Everett's speech become a jeremiad against slavery or anything else. See Edward Everett, "Dorchester in 1630, 1776, 1855," in *Orations and Speeches on Various Occasions* (Boston: Little, Brown, 1868–1870), III:292–348. On the Fourth of July genre, see Cedric Larson, "Patriotism in Carmine: 162 Years of July 4th Oratory," *Quarterly Journal of Speech* 26, no. 1 (1940): 12–25; Howard H. Martin, "The Fourth of July Oration," *Quarterly Journal of Speech* 44, no. 4 (1958): 393–401.

44. All volume and page references to Douglass's speeches are from the Blassingame compilation of his papers.

45. Douglass's reference to the founding fathers as men of peace who nonetheless went to war to defend their own liberties is an oblique reference to the abolitionists who eschewed the use of violent means to end slavery. Douglass is trying here to bridge the gap between these abolitionists and abolitionists like himself, who were (reluctantly) willing to use violent means to end slavery. For more on Douglass's views of violence, see II:89; II:347; II:390–91; II:459; III:316–17; III:339–40; III:417–19; III:562.

46. The bracketed material was added by the editor.

47. Of course, the choice of Douglass as the speaker for the occasion was not really a mockery, given the group that had invited him to speak.

48. Douglass often claimed to speak on behalf of the slaves or his race; see I:16; I:36; I:190; I:382; II:65; II:330; II:427; III:493–94. To varying degrees, Bell, Leroux, and Lucaites all stress this stance on Douglass's part as a way of distancing himself from his (white) audience. See Bell, "African-American Jeremiad," p. 149; Leroux, "Attention Shift," pp. 40, 46; Lucaites, "Irony of Equality," p. 57. Douglass himself always stressed the "American-ness" of African Americans; see II:165–66; II:210–11; II:310; II:341–42; II:524; III:93–95; III:505–8; IV:57–58.

49. This religious focus was foreshadowed in the first speech, in which Douglass compared the American Revolution to the Exodus (II:360, 362) and its end to a "jubilee" (II:365), the seventh year when the ancient Hebrews freed their native-born slaves. Then in the transitional phase of his speech, he compares the founding fathers with Abraham (II:366–67) and recites the tenth psalm on the Babylonian captivity (II:368), which signals that he will unequivocally adopt the perspective of the slaves in the second speech. All these references are obviously to the Old Testament. In the first volume of his study of New England Protestantism, Miller notes that placed a new emphasis on the Old Testament. See Perry Miller, *The New England Mind: The Seventeenth Century* (Boston: Beacon Press, 1961 [1939]), pp. 414–15.

50. The fact that Douglass makes the condemnation of the nation's churches the centerpiece of this count, however, does not mean that he condemns religion or religious institutions per se. Indeed, he observes that several prominent abolitionists are members of the clergy (II:380–81) and also that in Great Britain, unlike the United States, religious organizations spearheaded the antislavery crusade (II:381–82). In these passages, he is clearly reaching out to the evangelical abolitionists. Douglass and other nonevangelical abolitionists attacked the nation's churches not because they opposed religion but because so many religious leaders opposed abolition. See Fladeland, "Who Were the Abolitionists," pp. 111–13; Anne C. Loveland, "Evangelicalism and 'Immediate Emancipation' in American Antislavery Thought," *Journal of Southern History* 32, no. 2 (1966): 179; John R. McKivigan, "'Vote as You Pray and Pray as You Vote': Church-Oriented Abolitionism and Antislavery Politics," in *Crusaders and Compromisers: Essays on the Relationship of the Antislavery Struggle to the Antebellum Party System*, ed. Alan M. Kraut (Westport, Conn.: Greenwood Press, 1983), p. 180; Stewart, "Peaceful Hopes," pp. 305–7; John L. Thomas, "Antislavery and Utopia," in *The Antislavery Vanguard: New Essays on the Abolitionists*, ed. Martin Duberman (Princeton, N.J.: Princeton University Press, 1965), p. 249; Walters, *Antislavery Appeal*, pp. 41–52.

51. Again given the nature of the audience, this seems a fair assumption.

52. For a sampling of these arguments in Douglass's other speeches, see I:76; II:333; III:297; III:569 (slavery undercuts American exemplar) I:81; III:448; III:479; IIII:528 (slavery corrupts political process) I:46; II:199–200;

III:137; III:337 (slavery prostitutes churches) I:159; II:544; III:120; III:220 (slavery creates house divided) II:404; III:298; III:429–30; III:563 (free labor superior to slave labor) I:372; II:256; II:456; III:281 (slavery requires illiterate labor force) I:31; I:254; II:263–67; III:327 (slaveholders abuse slaves) I:120; I:122; II:404; III:326 (slavery impoverishes South).

53. It is also incumbent on Douglass to rebut the proslavery interpretation of the Constitution in this speech in order to restore the filiopiety with which he began the speech. (The way that the second "speech" undercuts filiopiety also was foreshadowed in the first speech. The founding fathers had fought for their own liberties but not for those of their slaves; see II:364.) Douglass actually was only a recent convert to the antislavery interpretation of the Constitution. As noted in chapter 1, his change in views was one of the major factors in his "break" with the Garrisonians, who at this time still subscribed to the proslavery interpretation of the Constitution. Both Jasinski and Lucaites, though, unduly focus on Douglass's views toward the Constitution and, more broadly, the founding fathers, ignoring the hybrid nature of the speech. See Jasinski, "Rearticulating History," pp. 72, 79–84; Lucaites, "Irony of Equality," pp. 51–55, 57, 61–63. Compare Leroux, "Attention Shift," pp. 38, 40, 42–45.

54. Douglass repeatedly emphasized the role of world opinion in condemning slavery in his speeches; see I:42; I:184; I:292–93; I:366–67; I:468; II:45; II:282–84; III:336–37. In this context, the abolition of slavery in the British colonies was particularly significant to Douglass, since British opinion was the "world" opinion that seemed to matter most to him and his fellow abolitionists; see I:75; I:475; II:70; II:332; III:188–91; III:194–95; III:216; III:367–69. Child, of course, had alluded to British colonial abolition *prospectively*.

55. Douglass also emphasized the argument that slavery was a dying institution in other speeches; see II:83; II:353; II:438; III:49; III:171; III:191–93; III:471–73; III:555.

56. In the exordium, Douglass expressed confidence in the eventual end of slavery in the United States because it was a young nation and therefore less resistant to changing its evil ways (II:360–61).

57. The lacuna in Douglass's theory of progress is, of course, the continuing presence of racial slavery on American soil. Welter's distinction between microhistory and macrohistory—a distinction central to the jeremiad—explains this lacuna. According to this distinction, only the general trajectory of history is progressive; on the "micro" level, regress is always possible. See Rush Welter, *The Mind of America, 1820–1860* (New York: Columbia University Press, 1975), pp. 26–27; Bercovitch, *American Jeremiad*, pp. 144–45.

58. See Garrison, *Selections from the Writings and Speeches of William Lloyd Garrison* (Boston: B. F. Wallcut, 1852), p. 316 ("The Triumph of Freedom," *Liberator*, January 10, 1845).

59. On Douglass's millennialism, see Blight, "Frederick Douglass and the American Apocalypse," pp. 315–17, 327–28; Howard-Pitney, *Afro-American Jeremiad*, pp. 20, 52; compare Mills, "Whose Fourth of July," pp. 126–33.

60. This tactic was presumably a reaction to the public fears that the abolitionists had encountered when they discussed their ultimate aims. See Martin Duberman, "The Northern Response to Slavery," in Duberman, ed., *Antislavery Vanguard*, pp. 405–6; Kraditor, *Means and Ends*, pp. 27–28.

NOTES TO CHAPTER 4

1. See Wendell Phillips, *Speeches, Lectures, and Letters* (Boston: Lee and Shepard, 1891), II:5 ("The Right of Petition," March 28, 1837). The speech was given in support of a resolution at the quarterly meeting of the Massachusetts Anti-Slavery Society in Lynn honoring John Quincy Adams and the other members of the Massachusetts congressional delegation who opposed the gag rule on abolitionist petitions to Congress. See Irving G. Bartlett, *Wendell Phillips: Brahmin Radical* (Westport, Conn.: Greenwood Press, 1961), p. 45; James Brewer Stewart, *Wendell Phillips: Liberty's Hero* (Baton Rouge: Louisiana State University Press, 1986), pp. 56–57.

2. See Ronald G. Walters, *The Antislavery Appeal: American Abolitionism after 1830* (New York: Norton, 1978), pp. 139–40.

3. See James B. Stewart, "Peaceful Hopes and Violent Experiences: The Evolution of Reforming and Radical Abolitionism, 1831–1837," *Civil War History* 17, no. 1 (1971): 293–309.

4. Although at the beginning of the war, uniting the house against slavery meant different things to the Garrisonians and Republicans, by the end of the war it meant the same thing.

5. My argument here is not that the abolitionists were not committed to racial equality but, rather, that their efforts to broaden the antislavery appeal prompted them to downplay that goal.

6. On this confluence, see especially Richard H. Sewell, *Ballots for Freedom: Antislavery Politics in the United States, 1837–1860* (New York: Oxford University Press, 1976). See also Merton L. Dillon, *The Abolitionists: The Growth of a Dissenting Minority* (DeKalb: Northern Illinois University Press, 1974), pp. 194, 211–12, 240; John R. McKivigan, "'Vote as You Pray and Pray as You Vote': Church-Oriented Abolitionism and Antislavery Politics," in *Crusaders and Compromisers: Essays on the Relationship of the Antislavery Struggle to the Antebellum Party System*, ed. Alan M. Kraut (Westport, Conn.: Greenwood Press, 1983), pp. 192–95; Gerald Sorin, *Abolitionism: A New Perspective* (New York: Praeger, 1972), pp. 136–37, 142–43; James B. Stewart, "The Aims and Impact of Garrisonian Abolitionism, 1840–1860," *Civil War History* 15, no. 3 (1969): 207–9.

7. Admittedly, the people of the North could conclude, as many people in the South did, that the real threat to the union was not slavery but antislavery agitation. Although the former were less likely to accept that conclusion than the latter were, the incidence of antiabolitionist mobs in the North suggests that not all people in the North rejected it. See especially Leonard L. Richards, *"Gentlemen of Property and Standing": Anti-Abolition Mobs in Jacksonian America* (New York: Oxford University Press, 1971).

8. Garrison disunionism still could have been a miscalculation or adopted on grounds of principle, regardless of its probable political impact. However, in my view, the Garrisonians were more political, in the broad sense of the term, as well as more nationalistic than they usually are credited with having been. See Stewart, "Aims and Impact," pp. 197–209.

9. A third rhetorical dynamic—toward liberalism—is not prominently featured in this chapter, since it already was examined in the last chapter through the comparison of Douglass's Fourth of July Oration and Child's *Appeal*. The dynamic toward contextualism can also be traced in Child's and Douglass's antislavery works. The dynamic toward unionism was not as pronounced in their two cases because they never embraced disunionism to the degree that, or as long as, Phillips did. On the dominance of the Garrisonian wing of the abolitionist movement, see Bertram Wyatt-Brown, "William Lloyd Garrison and Antislavery Unity: A Reappraisal," *Civil War History* 13, no. 1 (1967): 7, 11, 16, 20.

10. My references are to the reprint of the pamphlet published by the Negro Universities Press (New York, 1969). By 1844, the American Anti-Slavery Society had become a solely Garrisonian organization, following the 1840 schism and subsequent founding of the American and Foreign Anti-Slavery Society by the non-Garrisonian abolitionists. Garrison disunionism was one of several issues of contention between the two sides. See Walters, *Antislavery Appeal*, pp. 9–18.

11. In the introduction, Phillips stresses the importance of the long-delayed publication of James Madison's notes on the Federal Convention of 1787 to revealing the true proslavery nature of the Constitution (pp. 3, 7). He quotes extensively in the pamphlet from Madison's notes (pp. 14–33).

12. As evidence of the pamphlet's intended audience, Phillips ridicules the constitutional exegesis of the political abolitionists in his introduction (pp. 5–6). He soon responded to their champion in another American Anti-Slavery Society pamphlet: *Review of Lysander Spooner's Essay on the Unconstitutionality of Slavery* (New York: Arno, 1969 [1847]). Compare Lysander Spooner, *The Unconstitutionality of Slavery* (New York: Burt Franklin, 1965 [1845; rev. 1847]). The 1847 revision directly responds to Phillips's criticisms. William Wiecek usefully surveys the competing constitutional theories. See William M. Wiecek, *The Sources of Antislavery Constitutionalism in America, 1760–1848*

(Ithaca, N.Y.: Cornell University Press, 1977), chaps. 9–11. See also Robert M. Cover, *Justice Accused: Antislavery and the Judicial Process* (New Haven, Conn.: Yale University Press, 1975), chap. 9; Aileen S. Kraditor, *Means and Ends in American Abolitionism: Garrison and His Critics on Strategy and Tactics* (Chicago: Elephant, 1989 [1969]), pp. 185–212; Lewis Perry, *Radical Abolitionism: Anarchy and the Government of God in Antislavery Thought* (Ithaca, N.Y.: Cornell University Press, 1973), pp. 194–208; Jacobus tenBroek, *Equal under Law* (New York: Collier 1965 [1951]), chaps. 3–5.

13. Phillips, however, later claims that the founding fathers did not intend the Declaration's "all men are created equal" to apply to African Americans (p. 97). Throughout the address, he appears highly ambivalent toward the founding fathers; see also pp. 93–94, 100, 106–7, 109. As we will see, this ambivalence—which is resolved partially, but only partially, through the distinction between the "good" founders of 1776 and the "bad" founders of 1787—continually resurfaces in his antislavery works. Compare James Darsey, *The Prophetic Tradition and Radical Rhetoric in America* (New York: New York University Press, 1985), pp. 65–66.

14. We saw this same mix of religious and secular arguments in Douglass's Fourth of July oration and Child's *Appeal.*

15. For a contemporary debate over Phillips's constitutional exegesis, see Donald E. Fehrenbacher, "Slavery, the Framers, and the Living Constitution," and William M. Wiecek, "'The Blessings of Liberty': Slavery in the Constitutional Order," both in *Slavery and Its Consequences: The Constitution, Equality, and Race*, ed. Robert A. Goldwin and Art Kaufman (Washington, D.C.: American Enterprise Institute, 1988), pp. 1–44.

16. In favorably referring to the possibility of a violent end to Southern slavery, Phillips distinguishes himself from other Garrison abolitionists who were committed to nonviolence. Phillips does claim in the address, however, that he is committed to "universal love and peace" (p. 108) and that he does not believe violence will be necessary to abolish Southern slavery (p. 111). For more on Phillips's views on violence, see Phillips, *Speeches*, I:7 ("The Murder of Lovejoy," December 8, 1837); I:86 ("Sims Anniversary," April 12, 1852); I:279 ("Harper's Ferry," November 1, 1859).

17. Note Phillips's negative view of the "good" founders of 1776 in these passages. Douglass later made the same point in his Fourth of July oration.

18. Phillips also believes that the union was unnecessary to prevent Great Britain from reconquering the newly independent American states (pp. 95–96).

19. If disunion led to the end of Southern slavery, it obviously would usher in more drastic changes.

20. Here Phillips raises the collateral issue of free speech, which the abolitionists used effectively to build popular support for their cause by indicating exactly how Southern slavery threatened the rights and liberties of the people

of the North. See especially Russel B. Nye, *Fettered Freedom; Civil Liberties and the Slavery Controversy, 1830–1860* (East Lansing: Michigan State University Press, 1949 [rev. 1963]). The collateral issue, of course, was central to Phillips's "Right of Petition" speech. See also Phillips, *Speeches*, I:7 ("Murder of Lovejoy"); II:50–51 ("Kossuth," December 27, 1851); I:133–34 ("Philosophy of the Abolition Movement," January 27, 1853).

21. On Phillips's ambiguous disunionism, see Robert D. Marcus, "Wendell Phillips and American Institutions," *Journal of American History* 56, no. 1 (1969): 48–49. As noted earlier, this ambiguous disunionism included an ambivalent attitude toward the founding fathers.

22. According to Phillips, the four advantages of disunionism are (1) creating a solid North, (2) persuading the South to abolish slavery, (3) taking the offensive against the slave power, and (4) increasing the moral power of the abolitionists (pp. 111–12). The actions contemplated under Garrison disunionism even more strongly suggest its inward-looking character: (1) refusing to vote, (2) refusing to hold office in the federal and state governments, and (3) not voluntarily aiding those governments in any other way (though still paying taxes) (p. 111). See also Wendell Phillips, *Can Abolitionists Vote or Take Office under the United States Constitution?* (New York: American Anti-Slavery Society, 1845).

23. Antiabolitionist mobs targeted Thompson because he perfectly fit the role of "outside agitator." For the close personal connections between the British and American abolitionists, see especially Betty L. Fladeland, *Men and Brothers; Anglo-American Antislavery Cooperation* (Champaign-Urbana: University of Illinois Press, 1972), chap. 10.

24. My references are to the version of the speech reprinted in Phillips, *Speeches*, II:24–39.

25. In chapter 3, we saw how Douglass and Child also celebrated (or anticipated) British colonial abolition.

26. Phillips's public criticism of Curtis in this speech was part of a general tactic of subjecting Northern politicians to personal attack for their compromises with Southern slavery. As we shall see, Phillips repeatedly employed this tactic in his antislavery works. He defended the tactic, at some length, in his "Philosophy of the Abolition Movement" speech; see Phillips, *Speeches*, I:106–15.

27. In denouncing the new fugitive slave law, Phillips was outraged initially by Curtis's reference to fugitive slaves as foreigners (pp. 32–34).

28. For Phillips, this stream of progress accounts for, in particular, the Protestant Reformation, the Puritan revolution in Great Britain, and the Jeffersonian revolution in the United States (pp. 37–38).

29. Earlier in the speech, Phillips cited the losses that the pro-Compromise "Cotton" Whigs sustained in the recent congressional elections in Massachusetts as evidence of the growth of the antislavery appeal (pp. 26, 28).

30. Phillips both invokes the contextualist "American exemplar" and "human progress" arguments in this passage and joins deontology ("well-being") to consequentialism ("well-doing"). As yet another aspect of this seamless web, he earlier used the deontological "sectional purity" argument, claiming that antiabolitionist mobs were confessions of Northern guilt over Southern slavery (p. 25) and that the new fugitive slave law increased the North's complicity in the continued existence of the institution (p. 34).

31. Although both speeches represented attempts to reach broader audiences, it seems safe to assume that their audiences were still largely abolitionists.

32. My references to this speech are from the edition collected in *Pamphlets on Slavery in the United States* (Chicago: University of Chicago Library, n.d.), vol. 1.

33. Phillips returns to Wilson's letter several times during the speech; see also pp. 4, 10, 13, 15.

34. Here Phillips assumes that education and slavery are incompatible with each other but that an independent South will require an educated labor force to generate an adequate level of tax revenues. He also assumes that the Southern states currently can afford to undertax their citizens because of the, to him, disproportionate contributions of the Northern states to the federal coffers (pp. 12–13).

35. Phillips adds that while he is not a proponent of ending Southern slavery in this violent manner, he is willing to let "natural causes have free play" by withdrawing Northern support from the institution (p. 16).

36. Phillips later predicts that disunion will not materially affect North-South commerce, any more than the "disunion" of Great Britain and the American states materially affected Anglo-American commerce (p. 11).

37. Webster was a long-standing target of Phillips's barbs, even after his death in 1852. See also Wendell Phillips, *Review of Webster's Speech on Slavery* (Boston: American Antislavery Society, 1850); Phillips, *Speeches*, I:48–49 ("Public Opinion," January 28, 1852); I:247–49 ("Idols," October 4, 1859). Pierce was the outgoing president; Cushing, his attorney general. While in office, the two had attempted to vigorously enforce the new fugitive slave law.

38. Sumner had been one of Phillips's classmates at Harvard.

39. Phillips views this corruption as reciprocal because he views the slave power in the same terms. As he defines it, only the second of the three elements of the slave power is not intersectional: (1) the tremendous amount of capital invested in slaves, (2) the constitutional aristocracy created by the three-fifths clause, and (3) racial prejudice (p. 7).

40. My references are to the version of this speech reprinted in Phillips, *Speeches*, I:371–95.

41. See Phillips, *Speeches*, I:371 (n.); Bartlett, *Wendell Phillips*, pp. 226–35; Stewart, *Wendell Phillips*, pp. 213–15. For Phillips's own view of these mobs,

see also Phillips, *Speeches*, I:338–41 ("Mobs and Education," December 21, 1860); I:358–60 ("Disunion," January 20, 1861).

42. Phillips's reference to "Howard" is John Howard, an eighteenth-century British philanthropist and penal reformer. His reference to "Faust" is Johann Faust (or Fust), a pioneer in developing movable type.

43. Phillips once again draws the parallel to the Anglo-American "disunion" of 1776 (p. 374), apparently overlooking the fact that it twice led to war, not peace.

44. In recycling these disunionist arguments, Phillips now (wrongly) assumes that the North will not go to war to force the South back into the union and that North-South relations actually will improve with disunion (pp. 387–88). He also (wrongly) assumes that the South will become a house divided in itself between border states and Gulf states, which will prevent it from engaging in any wars (pp. 389–90). By border states, Phillips means Virginia, North Carolina, and Tennessee, as well as Delaware, Maryland, Kentucky, and Missouri. None of these states had yet seceded from the union, but Phillips seems to assume (again wrongly) that they all will. On the antebellum South as a house divided, see William W. Freehling, "The Divided South, Democracy's Limitations, and the Causes of the Peculiarly North American Civil War," in *The Reintegration of American History: Slavery and the Civil War* (New York: Oxford University Press, 1994), pp. 180–83.

45. Dana, however, was active in politics and soon thereafter was appointed a United States attorney.

46. Phillips then does attack a number of prominent Northern politicians in this speech, such as Seward and Charles Francis Adams, for their compromise efforts; see pp. 376, 379, 381, 383. The major compromise effort at this time was the Crittenden compromise, which would have extended the Missouri Compromise line to the Pacific.

47. Although he admits that the framers of the Constitution made these concessions with the expectation that slavery would die a natural death in the United States, Phillips claims that it still was (deontologically) wrong to make them. Moreover, the fact that the invention of the cotton gin confounded the framers' expectations proves that their concessions were wrong even on consequentialist grounds (pp. 377–78). See also Phillips, *Review of Lysander Spooner*, pp. 34–35. Again, one should note his ambivalence toward the founding fathers in these passages.

48. Phillips refuses even to discuss these subsequent compromises.

49. As we have seen, Phillips offers a less favorable view of Northern public opinion in the peroration. Probably most accurately, he asserts that both the people of the North and their leading politicians are now at least committed to blocking the further spread of slavery (p. 381)—which would explain why the Crittenden compromise failed to pass Congress.

50. Later in the speech, Phillips presents yet another scenario for the end of Southern slavery. In predicting that with disunion, the South will become a house divided between border states and Gulf states, he also predicts that the border states will continue to sell their slaves farther south until they reach the point at which they no longer have a sufficient stake in the institution to wish to maintain it. The Gulf states then will be forced to also abolish slavery because of their inability to sustain such large slave populations (pp. 389–90). Phillips's various scenarios for the end of Southern slavery in this and other works do not seem to have been fashioned with a view to their consistency with one another.

51. Phillips claims that ten years of slave insurrections would be preferable to one hundred more years of slavery (p. 383).

52. However, Phillips does mention that the continued existence of racial slavery in the South also adversely affects Southern whites (pp. 378, 385).

53. We have seen this lack of commitment to nonviolence many times before.

54. Here, Phillips criticizes Dana for expressing the contrary attitude. He also quotes Jefferson's *Notes on Virginia* on how God undoubtedly will take the side of the slaves in the eventuality of a race war (p. 386; see also p. 374). See Merrill D. Peterson, ed., *The Portable Jefferson* (New York: Viking, 1975), p. 215.

55. As already noted, Phillips presents a scenario for a peaceful end to Southern slavery later in the speech.

56. As we have seen, in the "human progress" argument of the exordium of the speech, Phillips also expresses confidence that the house will reunite on terms of liberty and equality (pp. 371–73).

57. In this respect, Phillips considers the separation between the North and South in a different light than the separation between Great Britain and the American states. Not surprisingly, manifest destiny flowed northward for Phillips, not southward, as it did for the Southern filibusters. Compare William W. Freehling, "The Complex Career of Slaveholder Expansionism," in *The Reintegration of American History: Slavery and the Civil War* (New York: Oxford University Press, 1994), pp. 158–75; Walters, *Antislavery Appeal*, pp. 142–43.

58. The passage also implies that racial slavery would have been abolished long ago in the South without the union to sustain it.

59. Phillips's ambivalence toward the founding fathers also persists; see pp. 375, 377–78, 379–80, 395.

60. My references are to the version of this speech reprinted in Phillips, *Speeches*, I:396–414. The speech was delivered nine days after the firing on Fort Sumter. In it, Phillips urges other abolitionists to support the war effort, too (p. 408). They largely did. See Dillon, *The Abolitionists*, pp. 251–53; Lawrence J. Friedman, *Gregarious Saints: Self and Community in American*

Abolitionism (Cambridge: Cambridge University Press, 1982), chap. 7; Carleton Mabee, *Black Freedom: The Nonviolent Abolitionists from 1830 through the Civil War* (Toronto: Macmillan, 1970), chap. 19; Perry, *Radical Abolitionism*, pp. 269–71; Sorin, *Abolitionism*, pp. 147–49; Walters, *Antislavery Appeal*, pp. 139–40. Although Phillips, unlike many other abolitionists, did not face the dilemma of whether to abandon "peace principles" during the war, he does remark in this speech that he had thought that "the age of bullets was over" (p. 398) and that the end of slavery would come peacefully in the United States, as it had in the British colonies (p. 410). We have noted that Phillips previously presented several different scenarios for a peaceful end to Southern slavery.

61. See Phillips, *Speeches*, I:396–97; Bartlett, *Wendell Phillips*, pp. 237–39; Stewart, *Wendell Phillips*, pp. 219–24.

62. Phillips quotes John Quincy Adams on the improbability of a permanent disunion (pp. 406–7).

63. Even after the firing on Fort Sumter, the North could have disregarded the incident instead of viewing it as a provocation for war.

64. Still, it is somewhat unfair of Phillips to reproach the Lincoln administration in this speech for having been too conciliatory to the South (pp. 401, 405–6), in view of Lincoln's refusal to recognize Southern independence and abandon Fort Sumner as well as Phillips's own statements in the "Progress" speech praising Lincoln for standing firm against compromise and urging him to let the South go in peace (p. 379). At that time, however, Phillips seemed to believe that trying to entice the South to reenter the union was being too conciliatory to the South but that letting it go in peace was not.

65. Phillips adds that the North's determination to see justice done to the Southern slaves has been fortified by its need to atone for seventy years of ignoring their plight (p. 407; see also p. 414).

66. Phillips points to British colonial abolition as the exception to this rule (p. 410). Some of the scenarios he presented earlier for the end of Southern slavery did contemplate the necessity of violence, but in terms of slave revolts, not interstate wars.

67. Indeed, Phillips now sounds very much like his erstwhile foil. See Spooner, *The Unconstitutionality of Slavery*, p. 89.

68. These changed circumstances would include a real, rather than a hypothetical, disunion; a Southern, rather than a Northern, secession; and the actual outbreak of hostilities.

69. Phillips also expresses much more favorable attitudes toward the founding fathers in this speech, but that change, too, could have been anticipated from his earlier antislavery works; see pp. 402, 405, 409, 412, 414.

70. Phillips referred to the heterogeneity of the union in his "Progress" speech (pp. 387–88).

71. In this context, Phillips clearly overstates the abolitionists' influence. At the end of the speech, he more cautiously, and accurately, states their influence in discussing the four segments of public opinion he sees in the North at the time, only the last of which is committed to immediate emancipation. The majority is instead committed to stopping the further aggressions of the Southern slavocracy (pp. 413–14). Again, one should compare his "Progress" speech.

72. Phillips's reference here to a working-class struggle is also somewhat hyperbolic, but it does point to the fact that of all the major abolitionists, he was probably the most sympathetic to the need for economic reform in the North. (After the Civil War, he was active in the labor movement.) His idea of economic reform, though, was hardly radical and, in fact, very liberal; he sought to enhance the competitive nature of the prevailing capitalist order by increasing the bargaining power of labor. See John Ashworth, *Slavery, Capitalism, and Politics in the Antebellum Republic: Volume 1: Commerce and Compromise, 1820–1850* (Cambridge: Cambridge University Press, 1995), pp. 161–62; Bartlett, *Wendell Phillips*, pp. 338–40, 348, 362; Richard Hofstadter, *The American Political Tradition and the Men Who Made It* (New York: Knopf, 1948), pp. 207–8; Marcus, "Wendell Phillips," pp. 50–58.

73. The passage is also a strong testament to how progressive liberalism and religious millennialism were intertwined in antislavery thought. For Phillips's faith in progress, see Hofstadter, *American Political Tradition*, pp. 177–78.

74. Phillips was plainly not an anti-institutionalist, as Elkins argues of the abolitionists, since he not only recognized the importance of institutions but also had a definite idea of the institutions he wanted to put in place of Southern slavery. Compare Stanley M. Elkins, *Slavery: A Problem in American Institutional & Intellectual Life* (New York: Grosset & Dunlap, 1963 [1959]), p. 175; Marcus, "Wendell Phillips," pp. 41–45, 47, 49–50.

75. See Dillon, *The Abolitionists*, pp. 211, 239–40; Robert F. Durden, "Ambiguities of the Antislavery Crusade of the Republican Party," in *The Antislavery Vanguard: New Essays on the Abolitionists*, ed. Martin Duberman (Princeton, N.J.: Princeton University Press, 1965), pp. 362–94; Larry Gara, "Slavery and the Slave Power: A Crucial Distinction," *Civil War History* 15, no. 1 (1969): 5–18; Sorin, *Abolitionism*, pp. 136–37, 141–42. The two groups also seem to have had different priorities between abolishing slavery and restoring the union, with the Republicans more committed to the latter and the abolitionists, to the former. Lincoln's frequently quoted letter of August 22, 1862, to Horace Greeley suggests these different priorities. See Roy B. Basler, ed., *The Collected Works of Abraham Lincoln* (New Brunswick, N.J.: Rutgers University Press, 1953), V:388 ("If I could save the Union without freeing *any* slaves, I would do it; and if I could save it by freeing *all* the slaves, I would do it."). But this contrast also is an ambiguous one. The abolitionists' commit-

ment to the union at this time cannot be attributed simply to political expediency, nor should Lincoln's commitment to abolishing slavery be dismissed simply as a wartime conversion. Both positions were predictable changes in their earlier positions, under dramatically altered circumstances.

76. The extent to which Reconstruction was a failure for the abolitionists is another matter cloaked with ambiguity. Compare Dillon, *The Abolitionists*, pp. 263–64, 271–75; Friedman, *Gregarious Saints*, chap. 9; Peter Kolchin, *American Slavery, 1619–1877* (New York: Hill & Wang, 1993), pp. 213–16, 224–25, 233–36; Mabee, *Black Freedom*, chap. 20; Duncan Rice, *The Rise and Fall of Black Slavery* (New York: Harper & Row, 1975), pp. 358–62, 399–400; Sorin, *Abolitionism*, chap. 8.

NOTES TO CHAPTER 5

1. As noted in both chapters 3 and 4, the extent of this institutional change is open to dispute.

2. See John Ashworth, *Slavery, Capitalism, and Politics in the Antebellum Republic: Volume 1: Commerce and Compromise, 1820–1850* (Cambridge: Cambridge University Press, 1995), p. 140; William J. Cooper Jr., *Liberty and Slavery: Southern Politics to 1860* (New York: Knopf, 1983), p. 34; David Brion Davis, *The Problem of Slavery in the Age of Revolution* (Ithaca, N.Y.: Cornell University Press, 1975), pp. 196–212; Gordon E. Finnie, "The Antislavery Movement in the Upper South before 1840," *Journal of Southern History* 35, no. 3 (1969): 319–42; Duncan J. Macleod, *Slavery, Race and the American Revolution* (Cambridge: Cambridge University Press, 1974), p. 44; Kenneth M. Stampp, "The Fate of the Southern Antislavery Movement," *Journal of Negro History* 28, no. 1 (1943): 10–17.

3. I demonstrated this proslavery liberalism in more synoptic terms in chapter 2.

4. Eugene D. Genovese outlines this proslavery progressivism in *The Slaveholders' Dilemma: Freedom and Progress in Southern Conservative Thought, 1820–1860* (Columbia: University of South Carolina Press, 1992). I believe that he exaggerates the extent to which proslavery figures divided their views toward progress in terms of material progress (which they welcomed) and moral progress (which they questioned). Such a stance is a standard American conservative stance, which is part of Genovese's point, but proslavery figures seemed confident, at least in their public pronouncements, that both material and moral progress eventually would shift in a proslavery direction.

5. In chapter 1, I conceded that these liberal proslavery arguments may well have been disingenuous, although determining whether or not they were is, I think, extremely difficult. In any case, they were liberal arguments according to the definition of liberalism I offered in chapter 2.

6. One exception is that unlike the abolitionists, the defenders of slavery did not have to be concerned with maintaining the internal unity of the proslavery movement, since the movement never assumed the organizational forms that the antislavery movement did. This point raises the question of whether there was a proslavery movement rather than merely some individual defenders of slavery. In *A Sacred Circle: The Dilemma of the Intellectual in the Old South* (Baltimore: Johns Hopkins University Press, 1977), Drew Gilpin Faust suggests that there was a proslavery movement, at least in terms of the identification of one circle of proslavery figures, which included Hammond, comparable to the Garrison abolitionists in the North.

7. The ultimate success of the proslavery movement is another one of those eminently debatable historical questions. As noted in chapter 2, some sources indicate that secession did not enjoy majority support in most of the Southern states. None of those sources, however, denies that during the antebellum period, there was significant movement in a proslavery direction in the South.

8. See Louis Hartz, *The Liberal Tradition in America: An Interpretation of American Political Thought since the Revolution* (New York: Harcourt Brace Jovanovich, 1955), chaps. 5–6; Rogers M. Smith, *Civic Ideals: Conflicting Visions of Citizenship in U.S. History* (New Haven, Conn.: Yale University Press, 1997), chap. 8. This is one point on which Smith agrees with Hartz.

9. See Eugene D. Genovese, *The Political Economy of Slavery: Studies in the Economy and Society of the Slave South* (New York: Vintage Books, 1967 [1961]), chap. 1; Ashworth, *Slavery and Capitalism*, chap. 2.

10. See James Oakes, *Slavery and Freedom: An Interpretation of the Old South* (New York: Knopf, 1990), chap. 2; Kenneth S. Greenberg, *Masters and Statesmen: The Political Culture of American Slavery* (Baltimore: Johns Hopkins University Press, 1985), chap. 5. I would interpret Greenberg's work as, again, showing that republicanism and liberalism are not clearly distinguished in the literature on American political thought.

11. Dew's *Review* was originally published as a separate pamphlet and later as part of the prominent proslavery collection: *The Pro-Slavery Argument; as maintained by the most distinguished writers of the Southern states, containing the several essays, on the subject, of Chancellor Harper, Governor Hammond, Dr. Simms, and Professor Dew* (New York: Negro Universities Press, 1968 [1852]), pp. 287–490. All page references to Dew's *Review* are from this source.

12. The pamphlet's antiabolitionist ("necessary evil") thrust is consistent with its relatively early status in the proslavery movement. In fact, some scholars argue that it inaugurated the movement. See Dickson D. Bruce Jr., *The Rhetoric of Conservatism: The Virginia Convention of 1829–1830 and the Conservative Tradition in the South* (San Marino, Calif.: Huntington Library, 1982), pp. 179–80; Ralph E. Morrow, "The Proslavery Argument Revisited,"

Mississippi Valley Historical Review 48, no. 1 (1961): 82; Joseph Clarke Robert, *The Road to Monticello: A Study of the Virginia Slavery Debate of 1832* (New York: AMS Press, 1971 [1941]), pp. v, 46. But compare Alison Goodyear Freehling, *Drift toward Dissolution: The Slavery Debate of 1831–1832* (Baton Rouge: Louisiana State University Press, 1982), pp. xii–xiii, 203; Kenneth M. Stampp, "An Analysis of T. R. Dew's *Review of the Debate in the Virginia Legislature*," *Journal of Negro History* 27, no. 4 (1942): 382–83; Larry E. Tise, *Proslavery: A History of the Defense of Slavery in America, 1701–1840* (Athens: University of Georgia Press, 1987), pp. 71–72, 288–89.

13. See Bruce, *Rhetoric of Conservatism*, p. 187; George M. Fredrickson, *The Black Image in the White Mind: The Debate on Afro-American Character and Destiny, 1817–1914* (Middletown, Conn.: Wesleyan University Press, 1987 [1971]), p. 44; Stampp, "An Analysis of Dew's *Review*," pp. 381–82; Tise, *Proslavery*, p. 71.

14. All page references to *Cannibals All* are from the 1960 reprint issued by the Belknap Press (Cambridge, Mass.).

15. In fact, Fitzhugh almost begged radical Northern abolitionists like Garrison to respond personally to his arguments, even wrote them letters to that effect, and was disappointed when they did not. In 1855, he took the unusual step of traveling north to visit one prominent abolitionist, Gerrit Smith (a distant cousin), and to speak jointly with another, Wendell Phillips. See Fitzhugh, *Cannibals All*, pp. 9–10, 97–106, 257–59.

16. Richard J. Ellis argues that two distinct proslavery groups emerged in the antebellum South: a seacoast group, to which Dew, Fitzhugh, and Hammond all belonged, and an interior group of more "democratic" defenders of slavery. See Richard J. Ellis, "Legitimating Slavery in the Old South: The Effect of Political Institutions on Ideology," *Studies in American Political Development* 5, no. 2 (1991): 340–51. I believe that he exaggerates the differences between the two groups. Dew, Fitzhugh, and Hammond each featured the "Herrenvolk democracy" argument that Ellis associates with the interior group. Smith also argues that Fitzhugh, in particular, was unrepresentative of the proslavery movement as a whole. He bases this argument on the premise that Fitzhugh did not defend slavery primarily on racial grounds but, rather, on class grounds. He then views the Southern ethnologists, who did defend slavery primarily on racial grounds, as more representative of the proslavery movement. See Smith, *Civic Ideals*, pp. 24–25, 203–5. However, as we have seen, the Southern ethnologists were marginalized in the antebellum South, and as we will see, Fitzhugh did defend slavery on racial grounds. I obviously view Fitzhugh as a more representative and a more liberal defender of slavery than Smith does. For other views of Fitzhugh's representativeness, see Ashworth, *Slavery and Capitalism*, p. 239; Eugene D. Genovese, *The World the Slaveholders Made: Two Essays in Interpretation* (New York: Pantheon Books, 1969), p.

243; Peter Kolchin, *American Slavery, 1619–1877* (New York: Hill & Wang, 1993), p. 196; James P. Young, *Reconsidering American Liberalism: The Troubled Odyssey of the Liberal Idea* (Boulder, Colo.: Westview Press, 1996), p. 111. Incidentally, Fitzhugh has generated much more of a secondary literature than either Dew or Hammond has, in part because he has become the fulcrum of debate over the liberal/illiberal nature of the proslavery movement.

17. For more scholarly reviews of the Virginia legislative debate, see A. G. Freehling, *Drift toward Dissolution*, chap. 5; Robert, *Road to Monticello*, chap. 3. The opening salvo in the debate was Thomas Jefferson Randolph's proposal that the state adopt a post-nati afterbirth) emancipation scheme patterned after the one his grandfather, Thomas Jefferson, had sketched in the 1780s but never proposed. The ensuing debate largely, though not solely, split the legislature along geographic lines between eastern, slaveholding Virginia and western, nonslaveholding Virginia, a split that eventually led to separate statehood for the latter. The debate ended with a token victory for the antislavery legislators—a resolution declaring slavery an evil institution—but with the defeat of all their specific proposals. A similar debate never again took place in Virginia or any other slave state.

18. Not surprisingly, then, scholars seem divided on the question of whether Dew was "necessary evil" or "positive good." Compare Bruce, *Rhetoric of Conservatism*, pp. 179–80; Fredrickson, *Black Image*, pp. 44–46; A. G. Freehling, *Drift toward Dissolution*, pp. xii–xiii, 203; Kolchin, *American Slavery*, p. 191; Ralph E. Morrow, "The Proslavery Argument Revisited," *Mississippi Valley Historical Review* 48, no. 1 (1961): 82; Robert, *Road to Monticello*, pp. v, 46; Stampp, "An Analysis of Dew's *Review*," pp. 382–83; Tise, *Proslavery*, pp. 71–72, 288–89.

19. The traditional explanation of this shift is that it was a response to the rise of Garrison abolitionism in the North. The problem with this explanation is that the "effect" seems to have preceded the "cause." (As we shall see, Dew himself appears unaware of the Garrison abolitionists.) A more likely explanation is that the shift was part of an elite attempt to stifle internal dissent against racial slavery as Southern political and intellectual leaders increasingly identified the institution with a distinctive Southern way of life. See Stanley M. Elkins, *Slavery: A Problem in American Institutional & Intellectual Life* (New York: Grosset & Dunlap, 1963 [1959]), pp. 211–12; Fredrickson, *Black Image*, pp. 43, 48; Hesseltine, "Some New Aspects," p. 71; Morrow, "Proslavery Argument Revisited," p. 94; Kenneth M. Stampp, "The Fate of the Southern Antislavery Movement," *Journal of Negro History* 28, no. 1 (1943): 13–14; Tise, *Proslavery*, pp. 286, 308.

20. Dew even believes that the Northern abolitionists agree that emancipation requires removals (p. 421), seemingly unaware of the Garrison abolitionists who advocated not only emancipation without removals but also im-

mediate emancipation. (It would not have been surprising if he had been unaware of the Garrisonians when he wrote his essay, given that they were only beginning to organize and publish antislavery tracts in 1832.) Although Dew's reference for "abolitionists" in the essay is the Virginia legislators who had proposed various gradual emancipation schemes during the recent legislative debate, today we would say, as the Garrisonians did, that they were not really abolitionists but colonizationists. See Lydia Maria Child, *An Appeal in Favor of Africans* (New York: Arno, 1968 [1833]), p. 101. Indeed, the following year, these same legislators sought, with temporary success, state funding for colonizing free blacks in Africa. See A. G. Freehling, *Drift toward Dissolution*, pp. 217–20. Both William Jenkins and Tise argue that Dew's primary target was the colonization movement and that his essay paralleled Garrison's *Thoughts on African Colonization* (Boston: Garrison and Knapp, 1832) in undercutting the movement in the United States. See William Sumner Jenkins, *Pro-Slavery Thought in the Old South* (Gloucester, Mass.: Peter Smith, 1960 [1935]), pp. 87–88; Tise, *Proslavery*, pp. 70, 72–73. Dew's essay did spark a defense of colonization from James Madison, who long had been associated with the American Colonization Society, the umbrella organization of the movement. See Marvin Meyers, ed., *The Mind of the Founder: Sources of the Political Thought of James Madison*, rev. ed. (Hanover, N.H.: Brandeis University Press, 1981), pp. 333–36 ("Letter to Thomas R. Dew," February 23, 1833). Colonization was not the only possibility for removals. Others included private manumissions with the requirement that the freed slaves leave the state and slaveholders selling their slaves farther south. (The former was imposed by Virginia law; the latter would result in removals without emancipation instead of emancipation with removals.) Dew, however, believes that these possibilities suffer from many of the same shortcomings as colonization does (pp. 379–84).

21. Compare Child, *Appeal*, pp. 127–28.

22. Dew insists that this plan will never work because "*mere philanthropy* . . . has never yet accomplished one great scheme." He goes on to cite Adam Smith to the effect that the slaveholders' self-interest must be engaged in any plan of emancipation in order for it to succeed (p. 380).

23. Dew points out that post-nati emancipation schemes suffer from the fact that they never can fully compensate slaveholders for the loss of their slaves; hence, slaveholders would have a strong incentive to flee the state or sell their slaves farther south (p. 382). Post-nati emancipation schemes then may succeed as plans of removals but not as plans of emancipation.

24. Dew emphasizes that the nonslaveholders of western Virginia, who constitute the natural constituency of the state's antislavery legislators, find emancipation without compensation especially appealing (pp. 385, 388). He, however, explains that emancipation without compensation would hurt both

eastern and western Virginia by unsettling all forms of property (pp. 390–91). He also thinks that the policy is fundamentally unjust (p. 387). Dew actually considers two other cost-shifting measures—reopening the slave trade with Latin America (p. 379) and securing federal subsidies for African colonization (pp. 413–14, 418–20)—but he rejects both as morally and/or politically objectionable.

25. Dew comments that all colonial enterprises, including the British settlement of North America, have required a long time to become self-sufficient because of the logistical difficulties they faced (pp. 393–94), difficulties that in the African case would be compounded by its climate (pp. 394–96).

26. Dew believes that the Southampton (Nat Turner) rebellion precipitated the legislative debate (pp. 289–90). He also believes that emancipation without removals in Virginia would encourage white flight from the state because of the increased threat of racial violence (pp. 443–44, 449). This eventuality would separate the two races inside—or, rather, outside—Virginia, but hardly in a way that Dew could have found acceptable.

27. Dew's supposition is that free white laborers will work no harder than free black laborers, or else they will flee the state rather than work with blacks (p. 443).

28. Dew contends that such a compulsory labor system already has been instituted in Haiti (pp. 441–42).

29. The abolitionists, in contrast, argued that racial slavery was the cause of racial prejudice and that the one would disappear with the other. See Child, *Appeal*, pp. 134–35.

30. Dew claims that many of the slaves themselves know they are better off than free blacks (p. 428); that slaves in border areas attempt to escape less often than slaves farther south because they are better acquainted with the wretched conditions of free blacks in the North (p. 428); and that West Indian slaves often reject offers of freedom from their masters and, when emancipated, welcome a return to slavery (pp. 424, 426–28, 437).

31. Indeed, these requirements could have come directly from Locke's *Second Treatise*. See John Locke, *Two Treatises of Government* (New York: New American Library, 1965), pp. 333 (para. 34), 343 (para. 48), 347–48 (para. 57), 350 (para. 60).

32. Dew does not even discuss the ability of the slaves to participate in their own *collective* self-government, as if that possibility was totally inconceivable to him.

33. Dew, in fact, offers internal improvements as a general panacea for all Virginia's problems, including the geographic divisions exposed by the recent legislative debate (pp. 479–80). His proposal suggests not only that he was an economic progressive but also that he was not a traditional Southern sectionalist (1) because, at least on the state level, he favored more, not less, government

(p. 478) and (2) because he envisioned Virginia's becoming a more urban and commercial state, more like the states to its north than to its south (pp. 478–79). The second count follows from his climatological theory: Virginia may well be too far north to sustain a prosperous slave economy (p. 484). Tise stresses that proslavery figures, in general, were not traditional Southern sectionalists. See Tise, *Proslavery*, pp. 323, 327–28, 334–35, 360–62. See also Hartz, *Liberal Tradition*, pp. 190–92; Jenkins, *Pro-Slavery Thought*, pp. 307–8; Donald L. Robinson, *Slavery in the Structure of American Politics, 1765–1820* (New York: Harcourt, Brace, 1971), p. 434; Jacobus tenBroek, *Equal under Law* (New York: Collier 1965 [1951]), pp. 121–22, 130–31.

34. In these passages, Dew often conflates the two ideas that the slaves are not ready for freedom (as if some day they might be) and that they are naturally unsuited for freedom (because they belong to an allegedly inferior race). As already suggested, this equivocation was typical of the defenders of slavery.

35. See also pp. 351, 354, 421. Dew also argued earlier that the British government was responsible for blocking Virginia's efforts to abolish the slave trade before independence (pp. 352–53).

36. As we have seen, Child cited this passage positively in her *Appeal.*

37. On this point, Dew offers an implicit critique of the people of the North for their narrowly utilitarian values (pp. 455–56). He appears highly ambivalent toward the North. While he is a defender of Southern slavery, he also admires Northern progress (pp. 429, 446–47, 478–79). See Genovese, *Slaveholders' Dilemma*, pp. 14–18, 46.

38. At one point, Dew refers to the Northern states as "what are called free States" (p. 466).

39. This passage is the same one McDuffie quoted in his 1835 gubernatorial message. For Dew's use of Burke, see Bruce, *Rhetoric of Conservatism*, p. 182; A. G. Freehling, *Drift toward Dissolution*, p. 205.

40. Here Dew presents his version of the "Herrenvolk democracy" argument.

41. Dew calculates that only three slave revolts have been attempted in the two hundred years of the existence of Southern slavery: one in Virginia (Nat Turner, 1831), one in South Carolina (Denmark Vesey, 1822), and (perhaps) one in Louisiana (a reference to the 1811 slave uprising near New Orleans?) (p. 471). See Herbert Aptheker, *American Negro Slave Revolts* (New York: International Publishers, 1963 [1943]), pp. 249–51, 268–72, 293–306.

42. In this comparison, Dew equates slave revolts in slave societies with lower-on-upper-class crime in free societies. By this highly tendentious measure, he claims that the South is much safer than the North (pp. 465–66). He also uncovers a series of flawed assumptions behind this objection, starting with the assumption that every slave secretly wishes to kill his or her master (pp. 462–63) and ending with the assumption that the size of Virginia's black

population is increasing relative to the size of its white population (pp. 472–77).

43. Dew has primarily the protective tariff in mind as a federal policy that he thinks unjustly (and unconstitutionally) benefits the North at the expense of the South (pp. 486–89). He contends that Louisiana is the most economically progressive Southern state precisely because it benefits from the tariff (p. 489). He also insists that the same type of damaging "imperial" interference with slave economies that has occurred in the American South has occurred in the British West Indies (p. 487; see also pp. 458–59). Yet he still cites Brazil and Cuba as prospering slave economies, presumably because of the lack of such interference (p. 487). Dew appears as a traditional Southern sectionalist in these passages. See Tise, *Proslavery*, p. 71.

44. As already noted, Dew admits that Virginia may be too far north to enjoy the optimal conditions for slave labor.

45. This first part of the *Review* is not consistently organized into sections and subsections; therefore, I refer to it as a whole.

46. Native-born slaves were freed every seventh year, but Dew observes that they could always choose to remain slaves (p. 318). He also notes that in densely populated areas where food is scarce, such as in China, people still sell themselves into slavery (pp. 318–19).

47. These natural-law theorists—Hugo Grotius, Thomas Rutherforth, Cornelis van Bynkershoek, Emmerich Vattel, as well as Locke—specify such circumstances as that the war is a just one and that the captives have committed acts for which they may be justly executed. Dew thus reminds us that despite his liberal principles and generally antislavery teachings, Locke did justify slavery under certain circumstances. See Locke, *Two Treatises*, pp. 325–26 (paras. 23–24). Locke's ambiguous treatment of slavery is consistent with David Brion Davis's thesis that the Enlightenment included both antislavery and proslavery tendencies. These points apparently are lost on those who argue that the institution is indefensible on liberal grounds. Interestingly, John Rawls, probably the most prominent contemporary liberal philosopher, discusses as a possible justification of slavery the historical shift from executing to enslaving captives of war. See John Rawls, *A Theory of Justice*, rev. ed. (Cambridge, Mass.: Belknap Press, 1999), p. 218.

48. Dew, in fact, believes the opposite: Southern slavery began in the injustices of the African slave trade (pp. 345–48). However, his claim that the people of the South were not themselves responsible for those original injustices becomes, once again, important in this context.

49. Dew notes that the status of slaves has historically been extremely common (pp. 294–95) and that statuses analogous to it remain so (pp. 295–96). He later pursues the most prominent of these analogues, that between slavery and serfdom (pp. 437–40).

50. This passage is reminiscent of Locke's statement that "a King of a large fruitful Territory [among the Native Americans] feeds, lodges, and is clad worse than a day Labourer in *England*." See Locke, *Two Treatises*, p. 339 (para. 41).

51. Part of Dew's point here is that the end of serfdom in Poland did not end the dependent relations between the parties involved; see also pp. 437–39.

52. Dew considers these legislators irresponsible for even broaching the slavery issue (p. 293).

53. On Fitzhugh's broad definition of slaves and slavery, see Eugene D. Genovese, *A Consuming Fire: The Fall of the Confederacy in the Mind of the White Christian South* (Athens: University of Georgia Press, 1998), pp. 79, 91, 101. Greenberg notes that proslavery figures even experimented with alternative words for slaves and slavery. See Greenberg, *Masters and Statesmen*, pp. 101–2.

54. Fitzhugh's two-pronged defense of Southern slavery has led to three confusions in the secondary literature. First, Fitzhugh does favor stronger government, even a stronger federal government (pp. 247–48). Although he never specifies exactly what he has in mind, it seems safe to assume that he, like Dew, was thinking of internal improvements and other policies that would "thicken" American society. His dedication of *Cannibals All* to Governor Henry Wise praises Wise's pursuit of internal improvements on the state level (p. 3), something Dew advocated more than twenty years earlier. While Fitzhugh is an excellent example of a defender of slavery who was not a traditional Southern sectionalist, William Freehling and Genovese clearly overstate the case in suggesting that he was a "statist." See William W. Freehling, "Beyond Racial Limits: Paternalism over Whites in the Thought of Calhoun and Fitzhugh," in *The Reintegration of American History: Slavery and the Civil War* (New York: Oxford University Press, 1994), p. 102; Genovese, *Slaveholders' Dilemma*, p. 26. Second, Fitzhugh does allude to the possibility of white or working-class slavery in *Cannibals All*. He quotes at length from two articles from British journals on this possibility. The first article, from *Jerrod's Magazine*, proposes working-class slavery with its tongue firmly in its cheek (pp. 153–57), and the second, from the *Edinburgh Review*, only remarks that British workers might be better off as slaves without proposing their actual enslavement (pp. 159–64). Similarly, Fitzhugh's 1858 essay, "Origin of Civilization," which is often cited in this context, asserts that whites would make (and have, in the past, made) better slaves than blacks (because they belong to the allegedly superior race), without offering any concrete proposal to that effect. See George Fitzhugh, "Origin of Civilization—What Is Property?—Which Is the Best Slave Race?" *DeBow's Review* 25 (1858): 662–63. See also "Southern Thought," *DeBow's Review* 23 (1857): 338–39, 347–48; "Southern Thought Again," *DeBow's Review* 23 (1857): 451; "The

White and Black Races of Men," *DeBow's Review* 30 (1861): 448–49, 454. It seems safe to conclude that for Fitzhugh, as in the articles from which he quotes, the idea of white or working-class slavery was rhetorical, not, as several scholars have suggested, something he seriously intended. See Ellis, "Legitimating Slavery," p. 349; Fredrickson, *Black Image*, pp. 59–60; Jenkins, *Pro-Slavery Thought*, p. 304; Smith, *Civic Ideals*, pp. 24, 205. Compare Ashworth, *Slavery and Capitalism*, pp. 228–29, 235–36; W. W. Freehling, "Beyond Racial Limits," pp. 97–100. Third, Fitzhugh makes some strikingly illiberal pronouncements in *Cannibals All*. Not surprisingly, then, Hartz singles out Fitzhugh as the exemplary proslavery polemicist who abandoned liberalism for the "feudal dream"; Wish, in his still-standard biography of Fitzhugh, and Woodward, in his critical introduction to the reprint of *Cannibals All*, also interpret Fitzhugh as choosing "Filmer over Locke"; and even scholars who are critical of Hartz and view the antebellum South as torn between slavery and liberalism place Fitzhugh on the illiberal side of that divide. See Genovese, *World the Slaveholders Made*, pp. 123–24, 127, 129–31, 157–58; Hartz, *Liberal Tradition*, pp. 145–46, 157, 164–65, 171, 182–83; Oakes, *Slavery and Freedom*, pp. 179–80; Charles Grier Sellers Jr., "The Travail of Slavery," in *The Southerner as American*, ed. Charles Grier Sellers Jr. (New York: Dutton, 1966), pp. 64–66; Harvey Wish, *George Fitzhugh: Propagandist of the Old South* (Gloucester, Mass.: Peter Smith, 1962 [1943]), pp. vii–viii, 32, 224, 301–3; C. Vann Woodward, editor's introduction to *Cannibals All*, pp. viii–xi, xix–xx, xxxi, xxxiv–v, xxxviii. Dispelling this third confusion is the main purpose of my analysis of Fitzhugh, not to deny his illiberal pronouncements, but to demonstrate the primacy of his liberal arguments.

55. Although Fitzhugh's timing of the South's shift from "necessary evil" to "positive good" seems in error, the shift was not a "clean" one. As we shall see, even Fitzhugh's own defense of slavery is not purely "positive good." None of this is to deny his hubris in estimating the impact of his first book.

56. Fitzhugh does assume Hobbes would have agreed with his "cannibals all" premise (pp. 215, 218) but not necessarily with his solution to the political problems that premise raises (p. 219).

57. Like Dew, Fitzhugh refers to free society as "what is falsely called Free Society" (p. 72). He also refers to the "so-called liberty and equality" in which free societies place men (p. 36) and contends that in free societies "miscalled freemen" perform the same offices that slaves perform in slave societies (p. 221). According to Fitzhugh, the fact that the British have resorted to importing Chinese laborers to replace the freed slaves in their colonies also suggests the futility of any attempt to eliminate such dependent statuses (pp. 232–33).

58. Dew made this same argument.

59. Here Fitzhugh supports Elkins's thesis regarding anti-institutionalism among the abolitionists and in the North. Elkins, however, also extended his

thesis to the South. See Elkins, *Slavery*, pp. 206–22. But compare Faust, *Sacred Circle*, pp. 89–90.

60. In chapter 10 of *Cannibals All* ("Our Best Witnesses and Masters in the Art of War"), Fitzhugh quotes the abolitionists ad nauseam on the failures of free society. But even as the abolitionists criticized Northern free society, they also vigorously defended it in opposition to Southern slave society. See Ashworth, *Slavery and Capitalism*, pp. 159–60; Jonathan A. Glickstein, "'Poverty Is Not Slavery': American Abolitionists and the Competitive Labor Market," in *Antislavery Reconsidered: New Perspectives on the Abolitionists*, ed. Lewis Perry and Michael Fellman (Baton Rouge: Louisiana State University Press, 1979), pp. 195–218; Daniel J. McInerney, "'A State of Commerce': Market Power and Slave Power in Abolitionist Political Economy," *Civil War History* 37, no. 2 (1991): 101–19; Walters, *Antislavery Appeal*, pp. 111–14, 120–22, 127. Similarly, the vast majority of abolitionists were not, *pace* Fitzhugh, anarchists, as Perry's definitive study of the subject has shown. See Lewis Perry, *Radical Abolitionism: Anarchy and the Government of God in Antislavery Thought* (Ithaca, N.Y.: Cornell University Press, 1973), pp. x–xi, 19–20, 55–56.

61. In these passages, Fitzhugh also seeks to debunk the abolitionists as racists, which would have been an odd strategy to pursue if he thought that appealing to racial inferiority was the best way of defending racial slavery. But he did not. As he wrote in one of his many *DeBow's* essays, "Inferiority of race is quite as good an argument against negro slavery as in its favor." See Fitzhugh, "Southern Thought Again," p. 451.

62. The abolitionists anticipated Fitzhugh with their own slippery-slope argument to the effect that the continued existence of racial slavery in the South was likely to lead to white slavery or at least to less freedom for all Americans. See Child, *Appeal*, pp. 74–75; John W. Blassingame, ed., *The Frederick Douglass Papers; Series One: Speeches, Debates, and Interviews* (New Haven, Conn.: Yale University Press, 1979–82), II:415 ("Northern Ballots and the Elections of 1852," October 14, 1852); Wendell Phillips, *Speeches, Lectures, and Letters* (Boston: Lee and Shepard, 1891 [1863]), I:52 ("Public Opinion, January 28, 1852). If Fitzhugh actually had advocated white slavery, he would have only strengthened his opponents' case. But, again, he did not. As he stated in an essay he wrote for the *Richmond Enquirer* (September 12, 1856), "no sane man in America proposes to makes slaves of white men" (quoted in W. W. Freehling, "Beyond Racial Limits," p. 100).

63. However, as we have seen, Fitzhugh identifies many analogues to slavery. He certainly never suggests that nations that have abolished serfdom should reinstitute it. (Nor did Dew, who made a similar comparison.) Fitzhugh's defense of serfdom is evidence that he believed protective institutions could increase the sphere of personal liberty, not that he believed in the

"feudal dream." See Hartz, *Liberal Tradition*, pp. 145–46, 157, 164–65, 171, 182–83.

64. In addition, Fitzhugh claims that British workers are worse off than the serfs of eastern Europe and central Asia (pp. 79–80); cites the *Edinburgh Review* to the effect that Russian serfs would be worse off if freed (p. 161); contends that before their emancipation, West Indian slaves were better off than British workers (pp. 24–25); quotes the *London Globe* to the effect that emancipation has significantly worsened the condition of West Indian workers (pp. 184–85); and asserts that West Indian workers formerly were freer as slaves than they currently are as free persons (p. 185).

65. Fitzhugh also argues that in this sense slaves are freer than their masters (pp. 16, 18, 80–81, 204, 235).

66. See Greenberg, *Masters and Statesmen*, pp. 90, 102.

67. While both Dew and Fitzhugh criticize Blackstone for his antislavery views, only Dew uses Locke's "just war" justification of slavery to criticize Blackstone. Fitzhugh instead criticizes Locke as the progenitor of laissez-faire philosophy. But whether or not Fitzhugh intentionally misinterprets Locke, he uses him not philosophically but polemically to criticize the abolitionists for (mis)using Lockean principles to attack Southern slavery. The central aim of chapter 7 of *Cannibals All* ("Liberty and Slavery"), which contains Fitzhugh's criticisms of Blackstone and Locke as well as of Montesquieu and Paley, is to denounce abstract philosophy and not modern philosophy as a whole, despite what he says here (pp. 71–72) and elsewhere (pp. 21, 53) about its deficiencies. Indeed, in his attacks on abstract philosophy, Fitzhugh likes to cite Thomas Carlyle (pp. 10–12, 66–67, 196, 213, 254–55, 261), who was similarly conflicted between past and present. (Dew, of course, had cited Burke in such contexts.) For Fitzhugh's use of Carlyle, see Wish, *George Fitzhugh*, pp. 73–74; Woodward, introduction to *Cannibals All*, p. xiv.

68. Again, Fitzhugh does not make clear what "more of protection" entails, although he does make clear that it means more than more government (pp. 247–48). He attributes the North's ability so far to sustain itself to the way that the frontier acts as a safety valve for its discontents, but he also emphasizes the short-term nature of that solution (pp. 11, 40, 199, 255, 259).

69. But note the reference to both religious and secular principles in this passage, as we have seen many times before on both the proslavery and antislavery sides.

70. Fitzhugh contends that racial prejudice also contributes to the present-day animus against racial slavery: whites hate black slavery because they hate blacks. He thus ascribes Northern antislavery sentiments to the fact that racial prejudice is stronger in the North than in the South (p. 201). (This claim is at least somewhat more credible than the similar claim he leveled against the abolitionists in trying to debunk their antislavery sentiments.) He ascribes the cru-

elty of West Indian slavery to the fact that in the West Indies, unlike in the American South, most of the slaves were "unseasoned" (pp. 79, 200). While Fitzhugh, like Dew, refuses to defend the African slave trade in *Cannibals All* and even accuses Northern merchants (instead of Southern slaveholders) of attempting to reinstitute it (pp. 79, 232–33), he endorsed Southern efforts to reinstitute the trade within a year of completing the book. Compare Fitzhugh, "The Conservative Principle, or, Social Evils and Their Remedies; Part II—The Slave Trade," *DeBow's Review* 22 (1857): 449–62; "The White Slave Trade," *DeBow's Review* 24 (1858): 273.

71. Fitzhugh's reference for white "slaves" is the serfs of eastern Europe and central Asia (p. 200).

72. Note that Fitzhugh blurs the source of racial inequality in this passage.

73. Fitzhugh clearly recognizes this conclusion as a generalization: not all blacks are, or should be, slaves; and not all whites are, or should be, free persons. He, nevertheless, does make a fairly sweeping racial generalization about who is best suited to which status.

74. In a private letter of April 11, 1855, to his friend and fellow proslavery polemicist, George Frederick Holmes, Fitzhugh confessed: "I assure you Sir, I see great evils in slavery, but in a controversial work, I ought not to admit them" (quoted in W. W. Freehling, "Beyond Racial Limits," p. 102). If nothing else, this confession betrays the essentially rhetorical nature of the proslavery argument. Fitzhugh's only reference to the possibility of abolishing Southern slavery in *Cannibals All* is to remark that it would be "a curse" to the slaves and those around them (p. 199). He, however, does refer twice to the, to him, disastrous consequences of abolition in the British West Indies (pp. 24–25, 184–85). As already noted, the abolitionists viewed the results of British colonial abolition in much more positive terms.

75. Fitzhugh, though, does not focus his proslavery consequentialism totally on nonslaveholding whites. He also claims broader benefits for whites, blacks, the North, the South, and the world as a whole (pp. 201–2, 221, 232). Still, Fitzhugh's focus made obvious sense, both politically and polemically. See Ashworth, *Slavery and Capitalism*, pp. 200, 281; Ellis, "Legitimating Slavery," pp. 346–51; Fredrickson, *Black Image*, pp. 68–70; William B. Hesseltine, "Some New Aspects of the Proslavery Argument," in *Sections and Politics: Selected Essays by William B. Hesseltine*, ed. Richard N. Current (Madison: State Historical Society of Wisconsin, 1968), pp. 79–83. But compare David Donald, "The Proslavery Argument Reconsidered," *Journal of Southern History* 37, no. 1 (1971): 6–8; Faust, *Sacred Circle*, pp. 115, 131; Morrow, "Proslavery Argument Revisited," pp. 81–83; Bertram Wyatt-Brown, "Proslavery and Antislavery Intellectuals: Class Concepts and Polemical Struggle," in *Antislavery Reconsidered: New Perspectives on the Abolitionists*, ed. Lewis Perry and Michael Fellman (Baton Rouge: Louisiana State University Press, 1979), pp. 323–24.

76. See Child, *Appeal*, p. 81; Douglass, *Papers*, II:289 ("Slavery's Northern Bulwarks," June 12, 1851); Phillips, *Speeches*, I:82 ("Simms Anniversary," April 12, 1852).

77. For Fitzhugh's faith in progress, see Genovese, *Slaveholders' Dilemma*, pp. 13, 21, 25–26.

78. Fitzhugh even suggests that this philosophical struggle has been a long-standing partisan struggle more than a sectional one (pp. 255–56); that it will be settled ultimately in the North rather than between the North and the South (p. 254); and that the loss of the frontier mandates the victory of the "more government" party, which is now the Democratic Party (pp. 30, 255).

79. Fitzhugh certainly displays more concern for the union in *Cannibals All* than Dew did in the *Review*, although Dew's lack of concern for the union in his essay was consistent with its early timing and intrastate focus and apparently not due to any disunionist sentiments. See Genovese, *Slaveholders' Dilemma*, p. 19. Fitzhugh's own commitment to the union seems evident. In praising Governor Wise in the dedication as someone who loves both his state and the union (p. 3), Fitzhugh undoubtedly was also speaking of himself. Later, he accuses the abolitionists of seeking to "involv[e] us in civil and fratricidal war" (p. 232). He also claims that Virginia intends to cling to the union "as long as honor permits" because it "cannot bear the thought of" disunion (p. 234). Fitzhugh did not support secession until *after* Lincoln's election; committed Southern secessionists had been working assiduously to precipitate the event throughout the year. Compare Fitzhugh, "Disunion within the Union," *DeBow's Review* 28 (1860): 1–7; "The Message, the Constitution, and the Times," *DeBow's Review* 30 (1861): 162–63. This is another aspect of the irony that some of the staunchest defenders of slavery were not traditional Southern sectionalists. See Tise, *Proslavery*, pp. 361–62.

80. See Gienapp, "Crisis of American Democracy," p. 120.

NOTES TO CHAPTER 6

1. Once Lincoln was elected president and South Carolina seceded from the union, Hammond moved in the opposite direction, honoring his pledge to follow his state wherever it went. See *Selections from the Letters and Speeches of the Hon. James H. Hammond of South Carolina* (New York: John F. Trow, 1866), p. 356 ("Speech delivered at Barnwell Court House, South Carolina," October 29, 1858) (all page citations in this chapter are from this volume unless otherwise indicated); *The Papers of James Henry Hammond* (Washington, D.C.: Library of Congress, 1823–1875), reel 14 (untitled speech, November 8, 1860), p. 2. Secession was a fait accompli for Hammond. He did not support the secession movement or the war effort. He died in 1864, an embittered man isolated on his South Carolina plantation. See Drew Gilpin Faust, *James Henry*

Hammond and the Old South: A Design for Mastery (Baton Rouge: Louisiana State University Press, 1982), chaps. 16–17.

2. See Faust, *Hammond*, pp. 287, 296, 349–52, 358–59; Eugene D. Genovese, *The Slaveholders' Dilemma: Freedom and Progress in Southern Conservative Thought, 1820–1860* (Columbia: University of South Carolina Press, 1992), pp. 86, 100–1; Lawrence T. McDonnell, "Struggle against Suicide: James Henry Hammond and the Secession of South Carolina," *Southern Studies* 22, no. 2 (1983): 109–37; Jon L. Wakelyn, "The Changing Loyalties of James Henry Hammond: A Reconsideration," *South Carolina Historical Magazine* 75, no. 1 (1974): 1–13.

3. In his study of the secession crisis in South Carolina, Channing refers to Hammond as a conditional unionist. See Steven A. Channing, *Crisis of Fear: Secession in South Carolina* (New York: Norton, 1974), pp. 170–71.

4. These considerations are not conclusive because (1) Hammond's professed antipathy to politics may have been insincere as a cultural stance; one was (is) more likely to succeed in American politics by appearing to be above politics; (2) he may have miscalculated how his shift toward unionism would affect his political prospects; (3) he also may have miscalculated the state of sectional controversy at the time; (4) the assumption that it was natural for those on the sectional extremes to move in a disunionist direction during periods of intense sectional controversy may be fallacious; perhaps just the opposite is the case. For Hammond's professed antipathy to politics, see p. 90 ("Message to the Senate and House of Representatives of the State of South Carolina," November 26, 1844); pp. 226–27 ("An Oration delivered before the Two Societies of the South Carolina College," December 4, 1849); pp. 267–68 ("An Oration on the Life, Character, and Services of John Caldwell Calhoun," November 21, 1850). McDonnell and, to a lesser extent, Faust handle Hammond's 1858–60 shift toward unionism as a case of "political suicide." See Faust, *Hammond*, pp. 350–51; McDonnell, "Struggle against Suicide," pp. 121–37. Greenberg assesses the cultural significance of the slaveholders' professed antipathy to politics. See Kenneth S. Greenberg, *Masters and Statesmen: The Political Culture of American Slavery* (Baltimore: Johns Hopkins University Press, 1985), chap. 3.

5. We also saw this rhetorical shift in the comparison of Fitzhugh with Dew as well as among the abolitionists. As a prominent politician, Hammond was compelled to focus more on the fate of the union than Fitzhugh and Dew were, but that does not explain the shift in his own rhetoric.

6. Nonetheless, I focus less on the dynamics toward liberal and "positive good" proslavery arguments in this chapter than on the dynamics toward contextualist arguments, since I treated the first two dynamics more fully in the previous chapter.

7. Hammond would have gone further than the procedure the House even-

tually adopted of receiving the abolitionist petitions only to immediately table them. He would have had the House not even receive the petitions; see pp. 48–49 ("On the Justice of Receiving Petitions for the Abolition of Slavery in the District of Columbia," February 1, 1836). He was heavily criticized, both inside and outside the House, for his aggressive stance on the issue. Faust believes that the resulting psychological stress caused him to suffer a physical collapse in late February, which led to his resignation from the House a couple of months later. See Faust, *Hammond*, pp. 169–85.

8. Hammond temporarily retired from politics in the mid-1840s at least partly to quell a brewing family scandal centering on allegations that he had sexually abused his nieces. His political career was resurrected in 1858 when he emerged as a compromise Senate candidate between the unionist and secessionist factions in South Carolina politics. See Faust, *Hammond*, pp. 241–45, 254, 258, 338–40.

9. Faust claims that it was the first "positive good" speech delivered in Congress. See Faust, *Hammond*, p. 176. The relevant comparison is with Phillips's speech honoring John Quincy Adams and the other Massachusetts congressmen who opposed the gag rule.

10. The abolitionist petitions also urged Congress to abolish the slave trade in the District of Columbia, which, according to Hammond, was equally unconstitutional (p. 18).

11. Hammond reads, or has the House clerk read, a number of abolitionist publications to expose their ultimate aims as well as their organizing efforts (pp. 20–31). As we will see, he is very impressed with the latter.

12. Hammond cites mob violence in the American North and western Europe as evidence of the validity of this claim while contending that only one serious slave insurrection (Nat Turner) had ever taken place in the American South (p. 32; see also p. 37). (Dew had counted three Southern slave insurrections, but he undoubtedly would have agreed to only one "serious" one.)

13. Hammond insists that slavery is abolished only when the institution no longer serves the interests of society, as when it was abolished in the American North and as when serfdom was abolished in western Europe (pp. 32–33).

14. Hammond exempts the South and possibly the North from this generalization (p. 36). Like Fitzhugh, he exhibits considerable reluctance to attack the North directly in his writings and speeches and usually targets Great Britain in his attacks on free society. Another parallel exists in his suggestion that free laborers in free societies are only "called" free (p. 32), although unlike Fitzhugh, he does not argue that slaves are freer than free laborers; only that they are better off. This is one sense in which Hammond's defense of slavery is deficiently liberal as compared with Fitzhugh's.

15. In this context, Hammond chides John Quincy Adams for accusing Southern slaveholders of frequently separating the families of their slaves. He

claims that slave families are at least as stable as "free" families once one takes into account the impact of westward expansion on the latter (p. 36).

16. Hammond constructs this idyll to argue that any abolitionist-inspired attempts to foment slave rebellions are likely to fail and that even if they do succeed, the rebellions themselves are bound to fail (pp. 35–37).

17. This passage also has a debunking purpose: Northern whites are at least as racially prejudiced as Southern whites are. Fitzhugh followed the same strategy.

18. Although Hammond again offers the North as a possible exception to this rule (p. 36), he also claims that it has been plagued by mob violence as much as western Europe has (p. 32) and that its upper classes have more reason to fear the lower classes than Southern slaveholders do (pp. 45–46).

19. Here Hammond, at least obliquely, attacks the Declaration of Independence. Earlier in the speech, he referred slightingly to the abolitionists' use of the document to attack slavery (pp. 27–28). He also views the abolitionists as part of the same leveling spirit that in the North could easily turn from attacking Southern slaveholders to attacking its own upper classes (pp. 41–46).

20. Hammond favorably compares the natural aristocracy of the American South with the hereditary aristocracies of western Europe (pp. 44–45).

21. Hammond leaves open the question of whether disunion is a matter of conscious intent on the part of the abolitionists or merely another potential consequence of their campaign that they have overlooked. He does, however, quote one abolitionist tract stating a determination to abolish slavery even at the cost of disunion (p. 24).

22. Hammond notes that other congressmen seem uncertain whether or not the abolitionist movement is significant (p. 19). His own estimate of its size is obviously a guesstimate but agrees with other such estimates. See John Ashworth, *Slavery, Capitalism, and Politics in the Antebellum Republic: Volume 1: Commerce and Compromise, 1820–1850* (Cambridge: Cambridge University Press, 1995), p. 129.

23. See Joel H. Silbey, "The Civil War Synthesis in American Political History," in *Beyond the Civil War Synthesis: Political Essays on the Civil War Era*, ed. Robert P. Swierenga (Westport, Conn.: Greenwood Press, 1975), pp. 9–10; C. Vann Woodward, "The Southern Ethic in a Puritan World," in his *American Counterpoint: Slavery and Racism in the North/South Dialogue* (New York: Oxford University Press, 1971), pp. 13–46.

24. This proposal also suggests the need for intersectional comity, which Hammond advocates more explicitly in subsequent works.

25. Hammond resigned his House seat a few months later because of illness. He also resigned a Senate seat twenty-four years later on the heels of Lincoln's election as president of the United States.

26. Hammond admits that it would be politically inexpedient for any

Northern politician to support laws muzzling the abolitionists, although the incidence of antiabolitionist mobs in the North suggests some support for such laws. His second-best solution is a congressional decision not to receive the abolitionist petitions (pp. 48–49). Perhaps as a third-best solution, he threatens the abolitionists with death if they ever come south to agitate against slavery (pp. 49–50).

27. Hammond sent Clarkson two letters because when he wrote the first letter, he had misplaced the copy of Clarkson's circular that a Northern minister had sent him. When he later found the circular, he wrote a second letter to address the arguments he had not addressed in the first; see pp. 114, 173–74. The letters are dated January 28 and March 24.

28. See Faust, *Hammond*, pp. 278–79.

29. In his two annual gubernatorial messages, Hammond accused the abolitionists as well as the British government of forestalling the annexation of Texas; see pp. 77, 100.

30. Greenberg stresses that the defenders of slavery appealed to national pride and, specifically, Anglophobia against the abolitionists, both British and American. See Greenberg, *Masters and Statesmen*, chap. 6. As we have seen, the American abolitionists did tend to be Anglophiles. Yet the proslavery strategy of attacking free society in Great Britain, instead of in the American North, was also a way for some defenders of slavery to preserve the image of a house united.

31. Genovese thus views Hammond's avowed refusal to defend slavery in the abstract in these letters as a rhetorical ploy. See Genovese, *Slaveholders' Dilemma*, p. 91.

32. Hammond quotes *The Anti-Slavery Record*, an early American Anti-Slavery Society publication, on this point. See also John W. Blassingame, ed., *The Frederick Douglass Papers; Series One: Speeches, Debates, and Interviews* (New Haven, Conn.: Yale University Press, 1979–82), II:284 ("Slavery's Northern Bulwark," January 12, 1851); Wendell Phillips, *Speeches, Lectures, and Letters* (Boston: Lee and Shepard, 1891), II:245 ("The Bible and the Church," May 28–30, 1850).

33. With particular reference to Clarkson and other British abolitionists, Hammond accuses them of being "silly enthusiasts" who have been manipulated by powerful men with ulterior motives (pp. 196–97). He also denounces Clarkson personally and the abolitionists generally for not being good Christians in holding men to higher standards than God would (pp. 124, 188, 196) and claims that they are doing the work of Satan, not God, in their crusade to abolish Southern slavery (pp. 152, 170).

34. Hammond quotes another famous British abolitionist, William Wilberforce, on "reason and order as the child of liberty" in suggesting that the dictum does not apply to African Americans (p. 168).

35. Accordingly, Hammond criticizes the British abolitionists for misplacing their charity from those nearby, whom they can help, to those far away, whom they cannot (pp. 154, 160, 196–97). The implication is that American abolitionists are using the same type of faulty logic.

36. Fitzhugh also impugned the abolitionists as heirs of the French Revolution who would return men to a barbaric state of nature. The antiabstractionist theme was, of course, central to both Fitzhugh's *Cannibals All* and Dew's *Review*; see also pp. 10–11 ("Report at a Meeting of the State Rights and Free Trade Party of Barnwell District, South Carolina, held at Barnwell Court-House, on Monday, July 7th, 1834").

37. Hammond's Clarkson letters display a similar mix of different types of arguments—religious and secular, ascriptive and liberal—that we have seen in other proslavery and antislavery figures.

38. Hammond insists that it is the abolitionists who would reduce the master-slave relationship to force by upsetting the relationship through their antislavery agitation (p. 184). For Hammond on slavery and consent, see Greenberg, *Masters and Statesmen*, p. 94.

39. Not surprisingly, given their addressee, Hammond once again singles out Great Britain more than the American North for criticism in these letters. Yet he, like Dew, shows considerable ambivalence toward the North in these letters as when he, again like Dew, criticizes the region for its overly utilitarian system of values (p. 187); see also pp. 127–28, 131, 134, 155, 162, 185–86; pp. 207, 221, 224 ("Oration before South Carolina College"). On the proslavery rejection of utilitarianism, see Daniel Kilbride, "Slavery and Utilitarianism: Thomas Cooper and the Mind of the South," *Journal of Southern History* 59, no. 3 (1993): 145–68.

40. The second letter actually ends with an *ad hominem* attack on the abolitionists (pp. 196–98).

41. Hammond offered the same prediction in the "gag rule" speech; see also p. 112 ("Letter to the Free Church of Glasgow, on the Subject of Slavery," June 21, 1844).

42. Hammond also contends that abolition has had a negative economic impact in Antigua and would have an even worse economic impact in the American South because it, unlike Antigua, was not a small island, and as a result, the freed slaves would roam the country rather than work on its plantations (p. 164). Hammond refers to the British resort to imported Indian laborers in its postemancipation colonies as further evidence of the difficulty of, in practice, abolishing slavery (pp. 163–64). Fitzhugh later made a similar reference.

43. In this passage, as he does throughout these letters, Hammond suggests both that blacks are naturally inferior to whites and that they are not; see also pp. 118, 165, 168. As already noted, Dew and Fitzhugh engaged in the same equivo-

cation which, I have argued, not only straddled the "necessary evil" and "positive good" positions on Southern slavery but also was a liberal equivocation.

44. Like Dew, Hammond even claims that the slave trade has yielded one great good in bringing Africans into contact with a "superior" civilization (p. 118), even though he, again like Dew, initially eschews defending the trade (p. 115). Similarly, he credits Clarkson for his work in abolishing the trade (p. 116) but then contends that even that achievement has spawned great evils in forcing it into illegal channels (pp. 116–18). In the second letter, he adds that Great Britain abolished the slave trade and, later, colonial slavery only when it was in its national interest to do so (p. 195).

45. Hammond's source for the low suicide and insanity rates of Southern slaves relative to those of free blacks was undoubtedly the flawed 1840 census. See William Stanton, *The Leopard's Spots: Scientific Attitudes toward Race in America, 1815–1859* (Chicago: University of Chicago Press, 1960), pp. 58–66.

46. In rebutting these antislavery arguments, Hammond variously accuses the abolitionists of exaggerating the incidence of the "abuses" in question or blames the abolitionists for causing them in the first place by "agitating" the Southern slaves.

47. Hammond contends that the causes of personal violence in the South lie in the frontier conditions still prevailing in many parts of the region rather than in slavery (pp. 130–31). He also contends that personal violence occurs less often in the South than in other societies, including the North (p. 131). He alleges a relative lack of interracial intercourse in the South as evidence that the region is not, *pace* the abolitionists, a cesspool of sexual immorality (pp. 136–37) and a disproportionate number of presidents and other prominent statesmen from the region as evidence that it is not lagging behind the North in formal education (p. 133). He also asserts that the South is at least as pious as the North is; the North, after all, has become fertile soil for all the latest religious fads (p. 134). Fitzhugh emphasized the last point; Dew, the disproportionate number of Southern statesmen.

48. Yet again, Hammond inverts the charge: the North and, even more, the rest of the world have a greater need of standing armies (p. 128).

49. Hammond's caveat is that slave revolts are unlikely to occur unless instigated by "outsiders" (pp. 128–29). In the "gag rule" speech, he used the relative lack of slave revolts in the South as an index of regional security.

50. Even as he suggests that the costs of a free-labor system to the community outweigh its benefits to individual employers, Hammond argues that the South would convert to the system if it could be assured of an adequate supply of free labor (pp. 139–40, 164–65). Dew made a similar argument.

51. Dew and (later) Fitzhugh also insisted on the importance of Southern cotton to the international economy and viewed the tariff as a tax on Southern exports.

52. Hammond seems more trusting of the North and, correspondingly, more confident that the South can protect its institution of racial slavery within the union in the Clarkson letters than he did in the "gag rule" speech.

53. Hammond is quoting Clarkson's circular, but he observes that many American abolitionists share Clarkson's disunionist sentiments (p. 192). Indeed, he could equally well have quoted Phillips's 1844 American Anti-Slavery Society pamphlet.

54. American abolitionists differ from British abolitionists in that their meddling violates intersectional comity rather than national pride (p. 192); see also p. 34 ("gag rule" speech); p. 106 ("Letter to Free Church of Glasgow").

55. Hammond goes on to argue that the very principles the abolitionists use to condemn slavery can be, and are, used to condemn other institutions, such as marriage and the family, which are generally considered essential to human society (pp. 176–77). This argument became one of Fitzhugh's mainstays.

56. Like Dew, Hammond considers the abolitionists the heirs of the French Revolution and places the defenders of slavery in the Burkean role of resisting a revolutionary movement (p. 194; see also pp. 170–72). But he does present his conservatism in a progressive, arguably liberal, light; see also pp. 211, 223 ("Oration before South Carolina College"). Genovese highlights Hammond's ambivalent attitudes toward progress. See Genovese, *Slaveholders' Dilemma*, pp. 89, 95–99, 106.

57. Unfortunately for Hammond, his chief rival as Calhoun's heir apparent, Robert Barnwell (Rhett), was chosen to deliver the other official funeral oration. See Faust, *Hammond*, p. 299. Recall that a family scandal had seriously set back Hammond's political career.

58. See Faust, *Hammond*, pp. 3, 154, 297, 300–1; McDonnell, "Struggle against Suicide," pp. 130–33.

59. See Faust, *Hammond*, p. 172.

60. Hammond does take a position in the speech on earlier intersectional compromises. He believes that the Constitution and Missouri Compromise were *bona fide* intersectional compromises and that the tariff of 1833 was an unqualified victory for the South (though subsequently undercut by the tariff of 1842); see pp. 263, 270, 278.

61. Actually, in his "Fourth of March" speech, Calhoun only hinted at the necessity of amending the Constitution in such a way as to offer the South more protection under it. See John C. Calhoun, *Works* (New York: D. Appleton, 1851–56), IV:572. One of his ideas for such a constitutional amendment was to create a dual presidency; one for the North and one for the South (I:392–95, "A Discourse on the Constitution and Government of the United States," n.d.).

62. See, for example, Calhoun, *Works*, IV:323–24 ("On 'The Three Million Bill,'" February 9, 1847).

63. Hammond's treatment of the slavery issue was foreshadowed by his repeated warnings against the dangers of sectional majorities; see pp. 245–46, 251, 255–56.

64. Hammond mentions three constitutional clauses as guarantees to slavery—the three-fifths, fugitive slave, and domestic insurrection clauses—as well as the fact that the Constitution is one of reserved powers (p. 278). Once more, one should compare Phillips's 1844 American Anti-Slavery Society pamphlet.

65. Interestingly, Hammond links this crisis to the nullification crisis, arguing that the tariff of 1833 made the North more receptive to antislavery agitation because it reduced the region's profits from slave labor (p. 279). He reasserts this linkage in subsequent works. Compare William W. Freehling, *Prelude to Civil War: The Nullification Controversy in South Carolina, 1816–1836* (New York: Harper & Row, 1968), pp. x, 49–52, 85–86, 257–59.

66. See Calhoun, *Works*, II:630–32 ("Abolition Petitions"). This is Hammond's only defense of slavery in the speech; thus it is not in his own voice.

67. In this speech, Hammond presents the North as being naturally antislavery in sentiment, more like in his "gag rule" speech than in his Clarkson letters.

68. According to Hammond, the Mexican War gave Northern antislavery politicians the concrete issue for which they had been searching: free soil (pp. 282–83).

69. Compare Calhoun, *Works*, IV:556–58.

70. Hammond's account of Calhoun's transition from progressive to conservative to philosophical statesman (as synthesizing the previous two) could well be self-referential; see pp. 297–99.

71. Calhoun most fully explicated his concurrent-majority theory in another posthumously published work: *A Disquisition on Government*. See Calhoun, *Works*, I:3–81.

72. Hammond's support for the Lecompton constitution is fairly tepid because he believes that both antislavery and proslavery forces in Kansas have engaged in fraudulent activities (pp. 307–8).

73. Hammond's principal target in the speech is Seward, not Douglas. He devotes only a few pages to attacking Douglas's "popular sovereignty" doctrine (pp. 305–6), whereas the whole speech is implicitly a response to Seward's "irrepressible conflict" doctrine. See Genovese, *Slaveholders' Dilemma*, p. 110 (n. 32); Mark J. Stegmaier, "Intensifying the Sectional Conflict: William Seward versus James Hammond in the Lecompton Debate of 1858," *Civil War History* 31, no. 3 (1985): 199, 208–10. Seward's "Irrepressible Conflict" speech was actually delivered in Rochester later in the year, but the doctrine is clearly adumbrated in his Senate speech. See George E. Baker, ed., *The Works of William H. Seward* (Boston: Houghton, Mifflin, 1884), IV:289–302 ("Irrepressible Conflict Speech," October 25, 1858); IV:574–604 ("Lecompton and

Kansas," March 3, 1858). (Hammond's speech was delivered the next day.) At the time, Seward was the leading contender for the 1860 Republican presidential nomination, and Douglas, for the Democratic nomination. Neither, of course, became the next president. Hammond's unexpected choice as the new South Carolina senator resurrected (briefly) his political career.

74. Seward had declared that the process of remaking the South in the North's image would occur peacefully through Northern control of the federal government which, he believed, was imminent. But he had used some stronger, martial language in his speech, eliciting this response from Hammond. Compare Seward, *Works*, IV:595; Hammond, *Selections*, pp. 310–11. See also Stegmaier, "Intensifying Sectional Conflict," pp. 205, 209–10.

75. Specifically, Hammond does not offer intersectional comity as a solution to increasing sectional conflict over the fate of Southern slavery as he had in earlier works. He also seems to place less trust in the North than he had in earlier works.

76. Hammond also expects an independent South not to be involved in wars because he believes that commerce is the leading cause of wars and that in the past, the South was drawn into wars only by Northern commerce (p. 316).

77. Hammond states this harmony as a general law and identifies the lack of such harmony as the cause of the American Revolution (p. 318); see also p. 287 ("Life of Calhoun").

78. Hammond quotes Cicero on how the common consent of mankind constitutes natural law (p. 319). He also argues that Africans make good "mud-sills," at least in the American South, because of their alleged ability to toil in warm climates (p. 318).

79. This revolution may occur through the ballot box—stressing the danger of "mud-sills" enjoying the right to vote—or by other means, hence Hammond's warning to the North that Southern politicians might start agitating its "mud-sills," just as Northern politicians are agitating the South's (p. 320).

80. Hammond claims that the South saved the North (as well as Great Britain) from financial ruin during the recent Panic of 1857 (p. 317). Fitzhugh also contended that the frontier acted as a safety valve for Northern discontents.

81. Hammond intends this argument as a rebuttal to Seward's assertion that slavery is a dying institution. See Seward, *Works*, IV:601.

82. Hammond contends that the South ruled the nation for its first seventy years, controlling the presidency for sixty of those years. (He obviously is counting Northern Democrats Martin Van Buren, Franklin Pierce, and James Buchanan as Southern-controlled presidents.) Hammond, however, agrees with Seward that the next president most likely will be a Northern Republican. Compare Seward, *Works*, IV:603; Hammond, *Selections*, p. 321.

83. The English bill, sponsored by Representative William English (D-Indiana), gave the people of Kansas the choice of immediately entering the union

under the Lecompton constitution or waiting until the territory had a minimum population of 90,000. Under the bill, which included a generous federal land grant to Kansas upon statehood, the Lecompton constitution was resubmitted to a popular vote and overwhelmingly defeated.

84. On the differences between these two speeches, see Genovese, *Slaveholders' Dilemma*, pp. 100–1; Stegmaier, "Intensifying Sectional Conflict," p. 219.

85. Hammond claims to have supported the Lecompton constitution only because his Southern colleagues in the Senate did (p. 327). (Recall his tepid support of the constitution in the "Mudsill" speech.) He also claims that Kansas never could have become a slave state anyway (p. 326); that the Republicans drummed up the whole issue only to exploit it for political gain (p. 326); and that the English bill, which he also supported, was fair because it required only the customary minimum population for statehood (p. 333).

86. Ironically, Hammond has again shifted in the same direction as the Garrisonians, directly questioning the assumption that the sectional extremes tended to become more extreme during times of sectional crisis.

87. In this part of the speech, Hammond suggests that his differences with other proslavery figures regarding the prospects for continued union reside in the fact that he, unlike they, does not want the federal government to act in a proslavery direction. He opposes reopening the slave trade (p. 335). He also opposes slavery extension, accepting the "natural limits on slavery" thesis with respect to the western territories (pp. 335–36) and, like Calhoun, viewing national expansion farther south into Latin America as a "forbidden fruit" for the South (pp. 336–38). See Faust, *Hammond*, p. 344; McDonnell, "Struggle against Suicide," p. 115. This is yet another aspect of the irony that proslavery figures tended not to be traditional Southern sectionalists, although Hammond here shows himself to be more of one than Fitzhugh was. See especially Arthur Bestor, "State Sovereignty and Slavery: A Reinterpretation of Proslavery Constitutional Doctrine, 1846–1860," *Journal of the Illinois State Historical Society* 54, no. 2 (1961): 117–80.

88. Hammond's history is somewhat suspect, but at least he is consistent. He presented the same historical argument in his funeral oration for Calhoun. Incidentally, Calhoun had long pressed the need for Southern unity. See, for example, Calhoun, *Works*, II:309 ("In Reply to Mr. Webster," February 26, 1833).

89. Hammond mentions George Washington, Thomas Jefferson, Henry Clay, John Marshall, and William Crawford as prominent Southern statesmen of the past who believed that slavery was a necessary evil (p. 344).

90. Hammond advances by-now-familiar claims about Southern slavery in the course of defending the institution: Africans constitute an inferior race perfectly suited to slavery (pp. 338, 346); the institution benefits both slaves and masters (p. 344); it has had a civilizing effect on mankind (pp. 344–45); and slave labor is the only form of labor suitable for staple production (p. 347).

91. As he had in the Clarkson letters, Hammond insists that Great Britain abolished slavery in its colonies only when it was in its national interest to do so (p. 346). He also alleges that at the same time Great Britain and France abolished slavery in their colonies, British and French capitalists were increasingly exploiting domestic laborers and that both countries subsequently reintroduced a type of slave trade (pp. 347–48).

92. Unfortunately for Hammond but fortunately for the nation, the Republicans won both of the next two presidential elections. In the "Mudsill" speech, Hammond predicted that the Republicans would win the next presidential election. On the broader claim, see William E. Gienapp, "The Crisis of American Democracy: The Political System and the Coming of the Civil War," in *Why the Civil War Came*, ed. Gabor S. Boritt (New York: Oxford University Press, 1996), p. 103.

93. Hammond issued a similar warning in the "gag rule" speech.

94. The implication is that the South controls Congress, despite Northern majorities in both chambers, through its faithful Northern allies and that President Buchanan is also such an ally. Hammond now (again) demonstrates more trust in the North than he did in the "Mudsill" speech.

95. Hammond emphasizes, however, that he is not a "mere" party man, since he will not sacrifice his inveterate states-rights principles to party expediency (pp. 354–55). Presumably, the "true" Democrats of the North share those principles.

96. See Channing, *Crisis of Fear*, chaps. 4–7.

97. In his cover letter, dated November 8, to a delegation from the state legislature that had invited him to speak on the current situation, Hammond claims to be too ill to speak and therefore is sending them a copy of a speech he had been preparing for precisely such an eventuality. The speech was suppressed by one of his political allies in the legislature because it seemed so incongruous with the prevailing secessionist temper of the body. See Faust, *Hammond*, pp. 357–58; McDonnell, "Struggle against Suicide," pp. 117–19, 134–36. My references are to the more accessible Library of Congress copy of the speech, even though p. 21 is missing. Fortunately, the missing page appears on pp. 28–29 of the copy of the speech in the South Caroliniana Library, microfilmed as part of *Records of Ante-Bellum Southern Plantations from the Revolution through the Civil War*, series A, Selections from the South Caroliniana Library, University of South Carolina; Part I: The Papers of James Henry Hammond, 1795–1865 (Frederick, Md.: University Publications of America, 1985), reel 10.

98. Hammond resigned from the Senate three days later, albeit reluctantly and only after the other South Carolina senator, James Chestnut, resigned. See Faust, *Hammond*, p. 358. Hammond spent the remaining four years of his life on his South Carolina plantation.

99. According to Channing, these were the positions the South Carolina

secessionists had forced the unionists into by late 1860. But whereas Channing argues that Hammond and the other South Carolina unionists were by this time really conditional *dis*unionists, I argue that Hammond, at least, remained a conditional unionist. Compare Channing, *Crisis of Fear*, pp. 240–44.

100. See p. 356 ("Barnwell" speech).

101. Hammond provides no date for this turning point in American history.

102. Hammond does not specify exactly why Northern politicians would no longer have an incentive to pursue antislavery agitation, but presumably it is because they, and, more important, their constituents, would no longer feel responsible for the continued existence of Southern slavery. He repeats the death threat of the "gag rule" speech against any abolitionists who come south to agitate against the institution (p. 23; see also p. 3).

103. Earlier, Hammond used this argument as a reason not to disrupt Lincoln's inauguration (pp. 13–15).

104. Recall that Hammond predicted in the "Barnwell" speech that the Republicans needed to win one of the next two presidential elections in order to survive as a major party. He now predicts that Lincoln will be only a one-term president, as all other Northern presidents have been. His explanation is that the nation has become too large and diverse for the spoils system, which, he believes, is the main motivating factor for Northern, as opposed to Southern, politicians (pp. 23–24).

105. Hammond thus clearly implies that from the very beginning, the union was a house divided.

106. Returning to a suggestion he made in the "gag rule" speech, Hammond argues that the Northern states abolished slavery only because of its unprofitability to them, and even then, individual slaveholders profited by selling their slaves farther south before they were to be freed (pp. 27–28). This practice was a significant problem in several Northern states that passed gradual emancipation acts. See Arthur Zilversmit, *The First Emancipation: The Abolition of Slavery in the North* (Chicago: University of Chicago Press, 1967), pp. 120, 151, 159, 201.

107. Hammond claims that this sectional party was also a response to population trends that worked to the North's advantage. He pinpoints immigration as the main reason that the North has outpaced the South in population growth (p. 28).

108. In this speech, unlike the "Barnwell" speech, Hammond does not insert any dicta about the South's still controlling Congress because the Republican Party "has crushed, apparently forever, all our Northern allies" (p. 28). His continued unionism therefore does not depend on continued trust in the North.

109. Hammond brackets this declaration by asserting that the South is likely to win any war with the North and, even if it were not, that it is better to perish than to submit to oppression (pp. 29–30, 31–32). He nevertheless does

not believe that the North will go to war to keep the South in the union (p. 21). Phillips expressed a similar belief even after South Carolina and five other Southern states had seceded from the union.

110. Hammond adds that the South owes it to Buchanan not secede while he is still president because he has been such a faithful ally (p. 34).

111. Hammond posits the inadvisability of single-state secession as one of the lessons of the nullification crisis (p. 11).

112. Hammond offered a similar prediction in the "Barnwell" speech.

113. Hammond voiced this same fear in the "Barnwell" speech (p. 333) and as early as the "gag rule" speech (pp. 43–46). See Faust, *Hammond*, pp. 331, 356–57; Wakelyn, "Changing Loyalties," pp. 11–13.

114. See Faust, *Hammond*, pp. 358–59; Genovese, *Slaveholders' Dilemma*, pp. 100–1; McDonnell, "Struggle against Suicide," pp. 134–35; Wakelyn, "Changing Loyalties," pp. 12–13.

115. See, for example, p. 187 ("Letters to Clarkson"). Compare James L. Huston, "The Experiential Basis of the Northern Antislavery Impulse," *Journal of Southern History* 56, no. 4 (1990): 609–40.

116. See Roy B. Basler, ed., *The Collected Works of Abraham Lincoln* (New Brunswick, N.J.: Rutgers University Press, 1953), II:454 ("Speech at Chicago, Illinois," July 10, 1858); III:439–40 ("Speech at Cincinnati, Ohio," Sept. 17, 1859); III:550 ("Address at Cooper Institute, New York City," February 27, 1860). Even in his first inaugural address, Lincoln promised not to interfere with slavery in those states where it already existed and signaled his support of a constitutional amendment to that effect (IV:270).

NOTES TO CHAPTER 7

1. See Roy B. Basler, ed., *The Collected Works of Abraham Lincoln* (New Brunswick, N.J.: Rutgers University Press, 1953), VII:301–2 ("Address at a Sanitary Fair, Baltimore, Maryland," April 18, 1864).

2. Lincoln, however, makes clear that the Southern definition has some currency "even in the North" and also that it is significant that in this case the sheep is "black." See Lincoln, *Works*, VII:302. Throughout this chapter, I assume a growing confluence among abolitionists and Republicans as disunion and civil war became more imminent and then occurred. This process was discussed in chapter 4.

3. See Robert W. Johannsen, ed., *The Lincoln-Douglas Debates of 1858* (New York: Oxford University Press, 1965), p. 14.

4. The Civil War did unite the house against slavery, but this is obviously not what Lincoln meant or intended.

5. However, as we have seen, not all the abolitionists concluded the argument in the same way.

6. It was also the position of the Constitutional Unionists, who received significant support in the border states.

7. For more extended analyses of the Lincoln-Douglas debates, see David F. Ericson, *The Shaping of American Liberalism: The Debates over Ratification, Nullification, and Slavery* (Chicago: University of Chicago Press, 1993), chaps. 7–8; Donald E. Fehrenbacher, *Prelude to Greatness: Lincoln in the 1850s* (Stanford, Calif.: Stanford University Press, 1962), chaps. 4–6; Harry V. Jaffa, *Crisis of the House Divided: An Interpretation of the Issues of the Lincoln-Douglas Debates* (New York: Doubleday, 1959); David Zarefsky, *Lincoln, Douglas and Slavery: In the Crucible of Public Debate* (Chicago: University of Chicago Press, 1990).

8. See Johannsen, *Lincoln-Douglas Debates*, pp. 54, 136, 313. Lincoln believed that those differences actually created a stronger union.

9. See Johannsen, *Lincoln-Douglas Debates*, pp. 44, 104, 126–27, 197, 218, 288, 326. Douglas also pointed out that if anything, the union was originally a house united for slavery, since at the time of the Federal Convention, twelve of the thirteen states were slave states (pp. 44–45, 218, 289, 326). Only Massachusetts had abolished slavery by 1787. See Arthur Zilversmit, *The First Emancipation: The Abolition of Slavery in the North* (Chicago: University of Chicago Press, 1967), pp. 113–16.

10. See Johannsen, *Lincoln-Douglas Debates*, pp. 54–55, 132, 277–78, 311–12. Lincoln thus suggested that the South's shift from a "necessary evil" to a "positive good" position on slavery was a recent one, although he again stressed that it was not strictly a sectional shift (pp. 219–20, 304–5).

11. See Johannsen, *Lincoln-Douglas Debates*, pp. 14–20; also pp. 55–61, 81–85, 231–32, 284. How seriously Lincoln took the conspiracy theory of his "house divided" speech is a matter of some dispute. Compare Ericson, *Shaping of Liberalism*, pp. 140–42; Fehrenbacher, *Prelude to Greatness*, pp. 80–82; Jaffa, *Crisis of the House Divided*, pp. 277–78; Zarefsky, *In the Crucible of Debate*, pp. 83–87.

12. See Johannsen, *Lincoln-Douglas Debates*, pp. 52, 131–32, 221, 278, 303. Lincoln was also very vague about the timetable for "extinguishing" Southern slavery, admitting that it could take as long as one hundred years (pp. 55, 200). This cautious gradualism was one factor that separated him and other Republican leaders from the abolitionists.

13. As noted in both chapters 2 and 5, it is not even clear that a majority of Southern voters supported secession.

14. Many Southern leaders, after all, seemed to discount Douglas's "purer" avowals of intersectional comity, for example, Hammond in his "Mudsill" speech. See James H. Hammond, *Selections from the Letters and Speeches of the Hon. James H. Hammond of South Carolina* (New York: John F. Trow, 1866), p. 306.

15. Some Southern proslavery figures such as Fitzhugh seemed determined to unite the house for slavery, but only on the basis of a very elastic definition of the institution.

16. Seward's "Irrepressible Conflict" speech was similarly attacked. See Steven A. Channing, *Crisis of Fear: Secession in South Carolina* (New York: Norton, 1974), pp. 230–32.

17. See David M. Potter, "The Historian's Use of Nationalism and Vice Versa," *American Historical Review* 67, no. 4 (1962): 943–48.

18. The supposition is that Northern, as well as Southern, whites ultimately could have accepted the view that racial slavery was a necessary means of race control in the South more readily than they could have accepted the view that it was a benign, liberal institution. This supposition is the premise of the "central theme of Southern history" literature. See Ulrich B. Phillips, "The Central Theme of Southern History," *American Historical Review* 34, no. 1 (1928): 30–43; Robert E. Shalhope, "Race, Class, Slavery, and the Antebellum Southern Mind," *Journal of Southern History* 37, no. 1 (1971): 557–74; George B. Tindall, "The Central Theme Revisited," in *The Southerner as American*, ed. Charles Grier Sellers Jr. (New York: Dutton, 1966), pp. 104–29. But as I have argued throughout this book, the dynamics of a national liberal consensus "required" this shift in rhetoric.

19. The "seepage" of the "house divided" argument from more extreme to less extreme groups in both sections of the country was also an important factor here.

20. See Johannsen, *Lincoln-Douglas Debates*, pp. 20–21; also pp. 67, 200, 233, 277, 319. In turn, Southern leaders began to define Douglas's position as an antislavery one. See Channing, *Crisis of Fear*, pp. 178–79.

21. The literature on civil-war causation is voluminous. For a recent overview, see Gabor S. Boritt, ed., *Why the Civil War Came* (New York: Oxford University Press, 1996).

22. See James G. Randall, "The Blundering Generation," *Mississippi Valley Historical Review* 27, no. 1 (1940): 3–28; Avery O. Craven, *The Coming of the Civil War* (Chicago: University of Chicago Press, 1957 [1942]). For a more recent revisionist account, see Lee Benson, "Explanations of American Civil War Causation: A Critical Assessment and Modest Proposal to Reorient and Reorganize the Social Sciences," *Toward the Scientific Study of History: Selected Essays of Lee Benson* (Philadelphia: Lippincott, 1972), pp. 225–333.

23. These fears supplied the substance of the conspiracy theories that David Brion Davis, among others, finds rampant at the time. See David Brion Davis, *The Slave Power Conspiracy and the Paranoid Style* (Baton Rouge: Louisiana State University Press, 1969). See also Channing, *Crisis of Fear*, chap. 1; William W. Freehling, "'Absurd' Issues and the Causes of the Civil War: Colonization as a Test Case," in *The Reintegration of American History: Slavery*

and the Civil War (New York: Oxford University Press, 1994), pp. 138–57; Larry Gara, "Slavery and the Slave Power: A Crucial Distinction," *Civil War History* 15, no. 1 (1969): 5–18; William E. Gienapp, "The Republican Party and the Slave Power," in *New Perspectives on Race and Slavery in America: Essays in Honor of Kenneth M. Stampp*, ed. Robert Abzug and Stephen E. Maizlish (Lexington: University of Kentucky Press, 1986), pp. 51–78.

24. See Arthur C. Cole, *The Irrepressible Conflict* (New York: Macmillan, 1934); Allan Nevins, *Ordeal of the Union* (New York: Scribner, 1947–50). For a more recent neo-Progressive account, see Kenneth M. Stampp, "The Irrepressible Conflict," in *The Imperiled Union: Essays on the Background of the Civil War* (New York: Oxford University Press, 1980), pp. 191–245.

25. See Bernard Bailyn, *The Ideological Origins of the American Revolution* (Cambridge, Mass.: Belknap Press, 1967), pp. 235–46; David Brion Davis, *The Problem of Slavery in Western Culture* (Ithaca, N.Y.: Cornell University Press, 1966), pp. 87–89, 255–62; William W. Freehling, "The Founding Fathers, Conditional Antislavery, and the Nonradicalism of the American Revolution," in *The Reintegration of American History: Slavery and the Civil War* (New York: Oxford University Press, 1994), pp. 17–18; Leon F. Litwack, *North of Slavery: The Negro in the Free States, 1790–1860* (Chicago: University of Chicago Press, 1961), pp. 3–15; Gary Nash, *Race and Revolution* (Madison, Wis.: Madison House, 1990), pp. 6–7, 31–35; Zilversmit, *First Emancipation*, pp. 226–29.

26. See Michael F. Holt, *The Political Crisis of the 1850s* (New York: Norton, 1978), especially chap. 1. For other "institutional failure" theses, see Thomas B. Alexander, "The Civil War as Institutional Fulfillment," *Journal of Southern History* 47, no. 1 (1981): 3–32; Arthur Bestor, "The American Civil War as a Constitutional Crisis," *American Historical Review* 69, no. 2 (1964): 327–52; Stanley M. Elkins, *Slavery: A Problem in American Institutional & Intellectual Life* (New York: Grosset & Dunlap, 1963 [1959]), chap. 2; William E. Gienapp, "The Crisis of American Democracy: The Political System and the Coming of the Civil War," in *Why the Civil War Came*, ed. Gabor S. Boritt (New York: Oxford University Press, 1996), pp. 79–124.

27. See Kenneth S. Greenberg, "Civil War Revisionism," *Reviews in American History* 7, no. 2 (1979): 206–7.

28. On institutional as opposed to cultural explanations of political change, see Karen Orren and Stephen Skowronek, "In Search of Political Development," in *The Liberal Tradition in American Politics: Reassessing the Legacy of American Liberalism*, ed. David F. Ericson and Louisa Bertch Green (New York: Routledge, 1999), pp. 29–41.

29. J. David Greenstone reinterpreted Hartz's thesis to argue that liberal principles established a "boundary condition" on American political practice, but he did not develop his view into a theory of civil-war causation. See J.

David Greenstone, *The Lincoln Persuasion: Remaking American Liberalism* (Princeton, N.J.: Princeton University Press, 1993), pp. 42–46.

30. Part of Lincoln's genius, however, was to combine theories of historical causation and political action. See Johannsen, *Lincoln-Douglas Debates*, p. 14.

Index

About the Author

David F. Ericson is an associate professor of political science at Wichita State University and the author of *The Shaping of American Liberalism: The Debates over Ratification, Nullification, and Slavery.*